Fodor's Seattle & Vancouver

Bernies

Signey Farms
Granger

Rummings Galley — Pioneer Sq 301 Occidental

Foster | White — Sixth & Pine

Legacy — 1003 1st

Reprinted from *Fodor's Pacific North Coast*

Fodor's Travel Publications, Inc.
New York • London • Toronto

ISBN 0–679–02202–3

Fodor's Pacific North Coast

Editor: Alison Hoffman
Contributors: Susan M. Bain, Robert Brown, Susan Brown, John Doerper, Eve Johnson, Philip Joseph, Marcy Pritchard, Glenn W. Sheehan, Loralee Wenger, Terri Wershler, Adam Woog
Art Director: Fabrizio La Rocca
Cartographer: David Lindroth
Illustrator: Karl Tanner
Cover Photograph: Eddie Hironaka/Image Bank

Design: Vignelli Associates

Special Sales

Contents

Foreword   *v*

Highlights   *viii*

Fodor's Choice   *ix*

Introduction   *xiv*

1 Essential Information   *1*

Before You Go *2*

Visitor Information *2*
Tour Groups *2*
Package Deals for Independent Travelers *3*
When to Go *4*
Festivals and Seasonal Events *5*
What to Pack *6*
Taking Money Abroad *7*
Getting Money from Home *7*
Currency *8*
What It Will Cost *8*
Passports and Visas *8*
Customs *9*
Traveling with Film *10*
Language *10*
Staying Healthy *10*
Insurance *11*
Car Rentals *11*
Rail Passes *12*
Bus Passes *12*
Student and Youth Travel *13*
Traveling with Children *14*
Hints for Disabled Travelers *14*
Hints for Older Travelers *16*
Further Reading *17*

Arriving and Departing *18*

From the U.S. by Plane *18*
From the U.S. by Car *19*
From the U.S. by Train *20*
From the U.S. by Bus *20*
From the U.K. by Plane *20*

Staying in Seattle and Vancouver *21*

Getting Around *21*
Telephones *24*
Mail *24*
Tipping *24*
Opening and Closing Times *25*
Shopping *25*

Ferries 23
(ʒr " 85

Participant Sports and Outdoor Activities *26*
Spectator Sports *28*
Beaches *29*
Dining *29*
Lodging *29*
Credit Cards *31*

2 Portraits of Seattle and Vancouver *33*

"In the Footsteps of the First Settlers,"
by Glenn W. Sheehan *34*

3 Seattle *40*

4 Vancouver *102*

Index *160*

Maps

Seattle and Vancouver *xi*
World Time Zones *xii–xiii*
Downtown Seattle *46–47*
Metropolitan Seattle *50*
Downtown Seattle Dining *62–63*
Metropolitan Seattle Dining *64*
Seattle Lodging *72–73*
Puget Sound *89*
Vancouver Exploring *104–105*
Tour 1: Downtown Vancouver *111*
Tour 2: Stanley Park *116*
Tour 3: Granville Island *118*
Downtown Vancouver Dining *130*
Greater Vancouver Dining *131*
Vancouver Lodging *138*
Downtown Victoria *147*

Foreword

We wish to express our gratitude to those who have helped with this guide, including Seattle/King County News Bureau, especially Barry Anderson and David Blandford; Elvira Quarin at Tourism Vancouver; Robert Brown with the Canadian Consulate General; and Hinda Simon.

While every care has been taken to ensure the accuracy of the information in this guide, the passage of time will always bring change, and consequently, the publisher cannot accept responsibility for errors that may occur.

All prices and opening times quoted here are based on information supplied to us at press time. Hours and admission fees may change, however, and the prudent traveler will avoid inconvenience by calling ahead.

Fodor's wants to hear about your travel experiences, both pleasant and unpleasant. When a hotel or restaurant fails to live up to its billing, let us know and we will investigate the complaint and revise our entries where the facts warrant it.

Send your letters to the editors of Fodor's Travel Publications, 201 E. 50th Street, New York, NY 10022.

Highlights and Fodor's Choice

Highlights

Seattle Known as one of the most liveable cities in the country, Seattle's tourism brings much money into the state, and the strong political contingent who are determined to maintain a balance between nature and development continues to grow. The city's cultural scene is flourishing, too, with repertories growing as quickly as its already solid world-class reputation for the progressive attitude toward the arts, dance, and theater. The **Seattle Art Museum,** scheduled to open in 1992, is a five-story post-modern-style building where Asian, Native American, Oceanic, African, and pre-Columbian art will be housed.

Vancouver Maintaining its speed in the fast lane, Vancouver prepares for the **Indy Vancouver,** part of the PPG Indy Car World Series. One of 16 international car races, the 1.7-mile circuit will run through downtown during Labour Day weekend. The city continues to make the headlines as plans for North America's largest urban development project gets underway, beginning with the former site of Vancouver's Expo 86. **International Village,** the first phase, sits adjacent to Chinatown and will be a mixture of condominiums, town houses, an office tower, hotels, parks, and commercial space. The entire project will not be completed for about 20 years.

Fodor's Choice

No two people will agree on what makes a perfect vacation, but it's fun and helpful to know what others think. We hope you'll have a chance to experience some of Fodor's Choices yourself in Seattle and Vancouver. For detailed information about each entry, refer to the appropriate chapter.

Seattle

Attractions International District

Pike Place Market

Seattle Aquarium

Space Needle

Hotels Alexis *(Very Expensive)*

Four Seasons *(Very Expensive)*

Edgewater *(Expensive)*

Sorrento *(Expensive)*

Inn at the Market *(Moderate–Expensive)*

Meany Tower Hotel *(Inexpensive)*

Restaurants Canlis *(Very Expensive)*

Cafe Alexis *(Expensive)*

Wild Ginger *(Moderate)*

Hien Vuong *(Inexpensive)*

Special Moments Sitting in on the "Out to Lunch" concert series at one of Seattle's parks

Seeing Seattle at night from the Space Needle's observation deck

Reading the hundreds of name tiles on the floor of the Pike Place Market

Seeing Mt. Rainier looming over Puget Sound on a clear day when "the mountain comes out"

Vancouver

Attractions Dr. Sun-Yat Sen Classical Garden, Chinatown

Granville Public Market, Granville Island

Museum of Anthropology, on University of British Columbia campus

Maritime Museum, Granville Island

Stanley Park Zoo

Hotels	Le Meridien *(Very Expensive)*
	Pan Pacific *(Very Expensive)*
	Wedgewood Hotel *(Expensive)*
	Georgia Hotel *(Moderate)*
	West End Guest House *(Moderate)*
	Sylvia Hotel *(Inexpensive)*
Restaurants	Chartwell *(Expensive)*
	Tojo's *(Expensive)*
	Kirin Mandarin Restaurant *(Moderate)*
	Rubina Tandoori *(Moderate)*
	Szechuan Chongqing *(Inexpensive)*
Shopping	Chinatown
	Fourth Avenue (between Burrard and Balsam streets)
	Pacific Centre Mall
	Robson Street

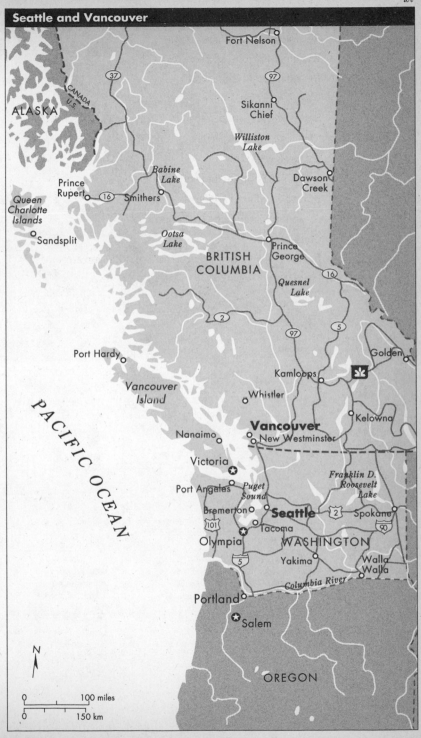

Seattle and Vancouver

Fort Nelson

37

97

Sikanni
Chief

CANADA
U.S

ALASKA

*Williston
Lake*

*Babine
Lake*

Dawson
Creek

Prince
Rupert

16

Smithers

*Queen
Charlotte
Islands*

Sandsplit

*Ootsa
Lake*

BRITISH
COLUMBIA

Prince
George

16

*Quesnel
Lake*

2

97

5

Golden

Port Hardy

Kamloops

*Vancouver
Island*

Whistler

Kelowna

Nanaimo

Vancouver
New Westminster

PACIFIC OCEAN

Victoria

*Franklin D.
Roosevelt
Lake*

Port Angeles

*Puget
Sound*

Bremerton

2

Seattle

Spokane

101

Tacoma

90

Olympia

WASHINGTON

5

Yakima

Walla
Walla

Columbia River

Portland

Salem

N

OREGON

0   100 miles

0   150 km

World Time Zones

Numbers below vertical bands relate each zone to Greenwich Mean Time (0 hrs.).
Local times frequently differ from these general indications,
as indicated by light-face numbers on map.

Algiers, **29**

Anchorage, **3**

Athens, **41**

Auckland, **1**

Baghdad, **46**

Bangkok, **50**

Beijing, **54**

Berlin, **34**

Bogotá, **19**

Budapest, **37**

Buenos Aires, **24**

Caracas, **22**

Chicago, **9**

Copenhagen, **33**

Dallas, **10**

Delhi, **48**

Denver, **8**

Djakarta, **53**

Dublin, **26**

Edmonton, **7**

Hong Kong, **56**

Honolulu, **2**

Istanbul, **40**

Jerusalem, **42**

Johannesburg, **44**

Lima, **20**

Lisbon, **28**

London (Greenwich), **27**

Los Angeles, **6**

Madrid, **38**

Manila, **57**

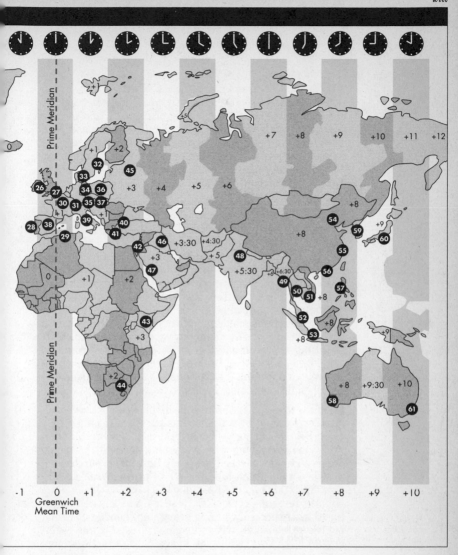

Mecca, **47**
Mexico City, **12**
Miami, **18**
Montreal, **15**
Moscow, **45**
Nairobi, **43**
New Orleans, **11**
New York City, **16**

Ottawa, **14**
Paris, **30**
Perth, **58**
Reykjavík, **25**
Rio de Janeiro, **23**
Rome, **39**
Saigon, **51**

San Francisco, **5**
Santiago, **21**
Seoul, **59**
Shanghai, **55**
Singapore, **52**
Stockholm, **32**
Sydney, **61**
Tokyo, **60**

Toronto, **13**
Vancouver, **4**
Vienna, **35**
Warsaw, **36**
Washington, DC, **17**
Yangon, **49**
Zürich, **31**

Introduction

A native New York native, Phil has found his way to Seattle where he is a freelance writer and editor.

The first time I visited Seattle, I took with me preconceived ideas about the Pacific Northwest. A friend who had moved here recently was full of stories about camping on the weekends, biking after work, and theater tickets that cost the same price as movies tickets in New York. Articles in the national press raved about the region's natural beauty, cultural vibrancy, and healthy economy. "America's Most Livable City," they touted, referring to Seattle. So I arrived with high expectations.

The weather was ideal. We went to Orcas Island—a short drive and ferry ride from Seattle—and camped on a bluff overlooking Puget Sound. My friend fell asleep, and I lay on my back in front of a dying fire, beneath stellar patterns I had rarely noticed before, and considered how inadequate my life in New York was, how suited I was to the natural, more wholesome lives people led in the Great Northwest. All of what I had heard seemed true: I felt I had found the ideal blend of natural splendor and urban sophistication, where a rain forest could mingle in perfect harmony with a modern metropolis. The next day we drove to the top of Mt. Constitution, the highest peak on the island. From this privileged perspective, I surveyed virtually the whole pristine region, including Puget Sound, Vancouver Island, and the Olympic Mountains. I decided to move west.

Needless to say, I suffered some disillusionment. I can remember waiting for a taxi at SeaTac Airport on my first day in Seattle, trying to decide if the mist demanded an umbrella and wondering why everything suddenly looked so dreary. Two days later I made my first major purchase in Seattle—a mountain bike. Eager to prove myself an outdoorsman, that evening I pedaled to a party on Queen Anne Hill; the terrain—typical for Seattle—was a little steeper than I had expected. Cursing every step, I ended up climbing the arduous hill, with bike alongside me. I was beginning to learn that, while the image of the great outdoors meeting the great metropolis evokes drama, if not romance, the two forces don't always create the most comfortable situations.

Last December, for instance, a snowstorm hit Seattle, leaving the steep hills sheathed in ice. As a New York native, I expected salt on the sidewalks, sand on the streets, and a fairly active city the next day. Not a chance. Many of the busiest streets hadn't been plowed, cars were abandoned by the side of the road, and businesses and schools were shut down. The message was clear: If you live on the Pacific North Coast, you must accept nature's tendency to disrupt and inconvenience you. Houses slide down eroded slopes into Puget Sound, volcanoes erupt, and it rains and rains and rains. Rigidity, outrage, obstinate determination, or any other form of hubris can get you into trouble. I was the only passenger on a bus one night, and the bus driver drove three blocks off his route to drop me at the door of my destination. Sure, he was being kind, but it's more than that. Native northwesterners are used to adjustments, and they make them without thinking twice.

My enchanted experience on Orcas Island was no fluke. If nature disrupts, its grace and power also inspires. On a clear day in Seattle, Mt. Rainier floats, dreamlike, over the industrial southern end of the city; the Cascade Mountains reign in the east, looming over Lake Washington; in the west, the Olympics rise over Bainbridge Island and Elliott Bay, and ragged clouds turn an evening sky into an explosion of color. Standing at the seawall in Vancouver's Stanley Park, the mountains rest at what seems like just an arm's reach across Burrard Inlet. Take just a few steps onto one of the park trails and you feel as though you're lost in a virgin forest, with no sign of city life.

If the weather has been especially depressing, I seize the first clear day and rent a canoe at the University of Washington waterfront in Seattle. The channels at the University Arboretum give way to Lake Washington, fringed by the Cascade Mountains. Inevitably, I feel serene, as I did on Orcas Island, and the Northwest once again becomes the ideal place to live.

But residents of Seattle and Vancouver don't just paddle away their days. Politics run hot here, and local leaders work hard to maintain legislation that has helped to protect the environment of the cities and their surroundings. Likewise, advocates deserve kudos for their efforts to restore some of the history that went into the makings of Seattle and Vancouver. In 1971, the Canadian Government bought Granville Island, which was originally used to store logging supplies. Today, only businesses that deal with maritime activities, the arts, and a public market are permitted to set up shop on the island. A walk around the island will lead you past produce stalls, crafts merchants, food vendors, and artists' studios. Around the same time as the Granville Island purchase, Vancouver embarked on the restoration of Gastown, a historic area by the waterfront and named for "Gassy" Jack Deighton, who opened the settlement's first saloon. By the time Deighton died in 1875, a bawdy and sometimes lawless townsite had sprouted in the vicinity of his saloon. In one way, the area remained faithful to his vision, as it proceeded for the next 100 years to attract an abundance of drunks. In 1960, more than two-thirds of all arrests in Vancouver were made in the vicinity of the old Deighton House. Some of the old buildings remain, but until the rehabilitation the squalor of the neighborhood was more prominent than its history. Today boutiques, galleries, restaurants, and a steam-powered clock line the cobblestone streets of this touted tourist spot—a worthy tribute to the old codger.

Vancouver's history predates Gassy Jack Deighton and the first white entourage. When the settlers arrived in Vancouver, there were, according to one witness, 10 Suquamish villages in the area. A few years later, most of the land had been claimed by the newcomers, and the villages had vanished. Fortunately, the native culture survived, and today Vancouver is the center for producing and selling native Pacific Coast crafts. Local Haida carver Bill Reid has his studio on Granville Island; galleries display the works of Inuit, Tlingit, Tsimshian, Kwakiutl, Haida, and Salish artisans; students can study the craft at the University of British Columbia; and the university's Museum of Anthropology houses one of the finest collections of native art in the world. Western techniques have been studied and incorporated into the works, but the dominant styles and the mythological references—usually related to the animal wildlife of the region—are firmly rooted in Pacific Coast cultures.

Seattle's early history began with the native Suquamish people, and the city has devoted much energy to preserving its historic neighborhoods. In the late 1800s, Seattle began to expand around a steam-powered lumber mill at the foot of a hill, in the area of what is now called Pioneer Square. Loggers cut the trees near the hilltop and skidded them down to the mill along a road that came to be known as "skid road." "Road" soon became "row," and the term lost its original significance.

By the early 1960s, Pioneer Square had lost its historic character, going the same sordid route as Gastown had in Vancouver. So Seattle undertook a massive rehabilitation of its own. Historic buildings were restored, shops and galleries moved in, and, in keeping with the theme, the city put 1890s-style uniforms on the police officers who walked the local beat.

Fortunately, Pioneer Square hasn't become overly sanitized. On my first visit to Seattle, a friend took me to a small bar on the block between the square and the waterfront. A quiet place to have a beer, she said. Soon after we sat down, a man with a gruff voice broke into a chorus of "Barnacle Bill the Sailor." When a younger man dressed in black told him to be quiet, a fight broke out. So much for the quiet beer. Most urban rehabilitations leave only the pure and clean, but Pioneer Square retains its old rowdiness, lending authenticity to the restoration. A church that feeds the homeless is right across the street from the Elliott Bay Bookstore, where well-known writers read from their latest works. On weekend nights, the OK Hotel (not really a hotel) may have slam dancing that appeals to a young, leather-adorned crowd, and just a few blocks away the busy Trattoria Mitchelli offers late-night pasta to a mixed-bag clientele. Seattle's unrefined elements nicely balance all the historical charm, making this part of town feel lived-in and real.

The city's other major restoration project was the Pike Place Market, which was originally built in 1907. The complex of lofts and stalls overlooking Elliott Bay nearly faced the demolition ball in the 1960s, but was saved by a voter referendum. Amid a maze of ramps and hallways, today's visitors shop for gourmet foods, spices, posters, jewelry, crafts, clothes, fish, and produce.

I go down to the market to get my hair cut. On my way, I pass a fish stall that's on the first level. A seller—I call him the fish-thrower—stands before an array of sea creatures displayed on beds of ice. Hoarsely, the man calls out the specials and jokes with a few potential customers. No takers, yet. Now the man is discussing a particular salmon with an older woman. He holds up the fish and lets it fly, over the heads of potential customers and into a piece of wax paper held by one of the counter merchants. Successful completion, as usual.

Now I walk down to the barbershop. Kim, my barber of choice, raises the radio volume, prattles for a while about her love life, and needles the owner, who is tending to the customer in the only other chair. He takes her ribbing in stride. The cut costs $7, and without fail there's a line out the door. My impulse is to ask the owner why he doesn't expand—get a bigger shop, with room for a new chair and another assistant. Clearly, there's a demand for it. But I can imagine his response: "You transplants are all the same, all bent on expansion." In this city, I remind myself, two chairs can be better than three. It's the same message that the Pike Place merchants are now sending to the Preservation and Development Authority, which manages the complex and nearly allowed it to slip into the control of a New York investor group. The market remains in the hands of the PDA, but merchants still worry about the future of the complex.

Of course, no one can deny that both cities have reaped at least some economic and cultural benefits from all the growth and renewal of the past few decades. Vancouver is among the busiest ports in North America, and Seattle—recognized in the past as the home of airline manufacturer Boeing—is now a center for computer technology as well, thanks to Bill Gates's Microsoft company. You can go to the theater for less than $10 in Seattle and, while a chandelier may not fall from the ceiling à la *Phantom of the Opera*, the performance is generally first-rate. Vancouver's Jazz Festival ranks among the best in the world.

All the success is also making people think. Highways are more crowded; sprawling suburbs encroach on the forests; and homelessness, drugs, and street gangs are on the rise.

In Seattle, some locals have responded by forming a group called Lesser Seattle, devoted to discouraging people from moving here. "Keep the Bastards Out," they say, only half-jokingly. But beneath the tough talk lies a simple wish they share with Vancouverites: to maintain at least some control over the recent changes in their cities. If you plan on spending some time in either Seattle or Vancouver, don't be too concerned with this talk. No one will blame you outright for all the congestion and untrammelled growth; folks out here are too polite for that. They may instead hint at it, or bait you into a statement that you'll later regret. "This rain can be depressing, huh?" A resident might feel you out with this kind of question, to see what kind of appreciation you really have. Keep your answers short, and remember that out here, two chairs are often better than three.

1 Essential Information

Before You Go

Visitor Information

For free travel information, contact the following tourism offices:

In the U.S. **Washington Tourism Development Division** (101 General Administration Bldg., Olympia, WA 98504, tel. 206/586–2088; for a *Destination Washington* travel guide, tel. 800/544–1800, ext. 2).

In Canada **Tourism British Columbia** (1117 Wharf St., Victoria, B.C. V8W 2Z2, tel. 800/663–6000).

In the U.K. For touring tips and brochures, contact the **United States Travel and Tourism Administration** (22 Sackville St., London W1X 2EA, tel. 071/439–7433), **Canadian High Commission, Tourism Division** (Canada House, Trafalgar Sq., London 5W1Y 5BJ, tel. 071/930–6857), or **Tourism British Columbia** (1 Regent St., London SW1Y 4NS, tel. 071/930–6857).

Tour Groups

Group tours pack a lot of sightseeing into a short period of time, hitting all the traditional tourist spots and some of the out-of-the-way places you might miss on your own.

Keep in mind, however, that these tours only permit you to spend as much time in any one place as the itinerary allows. If freedom and flexibility are important to you, pick up a map, decide where you want to go, plot a route, and experience the region at your own leisurely pace.

When evaluating any tour, be sure to find out: (1) exactly what expenses are included—particularly tips, taxes, service charges, side trips, meals, and entertainment; (2) the ratings of all hotels on the itinerary; (3) the cancellation policies for both you and the tour operator; and (4) if you are traveling alone, the additional cost of single, instead of double, accommodations.

Many tour companies offer reduced rates for their off-peak tours (i.e., May–June and September–October). These "shoulder season" rates can be bargains, and the weather and scenery is often just as good as in the peak summer season. Listed below is a sample of available operators and packages. For additional resources, contact your travel agent or the tourist office of the state or province you plan to visit. All may be booked through your travel agent.

General-Interest Tours **Westours** (300 Elliott Ave. W, Seattle, WA 98119, tel. 206/281–3535 or 800/426–0327) operates an extensive motorcoach tour program in Alaska and British Columbia. Itineraries are designed to coincide with the Vancouver departures and arrivals of Holland America Line cruise ships.

Princess Tours (2815 2nd Ave., Suite 400, Seattle, WA 98121, tel. 206/728–4202) offers motorcoach tours through Alaska and British Columbia that connect with Princess Cruise Line departures from Vancouver.

Brennan Tours (1402 3rd Ave., Suite 717, Seattle, WA 98101, Seattle, WA tel. 206/622–9155 or 800/237–7249) has 9- to 12-day motorcoach tours that begin and end in Seattle and travel through Washington, British Columbia, and Alberta.

Gadabout Tours (700 E. Tahquitz Way, Palm Springs, CA 92262, tel. 619/325–5556) offers a 12-day "Pacific Ports of Call" as well a 15-day tour of Oregon and Washington.

Globus–Gateway (150 S. Los Robles Ave., Pasadena, CA 91101, tel. 818/449–0919 or 800/556–5454) takes you from San Francisco to Vancouver in nine days.

Gray Line of Seattle (720 S. Forest St., Seattle, WA 98134, tel. 206/624–5813) features two- to seven-day tours of the region, including the "Northwest Triangle" of Seattle, Vancouver, and Victoria.

Maupintour (Box 807, Lawrence, KA 66044, tel. 913/843–1211 or 800/255–4266) explores Pacific Northwest seaports in eight days.

Britons The following U.K. tour operators feature tour packages to cities in the Pacific North Coast: **Canada Air Holidays** (50 Sauchiehall St., Glasgow G2 3AG, tel. 041/332–1511) makes group and individual flight arrangements to Canada in both summer and winter seasons.

All Canada Travel & Holidays (All Canada House, 90 High St., Lowestoft, Suffolk NR32 1XN, tel. 0502/585825), a full-service tour company offers escorted and independent tours to Western Canada.

Countrywide Holidays Association (109 Birch Heys, Cromwell Range, Manchester, England M14 6HU, tel. 061/257–2055) has wilderness programs to British Columbia that include hiking, mountain biking, and river rafting.

Jetsave Travel Ltd. (Sussex House, London Rd., East Grinstead, West Sussex RH19 1LD, tel. 0342/328231) offers fully inclusive tour packages featuring motorcoach tours, car and motorhome rentals with set itineraries throughout the Pacific Northwest, Alaska cruises, and rail tours.

Special-Interest **Cruise West** (4th and Battery Bldg., Suite 400, Seattle, WA Tours 98121, tel. 206/441–8687) allows you to see the San Juan Islands *Cruises* and towns on Vancouver Island as if you were on your own 82-passenger yacht. Ports of call include Friday Harbor, Roche Harbor, Deer Harbor and Port Townsend on Vancouver Island. The three-day cruise departs Seattle every Friday in April, May, September, and October, and costs $300–$600.

Package Deals for Independent Travelers

Americans **American Airlines** (tel. 800/433–7300) and **United Airlines** (tel. 800/328–6877) both offer independent fly/drive packages that start in the region's major cities.

Britons **Go Vacations** (95 High St., Burnham, Slough, Berks, England SL1 7JZ, tel. 06286/68061) books motorhome trips that originate in Vancouver and Seattle.

Air Canada (tel. 081/759–2636) offers a Flexipass that provides travel to and from any North American city served by the carrier. Passengers must be residents of the United Kingdom and purchase their passes within the commonwealth.

American Connections (7 York Way, Lancaster Rd., High Wycombe, Buckinghamshire HP12 3PY, tel. 0494/473173) offers clients a brochure of ground-only items that can be built up into a package including transatlantic flights or bought as separate arrangements for independent travelers to North America.

When to Go

June through September are the most popular months to visit Seattle and Vancouver because the region's mild, pleasant climate is at its best then. Summer temperatures generally range in the 70s, and rainfall is usually minimal. Nights, however, can be cool, so if you're going to enjoy the nightlife, take along a sweater or jacket.

Hotels in the major tourist destinations are often filled in July and August, so it is important to book reservations in advance.

Spring and fall are also excellent times to visit. The weather usually remains quite good, plus the prices for accommodations, transportation, and tours can be lower (and the crowds much smaller) in the most popular destinations.

In winter, the coastal rain turns to snow in the nearby mountains, making the region a skier's dream. As such, world-class ski resorts such as British Columbia's Whistler Village, north of Vancouver, are luring a growing number of winter visitors from around the world.

Climate Tempered by a warm Japan current and protected by the mountains from the extreme weather conditions found inland, the coastal regions of Washington and British Columbia experience a uniformly mild climate.

Average daytime summer highs are in the 70s; winter temperatures are generally in the 40s, with snow uncommon in the lowland areas. If it does snow (usually in December or January), everything grinds to a halt—but the children love it!

Seattle has an average of only 36 inches of rainfall a year—less than New York, Chicago, or Miami. The wetness, however, is concentrated during the winter months, when cloudy skies and drizzly weather persist. More than 75% of Seattle's annual precipitation occurs from October through March.

The following are average daily maximum and minimum temperatures for Seattle and Vancouver.

Seattle	**Jan.**	45F	7C	**May**	66F	19C	**Sept.**	69F	20C
		35	2		47	8		52	11
	Feb.	50F	10C	**June**	70F	21C	**Oct.**	62F	16C
		37	3		52	11		47	8
	Mar.	53F	12C	**July**	76F	24C	**Nov.**	51F	10C
		38	3		56	13		40	4
	Apr.	59F	15C	**Aug.**	75F	24C	**Dec.**	47F	8C
		42	5		55	13		37	3

Vancouver	Jan.	41F	5C	May	63F	17C	Sept.	64F	18C
		32	0		46	8		50	10
	Feb.	46F	8C	June	66F	19C	Oct.	57F	14C
		34	1		52	11		43	6
	Mar.	48F	9C	July	72F	22C	Nov.	48F	9C
		36	2		55	13		37	3
	Apr.	55F	13C	Aug.	72F	22C	Dec.	45F	7C
		41	5		55	13		34	1

Current weather information for more than 500 cities around the world can be obtained by calling **WeatherTrak** (tel. 900/370–8728). A taped message will instruct you to dial the three-digit access code for the destination you're interested in. For a list of access codes, send a stamped, self-addressed envelope to Cities, Box 7000, Dallas, TX 75209. For further information, call 214/869–3035 or 800/247–3282.

Festivals and Seasonal Events

Major cities of the Pacific North Coast come alive each year in a burst of colorful festivities. The following is a sample of noteworthy seasonal events. For dates and more details, contact the local tourism departments.

Seattle **Late May. Northwest Folklife Festival** lures musicians and artists to Seattle for one of the largest folk fests in the United States. Tel. 206/684–7200.

Mid-July. Bite of Seattle serves up sumptuous specialties from the city's finest restaurants. Tel. 206/232–2982.

Mid-July–early Aug. Seafair, Seattle's biggest event of the year, kicks off with a torchlight parade through downtown and culminates in hydroplane races on Lake Washington. Tel. 206/728–0123.

Late Aug.–early Sept. Bumbershoot, a Seattle festival of the arts, presents more than 400 performers in music, dance, theater, comedy, and the visual and literary arts. Tel. 206/684–7200.

Vancouver **Mid-May. Vancouver Children's Festival,** the largest event of its kind in the world, presents dozens of performances in mime, puppetry, music, and theater. Tel. 604/687–7697.

Late May. Swiftsure Race Weekend draws more than 300 competitors to Victoria's harbor for an international yachting event. Tel. 604/592–2441.

Late May. Victoria Day, a national holiday, is usually celebrated throughout Canada on the penultimate weekend in May.

Late June. Canadian International Dragon Boat Festival, Vancouver, is a multicultural festival featuring dragon boat races, which are based on Chinese legend; community and children's activities; dance; and visual arts. Tel. 604/684–5151.

Late June. Du Maurier International Jazz Festival celebrates a broad spectrum of jazz, blues, and related improvised music, with more than 200 performances in 20 locations in Vancouver. Tel. 604/682–0706.

July 1. Canada Day inspires celebrations around the country in honor of Canada's birthday.

Mid-July. Vancouver Sea Festival features water-related activities, such as a wooden- and heritage-boat festival, plus a parade, fireworks, entertainment, and a carnival. Tel. 604/684–3378.

Late July. International Bathtub Race takes to the high seas, from Nanaimo to Vancouver. Tel. 604/754–8474.

Mid-Aug.–early Sept. Pacific National Exhibition, western Canada's biggest annual fair, brings top-name entertainment and a variety of displays to Vancouver. Tel. 604/253–2311.

What to Pack

Clothing Residents of Seattle and Vancouver are generally informal by nature and wear clothing to match their disposition. During the summer, the days are warm but evenings can cool off substantially. Layered clothing is the local preference—sweatshirts, sweaters, and jackets are removed or put on as the day progresses. If you plan to explore the region's cities on foot, or if you choose to hike along mountain trails or beaches, bring comfortable walking shoes.

Dining out is usually an informal affair, although some restaurants require a jacket and tie for men and dresses for women. Residents tend to dress conservatively when going to the theater or symphony, but it's not uncommon to see some patrons wearing jeans. In other words, almost anything is acceptable for most occasions.

Passengers aboard cruise ships bound for Alaska should check with their travel agents about the dress code on board. Some vessels expect formal attire for dinner, while others do not. In all cases, you will need a waterproof coat and warm clothes if you plan to spend time on deck.

Miscellaneous It is often a good idea to pack an extra pair of eyeglasses, contact lenses, or prescription sunglasses when traveling. Also, be sure to pack any prescription medicines that you use regularly as well as any allergy medications you might need. Take along, too, a copy of any current prescription in case it needs to be refilled while you are away.

Carry-on Luggage Passengers aboard U.S. and Canadian airlines are usually limited to two carry-on bags. On U.S. carriers, bags stored under the seat must not exceed 9″ × 14″ × 22″; bags hung in a closet can be no larger than 4″ × 23″ × 45″; and bags in overhead bins must not exceed 10″ × 14″ × 36″ in total dimensions. Items exceeding these dimensions may be restricted from the cabin and sent through as checked baggage. Keep in mind that airlines adapt these rules to circumstances; on a crowded flight, you may be allowed only one carry-on bag.

In addition to two carryons, passengers may also bring aboard a handbag; an overcoat or wrap; an umbrella; a camera; a reasonable amount of reading material; an infant bag; and crutches, a cane, braces, or other prosthetic device. Infant/child safety seats can also be brought aboard if parents have purchased a ticket for the child or if there is space in the cabin.

Checked Luggage Passengers are generally allowed to check two or three pieces of luggage, none of which can exceed 62 inches (length + width + height) or weigh more than 70 pounds. Baggage allowances vary among airlines, so check with the carrier before departure.

Taking Money Abroad

To get the best exchange rate for your money, convert it into local currency at a bank or recognized currency exchange office (rather than at a hotel). It's a good idea to exchange at least a small amount of money before leaving home, because you may arrive at your destination when these offices are not open. Currency can be favorably exchanged at **Deak International** offices (630 5th Ave., New York, NY 10011, tel. 212/635–0515). Contact them for a list of their office locations.

Major credit cards and traveler's checks are widely accepted throughout the region. The most recognized traveler's checks are from American Express, Barclay's, Thomas Cook, and those issued through major commercial banks such as Citibank and Bank of America. Some banks will issue traveler's checks free to established customers, but most charge a 1% commission. Remember to take along addresses of offices where you can get refunds for lost or stolen traveler's checks.

It's a good idea to carry at least one major credit card when traveling, particularly for hotel and car rental payments, where you will probably be asked for a credit card in place of a cash deposit.

Getting Money from Home

There are at least three ways to get money from home: (1) Have it sent through a large commercial bank with a branch in the city you're visiting. The only stipulation is that you must have an account with the bank. If not, you'll have to go through your own bank and the process will be slower and more costly. (2) Have it sent through American Express. If you are a cardholder, you can cash a personal check or a counter check at an American Express office for up to $1,000. You can also receive money through an American Express Moneygram, which enables you to obtain up to $10,000 in cash—usually within 24 hours. For further information about this service, call 800/543–4080. (3) Have money sent through Western Union (tel. 800/325–6000). If you have a MasterCard or Visa, you can have money sent for any amount up to your credit limit. If not, have someone take cash or a certified cashier's check to a Western Union office. The money will be delivered to a bank in the town where you're staying. Fees vary with the amount of money sent and the location of the recipient.

Cash Machines Virtually all banks in the United States and Canada belong to a network of automated teller machines (ATMs) that dispense cash 24 hours a day. Cards issued by Visa and MasterCard may also be used in ATMs, but the fees are usually higher than the fees on bank cards, and there is a daily interest charge on the "loan," even if monthly bills are paid on time. Each network has a toll-free number you can call to locate machines in a given city. The number for the Cirrus system, owned by Master-

Card, is 800/4–CIRRUS; the number for the Plus system, affiliated with Visa, is 800/THE–PLUS.

Currency

The United States and Canada both use the same currency denominations—dollars and cents—although each currency has a different value on the world market. In the United States the most common paper currency comes in $1, $5, $10, and $20 bills. Common notes in Canada include the $2, $5, $10, and $20 bills. (Canada recently phased out its $1 bill, replacing it with a $1 gold-colored coin, nicknamed the "loonie" by Canadians because it has a picture of a loon on one side.) Coins in both countries come in denominations of 1¢ (penny), 5¢ (nickel), 10¢ (dime), 25¢ (quarter), and 50¢.

Traveler's checks can be purchased in either U.S. or Canadian dollars at banks and other financial institutions and are generally accepted by restaurants, hotels, and other businesses for payment of goods and services.

What It Will Cost

Prices for first-class hotel rooms in major cities range from $80 to $150 a night, although you can still find some "value" hotel rooms for $50–$60 a night. Most hotels offer weekend packages that offer discounts up to 50%. Don't look for these special deals during the peak summer season, however, when hotels are filled nearly to capacity. Compared with many other parts of the world, the Pacific North Coast is a travel bargain. The region is becoming increasingly popular with Japanese visitors, for example, who find prices for hotels, meals, and commodities to be quite a steal.

Prices in Canada are always quoted in Canadian dollars. When comparing rates with those in the United States, costs should be calculated via the current rate of exchange.

The amount of sales tax levied on goods and services varies among areas. The sales tax in Washington, for example, is 7.9%. The city of Seattle adds another 5% onto its hotel rooms. Canada's 7% Goods & Services Tax (GST) is added onto hotel bills, but will be rebated to foreign visitors. In British Columbia, consumers pay an 8% provincial tax. Where approved, an additional 2% is levied by local municipal governments.

Passports and Visas

Americans/ Citizens and permanent residents of the United States and
Canadians Canada do not require passports or visas to visit each other's country. However, native-born citizens should carry identification showing proof of citizenship, such as a birth certificate, a voter-registration card, or a valid passport. Naturalized citizens should carry a naturalization certificate or some other proof of citizenship. Permanent residents of the United States who are not U.S. citizens should carry their Alien Registration Receipt Cards. U.S. citizens interested in visiting Canada for more than 90 days may apply for a visa that allows them to stay for six months. For more information, contact the Canadian Embassy (501 Pennsylvania Ave., NW, Washington, DC 20001, tel. 202/682–1740).

Britons To enter the United States or Canada, you will need a valid, 10-year British passport (cost £15 for a standard 32-page passport, £30 for a 94-page passport). Note that a one-year British passport is not acceptable for entry under any circumstances. You can obtain passport application forms from most travel agents and major post offices, or from the **Passport Office** (Clive House, 70 Petty France, London SW1H 9HD, tel. 071/279–3434 or 071/279–4000).

You will not need a visa if you are staying in the United States for less than 90 days, have a return or onward ticket on a major airline, and complete a visa waiver form and an arrival/departure card. There are some exceptions to this, so check with your travel agent or with the Visa Unit of the **United States Embassy** (Visa and Immigration Dept., 5 Upper Grosvenor St., London W1A 2JB, tel. 071/499–3443 for recorded information or 071/499–7010). Visa applications must be made by mail. Britons are required, however, to have a visa for the United States if they are entering from Canada. Again, confirm requirements with the U.S. Embassy in London.

British visitors are not required to have a visa to enter Canada. Their stay in Canada, however, cannot exceed six months without authorization from Canadian immigration.

Customs

Customs regulations between the United States and Canada are among the most liberal in the world. Americans may bring home from Canada $400 in foreign goods, as long as you've been out of the United States for at least 48 hours and you haven't made an international trip in 30 days. Each member of the family is entitled to the same exemption regardless of age, and exemptions may be pooled. Visitors to Canada who meet the minimum age requirements of the province of entry (19 years in British Columbia) may take in either 1.1 liters (40 ounces) of liquor or wine or 24 12-ounce cans or bottles of beer. Visitors over 16 may take in 50 cigars, 200 cigarettes, and one kilogram (2.2 pounds) of manufactured tobacco. Gifts valued at less than C$40 each can also be brought into Canada, providing they do not contain tobacco or alcohol. Gifts valued at more than C$40 are subject to regular import duty on the excess amount.

Visitors age 21 or over can take into the United States 200 cigarettes or 50 cigars, or two kilograms of tobacco; one liter of alcohol; and duty-free gifts to a value of $100. For further information on United States customs regulations, write to the **United States Customs Service** (1301 Constitution Ave. NW, Washington, DC 20229).

Returning to the United Kingdom, you may bring home: (1) 200 cigarettes or 100 cigarillos or 50 cigars or 250 grams of tobacco; (2) two liters of table wine with additional allowances for (a) one liter of alcohol over 22% by volume (most spirits), (b) two liters of alcohol under 22% by volume (fortified or sparkling wine), or (c) two more liters of table wine; (3) 60 milliliters of perfume and 250 milliliters of toilet water; and (4) other goods up to a value of £32, but not more than 50 liters of beer or 25 lighters. For further information, contact **HM Customs and Excise** (Dorset House, Stamford St., London SE1 9PS, tel. 071/620–1313).

Canada has very strict gun control laws. Firearms with no legitimate sporting or recreational use are not allowed into the country. This includes all handguns, automatic weapons, and any rifle or shotgun that has been modified. For further information on Canadian customs regulations, write to **Revenue Canada** (Customs and Excise, Ottawa, Ont. K1A 0L5, tel. 613/993–6220)

Traveling with Film

If your camera is new, shoot and develop a few rolls of film before leaving home. Pack some lens tissue and an extra battery for built-in light meters. Invest about $10 in a skylight filter; it will protect the lens and also reduce haze in your pictures.

Hot weather can damage film, so if you're driving in summer, don't store film in the glove compartment or on the shelf under the rear window. Put it behind the front seat on the floor, on the side opposite the exhaust pipe. Try to avoid leaving film in a parked car on sunny days.

On a plane trip, never pack unprocessed film in checked luggage. If your bags get X-rayed, you can say goodbye to your pictures. Always carry undeveloped film with you through security and ask to have it inspected by hand. It helps to keep your film in a plastic bag, ready for quick inspection. Inspectors at U.S. airports are required to honor requests for hand inspection of film.

If your film gets fogged and you want an explanation, send it to the National Association of Photographic Manufacturers (550 Mamaroneck Ave., Harrison, NY 10528). Experts will try to determine what went wrong. The service is free.

Language

English is the language predominantly spoken in Seattle and Vancouver. It is not uncommon, however, to hear many other languages spoken on the street, both by visitors and by residents who have immigrated to the area in recent years. Partly because of the region's proximity to the Pacific Rim, the Asian influence is becoming increasingly widespread. Other ethnic groups also contribute to the populations of the region's major cities. Canada is officially a bilingual country (English and French). You will see many signs and services offered in both languages; however, little French is spoken on Canada's west coast.

Staying Healthy

There are no serious health risks associated with travel to Seattle and Vancouver, and no special shots are required before visiting the area. People with heart conditions may want to check the elevations of mountain passes on highways they plan to travel. Some passes may be higher than 5,000 feet and could affect people with respiratory problems. If you have a health problem that may require prescription drugs, have your doctor write a prescription using the generic name, because brand names can vary widely. The prescription can also help to eliminate delays at border crossings.

Insurance

Health and Accident **In the U.S.** Hospital and medical services are excellent in the United States and Canada, but hospital care in particular, can be very expensive, so before leaving home, be sure and check your existing health-insurance policy to see if it covers health expenses incurred while traveling or emergency medical-evacuation services abroad. If it does not, you can purchase a supplemental policy from one of the following companies: **Carefree Travel Insurance** (Box 310, 120 Mineola Blvd., Mineola, NY 11501, tel. 516/294-0220 or 800/323-3149), **International SOS Assistance** (Box 11568, Philadelphia, PA 19116, tel. 215/244-1500 or 800/523-8930), **Travel Assistance International** (1133 15th St. NW, Suite 400, Washington, DC 20005, tel. 202/331-1609 or 800/821-2828), **Travel Guard International** (1145 Clark St., Stevens Point, WI 54481, tel. 715/345-0505 or 800/782-5151), **Wallach and Company, Inc.** (Box 480, Middleburg, VA 22117, tel. 800/687-3166).

In the U.K. We recommend that to cover health and motoring mishaps, you insure yourself with **Europ Assistance** (252 High St., Croydon, Surrey CR0 1NF, tel. 081/680-1234). Also, travel insurance can be obtained from **Our Way Travel Ltd.** (Atlas House, Station Approach, Hayes, Kent BR2 7EQ, tel. 081/462-7746). It is wise to take out insurance to cover lost luggage (if your current homeowners' policies don't cover such loss). Trip-cancellation insurance is also a good idea. **The Association of British Insurers** (Aldermary House, 10-15 Queen St., London EC4, tel. 071/248-4477) will give you comprehensive advice on all aspects of holiday insurance and publishes a fact sheet on travel insurance, which can be obtained by sending a self-addressed envelope to ABI.

Lost Luggage On international flights, airlines are responsible for lost or damaged luggage of up to $9.07 per pound ($20 per kilo) for checked baggage, and up to $400 per passenger for unchecked baggage. On U.S. domestic flights, airlines are responsible for up to $1,250 per passenger in lost or damaged property.

If you're carrying valuables, take them with you on the plane or purchase additional insurance for lost, damaged, or stolen luggage. This type of coverage is available through travel agents or directly through various insurance companies. These policies may also include coverage for personal accidents, trip cancellation, default, and bankruptcy.

Two companies that issue luggage insurance are **Tele-Trip** (Box 31685, 3201 Farnam St., Omaha, NE 68131, tel. 800/228-9792) and **The Travelers Insurance Corporation** (Ticket and Travel Dept., 1 Tower Sq., Hartford, CT 06183, tel. 203/277-0111 or 800/243-3174).

Before you go, itemize the contents of each bag in case you need to file an insurance claim. Be certain to put your home or business address on each piece of luggage, including carry-on bags. If your luggage is lost or stolen and later recovered, the airline will deliver the luggage to your home free of charge.

Car Rentals

Renting a car can be a relatively inexpensive way to travel. If you're planning to do a lot of touring, check for rates that offer unlimited mileage. Most major car-rental firms have downtown and airport locations in main cities; some can be found in smaller towns as well. You can often rent a car in one location and return it to another in the same city without paying a penalty fee. However, if you return your car to a counter in another city, you may be hit with a hefty penalty charge.

A valid U.S., Canadian, or national driver's license is required to rent a car. An International Driving Permit is also accepted, but it must accompany a state or national license. In most cases, a major credit card is required as a security deposit for rentals. If you don't have a credit card, you may be asked to leave a large cash deposit as collateral.

When renting a vehicle, find out what the collision-damage waiver (usually an $8–$12 daily surcharge) covers and whether your personal insurance or credit card already covers damage to a rental car. If so, bring a photocopy of the benefits section along.

Taking a rental car across the U.S.–Canada border should not be a problem, especially if you keep a copy of the rental contract with you. It should bear an endorsement stating that the vehicle is permitted entry into the other country.

The following car rental companies have outlets throughout the Pacific North Coast: **Agency** (tel. 800/321–1972), **Avis** (tel. 800/331–1212), **Budget** (tel. 800/527–0700), **Dollar** (tel. 800/800–4000), **General** (tel. 800/327–7607), **Hertz** (tel. 800/654–3131), **National** (tel. 800/227–7368), **Rent-A-Wreck** (tel. 800/535–1391), and **Thrifty** (tel. 800/367–2277).

Rail Passes

For Britons, **Amtrak** (tel. 800/USA–RAIL) has USA Rail Passes that are good for unlimited coach travel throughout the United States for 45 days. The cost for these passes is: one region $189; two regions $269; whole country $339. Children (2–15) travel for half-fare. Rates may be slightly higher during peak season (late May–Sept.). The ticket must be purchased from a travel agent in the United Kingdom before departure. The offer does not apply to Americans or Canadians.

VIA Rail Canada (tel. 800/665–0200) offers a **Canrailpass** that is good for 30 days. Systemwide passes cost U.S. $427 (June 1–Sept. 30) and U.S. $287 (Oct. 1–May 31). Youth passes (age 24 and under) are U.S. $373 in peak season and U.S. $245 in the off-season. Tickets may be purchased in the United States or the United Kingdom from **Compass Travel** (9 Grosvenor Gardens, London SW1W 0BH, tel. 71/828–9028) or upon arrival in Canada. This offer does not apply to Canadian citizens.

Bus Passes

Greyhound offers the International Ameripass, which is good for unlimited travel throughout the United States and Canada. It is available for periods of 7, 15, and 30 days and can be purchased in the United Kingdom before you leave. Contact Greyhound International Travel (14–16 Cockspur St., London SW1Y 5BL, tel. 071/839–5591).

Student and Youth Travel

The **International Student Identity Card** (ISIC) entitles full-time students to rail passes, special fares on local transportation, student charter flights, and discounts at museums, theaters, sports events, and many other attractions. If purchased in the United States, the cost of the ISIC card gives the holder $3,000 in emergency medical insurance and a collect phone number to call in case of emergencies. Apply to the **Council on International Educational Exchange** (CIEE, 205 E. 42nd St., New York, NY 10017, tel. 212/661–1414), or in Canada, **Travel Cuts** (187 College St., Toronto, Ont. M5T 1P7, tel. 416/979–2406).

Travelers under age 26 can apply for a **Youth International Educational Exchange** (YIEE) **Card,** issued by the **Federation of International Youth Travel Organizations** (81 Islands Brugge, DK-2300 Copenhagen S, Denmark). It provides the same services and benefits as the ISIC card. The YIEE card is available in the United States from CIEE and in Canada from the **Canadian Hostelling Association** (CHA, 1600 James Naismith Dr., Suite 608, Gloucester, Ont. K1B 5N4, tel. 613/748–5638) or the **Canadian Hostelling Association, B.C. Region** (1515 Discovery St., Vancouver, B.C. V6R 4K5, tel. 604/224–7111).

An **International Youth Hostel Federation** (IYHF) membership card is the key to inexpensive dormitory-style accommodations at thousands of youth hostels around the world. Hostels aren't only for young travelers on a budget; many have accommodations for families. Most, however, provide separate sleeping quarters for men and women at rates of $7–$20 a night per person. IYHF memberships, valid for 12 months from the time of purchase, are available in the United States through **American Youth Hostels** (AYH, Box 37613, Washington, DC 20013, tel. 202/783–6161). The cost for a first-year membership is $25 for adults 18–54. Renewal thereafter is $15. For youths (age 17 and under) the rate is $10, and for senior citizens (age 55 and older) the rate is $15. Family membership is available for $35. National hostel associations can arrange special reductions for members, such as discounted rail fares or free bus travel.

Council Travel, a CIEE subsidiary, is the foremost U.S. student travel agency. It specializes in low-cost charters and serves as the exclusive U.S. agent for many student airfare bargains and student tours. CIEE's 80-page *Student Travel Catalogue* and "Council Charter" brochure are available free from any Council Travel office in the United States. In Seattle, the organization is located at 1314 N.E. 43rd Street, tel. 206/632–2448; in Portland, it is at 715 S.W. Morrison Street, Suite 600, 97205, tel. 503/228–1900.

The **Educational Travel Center** (438 N. Frances St., Madison, WI 53703, tel. 608/256–5551) is another travel specialist for student tours, bargain fares, and bookings.

Students who would like to work abroad should contact CIEE's **Work Abroad Department,** at the CIEE address given above. Various types of paid and voluntary work experiences can be arranged for up to six months. CIEE also sponsors study programs in Europe, Latin America, Asia, and Australia, and publishes many books of interest to the student traveler. These include *Work, Study, Travel Abroad: The Whole*

World Handbook and *Volunteer! The Comprehensive Guide to Voluntary Service in the United States and Abroad.*

The Information Center at the **Institute of International Education** (809 United Nations Plaza, New York, NY 10017, tel. 212/984-5413) has reference books, foreign university catalogues, study-abroad brochures, and other materials that may be consulted by students and nonstudents alike, free of charge.

Traveling with Children

Regulations about infant travel are in the process of changing. Until they do, however, if you want to be sure your infant is secure and traveling in his or her own safety seat, you must buy a seperate ticket and bring your own infant car seat. Check with the airline in advance to be sure your seat meets the required standard. For more information, write for the booklet "Child/Infant Safety Seats Acceptable for Use in Aircraft" from the **Federal Aviation Administration** (APA-200, 800 Independence Ave. SW, Washington, DC 20591, tel. 202/267-3479).

Most large hotels offer licensed baby-sitters or referrals. Hyatt Hotels, for example, feature children's programs and activities. Resorts are more likely to provide children's services than downtown hotels, which are geared to business travelers. Contact individual hotels for specifics, as facilities vary widely.

There are many exciting activities for children throughout the Pacific North Coast. Museums designed especially for children, science centers, zoos, aquariums, and parks offer children endless opportunities to use their imaginations and burn off excess energy.

Many local organizations, such as public libraries, museums, parks and recreation departments, and YMCA/YWCAs, also have special events throughout the year for children of all ages. Check local newspaper listings for activities such as plays, storytelling, sporting events, and so forth.

The Vancouver Children's Festival, held annually in May, is the largest event of its kind in the world, with dozens of troupes presenting mime, puppetry, theatrical performances, and music.

Family Travel Times, a newsletter published 10 times a year, also offers ideas for having fun with children, although not all data is specific to the Pacific North Coast area. To order the newsletter, contact **Travel with Your Children** (45 W. 18th St., 7th floor Tower, New York, NY 10011, tel. 212/206-0688).

Hints for Disabled Travelers

The **Information Center for Individuals with Disabilities** (Ft. Point Pl., 1st floor, 27-43 Wormwood St., Boston, MA 02210, tel. 617/727-5540; TDD 617/727-5236) offers useful problem-solving assistance, including lists of travel agents who specialize in tours for the disabled.

Moss Rehabilitation Hospital Travel Information Service (1200 W. Tabor Rd., Philadelphia, PA 19141-3009, tel. 215/456-9602) provides information on tourist sights, transportation, and accommodations in destinations around the world for a nominal fee.

Travel Industry and Disabled Exchange (5435 Donna Ave., Tarzana, CA 91356, tel. 818/368–5648), for a $15-per-person annual membership fee, issues a quarterly newsletter and information on travel agencies and tours.

Mobility International USA (Box 3551, Eugene, OR 97403, tel. 503/343–1284) coordinates exchange programs for disabled people around the world. For a $20 annual fee, the organization offers information on accommodations and organized study programs.

Evergreen Travel/Wings on Wheels (4114 198th SW, Lynnwood, WA 98036–5699, tel. 206/776–1184) is a recognized tour operator specializing in domestic and international travel for the disabled. Group and individual trips can be arranged.

The **Canadian Paraplegic Association** (780 S.W. Marine Dr., Vancouver, B.C. V6P 5Y7, tel. 604/324–3611) provides information to the disabled traveler about touring British Columbia. Information for the hearing-impaired is available from the **Western Institute for the Deaf** (2125 W. 7th Ave., Vancouver, B.C. V6K 1X9, tel. 604/736–7391 [voice] or 604/736–2527 [TDD]). The annual *British Columbia Accommodation Guide* (tel. 800/663–6000) includes a list of hotel facilities for persons with disabilities.

Greyhound/Trailways (tel. 800/752–4841; TDD 800/345–3109) "Helping Hand" program will carry a disabled person and companion for the price of a single fare. You must have a doctor's certificate verifying the need for assistance.

Amtrak (tel. 800/USA–RAIL) advises that you request redcap service, special seats, or wheelchair assistance when making reservations. Not all stations are equipped to provide these services. All handicapped passengers are entitled to a 25% discount off regular coach fares. A special children's handicapped fare is also available, offering qualifying children, ages 2–12, a 50% discount on already discounted children's fares. For a free copy of *Access Amtrak*, a guide to its services for elderly and handicapped travelers, write to Amtrak (400 N. Capitol St. NW, Washington, DC 20001, tel. 800/872–7245).

VIA Rail Canada (tel. 800/665–0200) will arrange preboarding for people in wheelchairs or with other special needs if given at least 24 hours notice.

Publications Twin Peaks Press publishes several useful books: *Travel for the Disabled* ($9.95), *Directory of Travel Agencies for the Disabled* ($12.95), and *Wheelchair Vagabond* ($9.95). You can order them through your local bookstore or from the publisher (Box 129, Vancouver, WA 98666, tel. 206/694–2462). Add $2 per book for postage if you are requesting the books by mail.

Access to the World: A Travel Guide for the Handicapped, by Louise Weiss, provides general information on transportation, hotels, travel agents, tour operators, and travel organizations. It is available at your local bookstore or from Henry Holt & Co. (tel. 800/247–3912) for $12.95.

Access America: An Atlas and Guide to the National Parks for Visitors with Disabilities (National Cartographic, Box 133, Burlington, VT 05402, tel. 802/655–4321) contains detailed information about access to the 37 most-visited national parks in the United States. This award-winning book is available directly from the publisher for $44.95 plus $5 shipping.

"Fly Rights," available free from the U.S. Department of Transportation (tel. 202/366–2220), offers airline service information for the handicapped.

The Easter Seal Society (521 2nd Ave. W, Seattle, WA 98119, tel. 206/281–5700) publishes *Access Seattle,* a free guide to the city's services for the handicapped.

Hints for Older Travelers

The **American Association of Retired Persons** (AARP, 601 E St. NW, Washington, DC 20049, tel. 202/434–2277) has two programs for independent travelers: (1) the Purchase Privilege Program, which offers discounts on hotels, airfare, car rentals, RV rentals, and sightseeing; and (2) the AARP Motoring Plan, provided by Amoco, which furnishes emergency road-service aid and trip-routing information. AARP also arranges group tours and cruises at reduced rates through **AARP Travel Experience from American Express Vacations** (400 Pinnacle Way, Suite 450, Norcross, GA 30071, tel. 800/927–0111). AARP members must be 50 years of age or older. Annual dues are $5 per person or per couple.

If you're planning to use an AARP or other senior-citizen identification card to obtain a reduced hotel rate, mention it at the time you make your reservation. At participating restaurants, show your card before you are seated, because discounts may be limited to certain menus, days, or hours. When renting a car, be sure to ask about special promotional rates, which may offer greater savings than the available discount.

Elderhostel (75 Federal St., 3rd floor, Boston, MA 02110–1941, tel. 617/426–7788) is an innovative program for people age 60 or older. Participants live in dormitories on some 1,200 campuses around the world. Mornings are devoted to lectures and seminars; afternoons to sightseeing and field trips. The Elderhostel catalogue is free for the first year, if you participate in a program, and costs $10 a year thereafter.

Saga International Holidays (120 Boylston St., Boston, MA 02116, tel. 800/343–0273) specializes in group travel for people age 60 or older. A selection of variously priced tours allows travelers to choose the package that meets their needs.

National Council of Senior Citizens (1331 F St. NW, Washington, DC 20004, tel. 202/347–8800) is a nonprofit advocacy group with about 5,000 local clubs across the country. Annual membership is $12 per person or couple. Members receive a monthly newspaper with travel information and an ID card that entitles them to reduced rates on hotels and car rentals.

Mature Outlook (6001 N. Clark St., Chicago, IL 60660, tel. 800/336–6330) is a travel club for people over age 50, offering discounts at participating hotels and motels and a bimonthly newsletter. Annual membership is $9.95 per person or couple. Instant membership is available at participating Holiday Inns.

Golden Age Passport is a free lifetime pass to all parks, monuments, and recreation areas run by the federal government. Travelers age 62 or older can pick one up at any national park that charges admission. The passport also provides a 50% discount on camping, boat launching, and parking.

September Days Club (tel. 800/241-5050) is run by Days Inns of America. The $12 annual membership fee for individuals or couples over 50 entitles them to reduced car-rental rates and to reductions of 15%-50% at most of the chain's 350 motels.

Greyhound/Trailways (tel. 800/752-4841; TDD 800/345-3109) offers special fares for senior citizens, subject to date and destination restrictions.

Amtrak (tel. 800/USA-RAIL) requests advance notice to provide redcap service, special seats, or wheelchair assistance at stations that are equipped to provide these services. Elderly passengers are entitled to a 25% discount on regular coach fares. There are some exceptions to these discounts; always check with Amtrak before traveling.

VIA Rail Canada (tel. 800/665-0200) offers senior citizens (60 and over) a 10% discount on basic transportation throughout its system for travel anytime and with no advance-purchase requirement. This 10% discount can also apply to off-peak reduced fares that do have advance-purchase requirements.

Publications **The International Health Guide for Senior Citizen Travelers,** by W. Robert Lange, MD, and **The Senior Citizens Guide to Budget Travel in the United States and Canada,** by Paige Palmer, are available for $4.95 and $3.95, respectively, plus $1 shipping from Pilot Books (103 Cooper St., Babylon, NY 11702, tel. 516/422-2225).

The Discount Guide for Travelers Over 55, by Caroline and Walter Weintz, lists helpful addresses, package tours, reduced-rate car rentals, and so forth, in the United States and abroad. If unavailable from your local bookstore, send $7.95 plus $1.50 shipping to Penguin USA/NAL (120 Woodbine St., Bergenfield, NJ 07621, tel. 800/526-0275).

"Fly Rights," a free brochure issued by the U.S. Department of Transportation (tel. 202/366-2220), provides information on airline services that are available to elderly passengers.

Further Reading

The late Bill Spiedel, one of Seattle's most colorful characters, wrote about the early history of the city in books full of lively anecdotes and legends; *Sons of the Profits* and *Doc Maynard* are two of his best. *Washingtonians, A Biographical Portrait of the State,* edited by David Brewster and David M. Buerge, is a series of essays on well-known and influential residents who have left their mark on the state. *Skookum,* by Shannon Applegate, is the history of an Oregon pioneer family.

At the Field's End, by Nicolas O'Connell, features interviews with 20 leading writers who are all closely connected to the Pacific North Coast and reflect the character of the region. *Whistlepunks and Geoducks—Oral Histories from the Pacific Northwest,* by Ron Strickland, is a collection of stories told by old-timers from all walks of life in Washington State. Gloria Snively's *Exploring the Seashore* offers a guide to shorebirds and intertidal plants and animals in Washington, Oregon, and British Columbia. The *Northwest Sportsman Almanac,* edited by Terry W. Sheely, provides an in-depth guide to fishing and hunting in the Pacific North Coast.

Well-known fiction writers of the region include Raymond Carver, Ursula LeGuin, Jean Auel, Ken Kesey, W. P. Kinsella, Tom Robbins, William Stafford, Walt Morey, and Norman Maclean.

Other magazines that focus on life and travel in the Pacific North Coast are *Pacific Northwest* magazine (Dexter Ave. N, Suite 101, Seattle, WA 98109, tel. 206/284–1750), *Beautiful B.C.* (929 Ellery St., Victoria, B.C. V9A 7B4, tel. 604/384–5456), and *Northwest Travel* and *Oregon Coast* (Box 18000, Florence, OR 97439, tel. 503/997–8401).

Arriving and Departing

From the U.S. by Plane

There are three types of flights: nonstop—no stops or changes of aircraft; direct—one or more stops but no change of aircraft; and connecting—at least one change of aircraft and possibly several stops as well.

Airports and Airlines There are international airports in Seattle and Vancouver. All major U.S. carriers—**Alaska** (tel. 800/426–0333), **American** (tel. 800/433–7300), **Continental** (tel. 800/525–0280), **Delta** (tel. 800/221–1212), **Northwest** (tel. 800/225–2525), **TWA** (tel. 800/221–2000), **United** (tel. 800/241–6522), and **USAir** (tel. 800/428–4322)—offer regular flights into Seattle from points throughout the United States. Nonstop flying time from New York to Seattle is approximately five hours; flights from Chicago to Seattle are about 4–4½ hours; flights between Los Angeles and Seattle take 2½ hours.

Air Canada (tel. 800/663–8868) and **Canadian Airlines International** (tel. 800/426–7000) offer frequent service from all major Canadian cities to Vancouver. **American Airlines, Continental, Delta,** and **United** fly direct to Vancouver from various points in the United States. Flying time from New York to Vancouver is about 8 hours with connections; from Chicago to the city takes about 4½ hours nonstop; and flights from Los Angeles to Vancouver are about 3 hours nonstop.

Enjoying the Flight Unless you're flying to the United States or Canada from Europe, jet lag shouldn't be a problem. There is only a three-hour time difference between the East Coast and West Coast of the United States. Because the air on a plane is dry, it helps, while flying, to drink nonalcoholic beverages. Drinking alcohol contributes to jet lag, as does eating heavy meals. Feet swell at high altitudes, so it's a good idea to remove your shoes at the beginning of the flight. Sleepers usually prefer window seats to curl up against; those who like to move about the cabin should ask for aisle seats. Bulkhead seats (located in the front row of each cabin) have more legroom. But generally, these seats are reserved for the disabled, the elderly, or parents traveling with babies.

Discount Flights The major airlines offer a range of tickets that can vary the price of any given seat by more than 300%, depending on different conditions. As a rule, the further in advance you buy the ticket, the less expensive it is but the greater the penalty (up to 100%) for canceling.

APEX (advanced purchase) tickets on any of the major airlines carry certain restrictions. They must be bought in advance (usually 21 days); they restrict your travel, usually with a minimum stay of seven days and a maximum of 90; and they also penalize you for changes—voluntary or not—in your travel plans. But if you can work around these drawbacks (and most travelers can), they are among the best-value fares available.

Other discounted fares—up to 50% below the cost of APEX tickets—can be found through consolidators, companies that buy blocks of tickets on scheduled airlines and sell them at wholesale prices. Tickets are subject to availability, so passengers must have flexible travel schedules. Also, be aware that if you change your plans, you could lose all or most of your money. As a precaution, purchase trip-cancellation insurance. Consolidators advertise in Sunday newspaper travel sections.

Another option is to join a travel club that offers special discounts to its members. Several such organizations are **Discount Travel International** (114 Forrest Ave., Narbeth, PA 19072, tel. 215/668–7184 or 800/334–9294), **Moment's Notice** (40 E. 49th St., New York, NY 10017, tel. 212/486–0503), **Traveler's Advantage** (CUC Travel Service, 40 Oakview Dr., Trumbull, CT 06611, tel. 800/648–4037), and **Worldwide Discount Travel Club** (1674 Meridien Ave., Miami Beach, FL 33139, tel. 305/534–2082).

Smoking As of 1990, smoking is banned on all routes within the 48 contiguous states, within the states of Hawaii and Alaska, to and from the U.S. Virgin Islands and Puerto Rico, and on flights of less than six hours to and from Hawaii and Alaska. The rule applies to both domestic and foreign carriers.

Canadian regulations are similar and ban smoking on all flights of less than six hours.

On a flight where smoking is permitted, you can request a no-smoking seat during check-in or when booking your ticket. If the airline tells you there are no seats available in the no-smoking section, insist on one. Department of Transportation regulations require carriers to find seats for all nonsmokers, provided they meet check-in time restrictions. These regulations apply to all international flights on U.S. domestic carriers; however, the Department of Transportation does not have jurisdiction over foreign carriers traveling out of, or into, the United States.

From the U.S. by Car

The U.S. interstate highway network provides quick and easy access to the Pacific North Coast in spite of imposing mountain barriers. From the south, I-5 runs from the U.S.–Mexico border through California, into Oregon and Washington, and ends at the U.S.–Canada border. Most of the population and economic development of Oregon and Washington is clustered along this corridor. From the east, I-90 stretches from Boston to Seattle. I-84 runs from the Midwest states to Portland.

The main entry point by car into Canada is on I-5 at Blaine, Washington, just 30 miles south of Vancouver. Two major highways enter British Columbia from the east—the Trans-Canada Highway (the longest highway in the world, running more than 5,000 miles from St. John's, Newfoundland, to Victoria, British Columbia) and the Yellowhead Highway, which runs through northern British Columbia from the Rocky Mountains to Prince Rupert.

Border-crossing procedures are usually quick and simple (*see* Passports and Visas and Customs, *above*). The I–5 border crossing at Blaine, WA, is one of the busiest anywhere between the United States and Canada. Peak traffic times at the border northbound into Canada are daily at 4 PM. Southbound, delays can be expected evenings and weekend mornings. Try to plan on reaching the border at off-peak times.

From the U.S. by Train

Amtrak (tel. 800/USA–RAIL), the U.S. passenger rail system, has daily service to the Pacific North Coast from the midwestern United States and California. The *Empire Builder* takes a northern route from Chicago to Seattle. The *Coast Starlight* begins in Los Angeles, makes stops throughout western Oregon and Washington, and terminates its route in Seattle. There are no trains that cross the border from Seattle into Canada.

Canada's passenger service, **VIA Rail Canada** (tel. 800/665–0200), operates transcontinental routes on the *Canadian* three times weekly between eastern Canada and Vancouver. During the summer months, this service expands to six weekly trips on the western leg of the trip between Jasper, Alberta, and Vancouver.

From the U.S. by Bus

Greyhound/Trailways (local listings only) operates bus service to Washington and British Columbia from various points in the United States and Canada. Bus service in North America—though fairly economical—has not been a first-class means of travel in recent years. But Greyhound and other bus companies are putting a major effort into improving service. New amenities may include an on-board host/hostess, meals, and VCRs.

From the U.K. by Plane

Airlines and Airfares British travelers coming into the Pacific North Coast can enter the main international gateways of Seattle and Vancouver.

At press time **British Airways** (tel. 081/897–4000) services Seattle from Heathrow. **KLM** (tel. 081/751–9000 in U.K., 800/777–5553 in U.S.) flies to Vancouver from 25 U.K. and Irish airports via Amsterdam. Also to Vancouver, **Air Canada** (tel. 081/759–2636) and **British Airways** departed from Heathrow; **Canadian Airlines International CAIL** (tel. 081/667–0666 in London, 0345/616–767 outside London) services Gatwick.

Fares on scheduled flights vary considerably. January to March are the cheapest months to fly, and mid-week flights nearly always offer some reductions. Round-trip, peak-season fares to Seattle begin at £530 and climb to £3,690 for a first-class ticket.

Charters **Globespan Ltd.** (tel. 0293/562690), **ASAT** (tel. 0737/778560), and **Unijet** (tel. 0444/459100) with weekly flights to Vancouver, offer sizable reductions on fares. At press time, prices began at £425 round-trip. You can also find good deals through specialized ticket agencies such as **Travel Cuts** (tel. 071/637–3161). Round-trip fares to Seattle start at about £300 in the off-season.

Staying in Seattle and Vancouver

Getting Around

By Plane In the past few years, regional air travel has changed considerably in North America. Large national carriers have given up many of their shorter routes to secondary cities. But smaller, regional companies, which are often owned by, or have joint marketing and reservation systems with, larger airlines, have taken up the slack. Instead of operating jets, they often fly turboprop planes that hold 10–50 passengers.

Leading regional carriers in the U.S. Pacific North Coast are **Horizon Air** (tel. 800/547–9308) and **United Express** (tel. 800/241–6522). The two airlines provide frequent service between cities in Washington and Oregon. Horizon Air also flies from Seattle to Vancouver and Victoria.

The two major regional carriers in Canada are **Air BC** (tel. 800/663–0522) and **Time Air** (tel. 800/426–7000). They serve communities throughout western Canada and have daily flights from Vancouver and Victoria to Seattle.

With all the water surrounding the Pacific North Coast, float planes are a common and convenient means of transportation. Accommodating 5–15 passengers, the planes fly at fairly low elevations and provide a great way to see the scenery.

Air BC has float-plane service between Vancouver and Victoria harbors in addition to its regular airport service. **Lake Union Air** (tel. 800/826–1890) operates scheduled flights and charters from Seattle to Vancouver, Victoria, and other points on Vancouver Island, and the San Juan Islands. **Kenmore Air Harbor** (tel. 800/543–9595) flies charters from Seattle to many points within the region.

By Train The Pacific North Coast has a number of scenic train routes in addition to the ones operated by Amtrak and VIA Rail Canada. The **Rocky Mountaineer** (Great Canadian Railtour Co., Ltd., 340 Brooksbank Ave., Suite 104, North Vancouver, B.C. V7J 2C1, tel. 800/665–7245) is a two-day rail trip between Vancouver and the Canadian Rockies, May–October. There are two routes—one to Banff/Calgary and one to Jasper—through landscapes considered the most spectacular in the world. An overnight hotel stop is made in Kamloops.

On Vancouver Island, VIA Rail (tel. 604/383–4324) runs the *E&N Railway* from Victoria north to Nanaimo. **BC Rail** (Box 8770, Vancouver, B.C. V6B 4X6, tel. 604/631–3500) operates daily service from its North Vancouver terminal to the town of Prince George.

By Bus   **Greyhound/Trailways** (local listings only) operates regular intercity bus routes to points throughout the region. Smaller bus companies provide service within local areas. One such service, **Pacific Coach Lines** (tel. 604/662–8074), runs from downtown Vancouver to Victoria (via the British Columbia ferry system).

Several companies operate charter bus service and scheduled sightseeing tours that last from a few hours to several days in length. Most tours can be booked locally and provide a good way for visitors to see the sights comfortably in a short period of time. **Gray Line** companies in Seattle (tel. 206/624–5077), Vancouver (tel. 604/681–8687), and Victoria (tel. 604/388–5248) run such sightseeing trips.

By Car   Highway travel in the Pacific North Coast is largely determined by the geography of the region. In Washington and British Columbia, roads that run east to west are limited to a few mountain passes.

The speed limit on U.S. interstate highways is 65 miles per hour in rural areas and 55 miles per hour in urban zones and on secondary highways. In Canada (where the metric system is used), the speed limit is usually 100 kilometers per hour on expressways and 80 kilometers per hour on secondary roads.

Vehicle insurance is compulsory in the United States and Canada. Motorists are required to produce evidence of insurance should they be involved in an accident. Visitors from other countries who plan to bring their own cars to the United States or Canada may find it difficult to get the proper insurance before leaving home. Upon arrival, they should contact an insurance agent or broker to obtain the necessary insurance for North America. Drivers who can prove (in writing) that they have had no claims in recent years will be eligible to purchase insurance at the lowest price.

Winter driving in the Pacific North Coast can sometimes present some real challenges. In coastal areas, the mild, damp climate contributes to roadways that are frequently wet. Winter snowfalls are not common (maybe only once or twice a year), but when snow does fall, traffic grinds to a halt. Road departments and municipalities simply do not have the equipment to handle snow, so the roadways quickly become treacherous and stay that way until the snow melts.

Tire chains, studs, or snow tires are essential equipment for winter travel in mountain areas. If you're planning to drive into high elevations, be sure to check the weather forecast beforehand. Even the main highway mountain passes can close because of snow conditions. The state or provincial highway departments operate snow advisory telephone lines during the winter months to give pass conditions.

Driving a car across the U.S.–Canada border is a simple process. Personal vehicles are allowed entry into the neighboring country, provided they are not to be left behind. Drivers of rental cars should bring along a copy of the rental contract, bearing an endorsement that states that the vehicle is permitted to cross the border.

The **American Automobile Association** (AAA) and the **Canadian Automobile Association** (CAA) provide full services to members of any of the Commonwealth Motoring Conference (CMC) clubs, including the Automobile Association, the Royal Automobile Club, and the Royal Scottish Automobile Club. Services are also available to members of the Alliance Internationale de l'Automobile (AIT), the Federation Internationale de l'Automobile (FIA), and the Federation of Interamerican Touring and Automobile Clubs (FITAC). By presenting membership cards, motorists are entitled to travel information, itineraries, maps, tour books, information about road and weather conditions, emergency road services, and travel-agency services.

By Ferry Ferries play an important part in the transportation network of the Pacific North Coast. In some areas, ferries provide the only form of access into and out of communities. In other places, ferries transport thousands of commuters a day to and from work in the cities. For visitors, ferries are one of the best ways to get a feel for the region and its ties to the sea. The busiest ferries operate between the mainland and Vancouver Island, carrying passengers, cars, campers, RVs, trucks, and buses.

The **British Columbia Ferry Corporation** (1112 Fort St., Victoria, B.C. V8V 4V2, tel. 604/386–3431 in Victoria; for 24-hour recorded schedule information, 604/656–0757 in Victoria or 604/685–1021 in Vancouver) operates one of the largest and most modern ferry fleets in the world, with 38 ships serving 42 ports of call along the British Columbia coast. More than 15 million passengers ride this fleet each year.

The **Washington State Ferry System** (Colman Dock, Seattle, WA 98104, tel. 800/542–7052 in WA or 206/464–6400 out of state) has 23 ferries in its fleet, which carries more than 18 million passengers a year between points on Puget Sound and the San Juan Islands. Reservations are not available on any domestic routes.

If you are planning to take a ferry, try to avoid peak commuter hours. The heaviest traffic flows are eastbound in the mornings and on Sunday evenings, and westbound Saturday mornings and on weekday afternoons. The best times for travel are 9 AM–3 PM and after 7 PM on weekdays. In July and August, you may have to wait up to two hours to take a car aboard one of the popular San Juan Islands ferries. Walk-on space is always available; if you can, leave your car behind.

Clipper Navigation (2701 Alaskan Way, Pier 69, Seattle, WA 98121, tel. 800/888–2535) operates three passenger-only jet catamarans between Seattle and Victoria; each facilitates 300 people. The *Victoria Clipper* makes the scenic crossing in just 2½ hours; the *Victoria Clipper 2* does it in less than 3 hours; and the *Victoria Clipper 3*, which stops in Friday Harbor and Port Townsend, does the trip in 5 hours.

By Cruise Ship Cruise ships travel British Columbia's Inside Passage to Alaska from mid-May through early October. Most ships start or end their seven-day journeys in Vancouver, making stops at several Alaskan ports along the way. A few companies provide land tours in conjunction with their week-long cruises into the Yukon Territory and other parts of Alaska.

More than 18 ships offer cruises to Alaska, including those operated by **Holland America Line, Princess Cruises, Cunard Line, Costa Cruises, Regency Cruise Line, Admiral Cruises, Crystal Cruises, Kloster Cruise Line,** and **World Explorer**

Cruises. For more information, contact your travel agent or the Cruise Lines International Association (CLIA, 17 Battery Pl., Suite 631, New York, NY 10004, tel. 212/425–7400).

Telephones

The telephone area codes in the Pacific North Coast are 206 for western Washington, including Seattle, and 604 for British Columbia.

Pay telephones cost 25¢ for local calls. Charge phones are also found in many locations. These phones can be used to charge a call to a telephone company credit card, your home phone, or the party you are calling: You do not need to deposit 25¢.

To reach an operator for a telephone number, dial the area code for the community you wish to call, followed by 555–1212. To obtain a local number, dial 1 followed by 555–1212. You can dial most international calls direct, but if you need assistance, dial "0" to reach an operator.

Many hotels place a surcharge on local calls made from your room and include a service charge on long-distance calls. It may be cheaper for you to make your calls from a pay phone in the hotel lobby, rather than from your room.

Mail

Postal Rates Because postage rates vary for different classes of mail and destinations, it is advisable to check with local postal authorities before mailing a letter or parcel. At press time, it costs 29¢ to mail a standard letter anywhere within the United States. Mail to Canada costs 40¢ per first ounce, and 23¢ for each additional ounce; mail to Great Britain and other foreign countries costs 50¢ per half-ounce.

First-class rates in Canada are 40¢ + 3¢ GST tax for up to 1.6 ounces of mail delivered within Canada, 46¢ + 3¢ GST tax for mail to the United States, and 80¢ + 6¢ GST tax for mail to other foreign destinations.

Receiving Mail Visitors can have letters or parcels sent to them while they are traveling by using the following address: Name of addressee, c/o General Delivery, Main Post Office, City and State/Province, U.S./Canada, Zip Code (U.S.) or Postal Code (Canada). Contact the nearest post office for further details. Any item mailed to "General Delivery" must be picked up by the addressee, in person, within 15 days or it will be returned to the sender.

Tipping

Tips and service charges are usually not automatically added to a bill in the United States or Canada. If service is satisfactory, customers generally give waiters, waitresses, taxi drivers, barbers, hairdressers, and so forth, a tip of 15%–20% of the total bill. Bellhops, doormen, and porters at airports and railway stations are generally tipped $1 for each item of luggage.

Opening and Closing Times

Most retail stores in Washington are open 9:30–6 seven days a week in downtown locations and later at suburban shopping malls. Downtown stores sometimes stay open late Thursday and Friday nights. Normal banking hours are weekdays 9–6; some branches are also open on Saturday morning.

In British Columbia, many stores close on Sunday. Outlets that cater to tourists are the notable exception. Normal banking hours in Canada are 10–3 on weekdays, with extended hours in many locations. Some banks in major cities are now open on Saturday morning.

Shopping

Seattle and Vancouver offer shoppers quite a cache of regionally made crafts and souvenirs. Some of the most distinctive items are produced by Northwest Native American artists, who manufacture prints, wood carvings, boxes, masks, and so forth. Shops in Seattle and Vancouver carry a wide variety of these objects, but art collectors can find the best selection and prices in the small communities located on Vancouver Island.

Another popular "souvenir" for visitors is freshly caught salmon. Fish vendors can pack a recent catch in a special airlines-approved box that will keep the fish fresh for a couple of days. A package of smoked salmon—which will keep even longer—is another alternative.

Public markets are among the best places to purchase salmon and other gifts. Seattle's historic Pike Place Market and Vancouver's Granville Island Market offer a wonderful array of fish stalls, fresh fruit and vegetable stands, arts and crafts vendors, and small shops that sell practically everything.

Because residents of the Pacific North Coast have such an active lifestyle, many leading manufacturers and retailers of outdoor equipment and apparel have their headquarters here. Recreation Equipment Inc. (REI) has several stores in the Seattle area that sell everything from high-quality sleeping bags and backpacks to freeze-dried food and mountain-climbing equipment. Eddie Bauer, the famous recreational clothing and equipment catalogue distributor and retailer, was founded in Seattle and still has outlets here.

Sales taxes vary depending on state or province. Washington's tax varies between 7% and 8.2%, depending on municipality; provincial sales tax in British Columbia is 6%. Canada's Goods and Services Tax (better known as GST) is a value-added tax of 7%, applicable on virtually every purchase except basic groceries and a small number of other items. Visitors to Canada, however, may claim a full rebate of the GST on any goods taken out of the country as well as on short-term accommodations. At press time, rebates could be claimed either immediately on departure from Canada at participating Duty Free Shops or by mail. Rebate forms can be picked up at most stores and hotels in Canada or can be obtained by writing to **Revenue Canada** (Visitor's Rebate Program, Ottawa, Ontario, Canada K1A 1J5). Claims must be for a minimum of $7 and can be submitted up to a year from the date of purchase. Purchases made during multiple visits to Canada can be grouped together for rebate purposes.

Participant Sports and Outdoor Activities

Bicycling   Bicycling, a popular sport in the Pacific North Coast, appeals to both families out for a leisurely ride and avid cyclists seeking a challenge on rugged mountain trails.

Several cycling organizations sponsor trips of various lengths and degrees of difficulty. For further information, contact: **Washington State Bicycle Association** (tel. 206/329–BIKE) or the **Bicycling Association of British Columbia** (1200 Hornby St., Vancouver, B.C. V6Z 2E2, tel. 604/669–BIKE).

Rentals are available from bicycle shops in most cities.

Boating   The sheltered waters of Puget Sound plus the area's many freshwater lakes, make boating one of the most popular outdoor activities in the Pacific North Coast. On sunny days, a virtual fleet of boats dot the waterways; in fact, some claimants say that there are more boats per capita in the Puget Sound area than anywhere else in the world.

Because of the region's mild climate, it is possible to enjoy boating throughout the year. Charters, which are available with or without a skipper and crew, can be rented for a period of a few hours up to several days. The calm waterways are also rated as among the best in the world for sea kayaking, an appealing way to explore the intertidal regions.

The area's swift rivers also provide challenges to avid canoers and kayakers. A word of warning, however: Many of these rivers should be attempted only by experienced boaters. Check with local residents about what dangers may lie downstream before taking to the waterways.

Climbing/   The mountains of the Pacific North Coast have given many an
Mountaineering   adventurer quite a challenge. It is no coincidence that many members of the U.S. expedition teams to Mt. Everest have come from this region.

With expert training and advanced equipment, mountaineering can be a safe sport, but you should never go climbing without an experienced guide. Classes are available from qualified instructors. For more information, contact: **The Mountaineers** (300 3rd Ave. W, Seattle, WA 98119, tel. 206/284–8484) or **Rainier Mountaineering Inc.** (Paradise, WA 98397, tel. 206/569–2227).

Fishing   The coastal regions and inland lakes and rivers of the Pacific North Coast are known for their excellent fishing opportunities. Fishing lodges, many of which are accessible only by float plane, cater to anglers looking for the ultimate fishing experience.

Visiting sportsmen must possess a nonresident license for the state or province in which they plan to fish. Licenses are available at sporting goods stores, bait shops, and other outlets in popular fishing areas.

For information on fishing regulations, contact: **Washington Department of Fisheries** (Administration Bldg., Room 115, Olympia, WA 98505, tel. 206/753–6600 for salmon-fishing or marine licenses, tel. 206/753–5700 for freshwater licenses). In British Columbia, separate licences are required for saltwater and freshwater fishing. Information and licences for saltwater fishing can be obtained from the **Department of Fisheries and Oceans** (555 W. Hastings St., Vancouver, B.C. V6B 5G2, tel. 604/666–3545). For freshwater fishing, contact the **Ministry of Environment, Fish and Wildlife Information** (Parliament Buildings, Victoria, B.C. V8V 1X5 tel. 604/387–9737).

Most coastal towns have charter boats and crews that are available for deep-sea fishing. State and provincial tourism departments can provide further information on charters.

Golf   The Pacific North Coast has many excellent golf courses, but not all of them are available to the public. Consequently, visitors may find it difficult to arrange a tee time at a popular course. If you are a member of a golf club at home, check to see if your club has a reciprocal playing arrangement with any of the private clubs in the areas that you will be visiting.

Hiking   There are many trails in the Pacific North Coast that are geared to both beginning and experienced hikers. The **National Parks and Forests Outdoor Recreation Information Center** (915 2nd Ave., Room 442, Seattle, WA 98174, tel. 206/553–0170) can provide maps of trails that are well marked and well maintained. Guidebooks that describe the best trails in the area are readily available in local bookstores. The *Footsore* series of books, published by The Mountaineers (306 2nd Ave. W, Seattle, WA 98119, tel. 206/285–2665), are among the best.

Hunting   Autumn visitors to the Pacific North Coast will find opportunities for deer hunting and waterfowl hunting in the coastal areas and around inland lakes. Big-game hunters, who are on the trail for elk, moose, and bear, should go to British Columbia or Alaska where outfitters are available to act as guides.

For more information on hunting facilities and licenses contact: **Washington State Game Department** (600 N. Capitol Way, Olympia, WA 98504, tel. 206/753–5700) or **British Columbia Ministry of Environment, Wildlife Branch** (780 Blanshard St., Victoria, B.C. V8W 2H1, tel. 604/387–9737).

Skiing   Skiing is by far the most popular winter activity in the area. Moist air off the Pacific Ocean dumps snow on the coastal mountains, providing excellent skiing from November through the end of March and sometimes into April. Local newspapers regularly carry snow conditions for ski areas throughout the region during the winter season.

The Whistler and Blackcomb mountains, north of Vancouver, comprise the biggest ski area in the region. Whistler Village Resort boasts the longest and second-longest vertical drops (more than a mile each) of any ski area in North America. Aside from Whistler/Blackcomb, British Columbia has many other excellent ski resorts scattered throughout the province, including several only minutes from downtown Vancouver.

Washington has 16 ski areas, several of which are located just 45 miles east of Seattle in the Cascade Mountains. Other major ski resorts include Mt. Baker, Crystal Mountain, Stevens Pass, and Mission Ridge.

Cross-country skiing is a popular and less-expensive way to enjoy the winter wilderness. Many downhill ski resorts also feature well-marked and well-groomed cross-country trails. Washington operates a system of **SnoParks** (Office of Winter Recreation, Parks and Recreation Commission, 7150 Clean-water La., KY-11, Olympia, WA 98504), which provides access to trails in 70 locations statewide.

Swimming Despite all the water surrounding the region, there is not as much swimming as one might expect in the Pacific North Coast. While the sandy ocean beaches attract throngs of people during the summer, most sun-worshipers spend little time in the water—it's simply too chilly!

Similarly, the waters of Puget Sound are generally too cold for swimming, and the beaches are mostly rocky. The best swimming beaches can be found around the Parksville area of Vancouver Island, where the combination of low tide, sandy beaches, and shallow water create fairly warm swimming conditions.

Many communities throughout the region have public swimming pools. Locations and hours are posted locally.

Wildlife Viewing The Pacific North Coast offers ample opportunities for viewing wildlife, both on land and on water. The best way to identify the wide range of native creatures is with a pair of binoculars and a good nature guide in hand. Books featuring regional wildlife can be found in local bookstores. Bald eagles, sea lions, dolphins, and whales are just a few of the animals that can be observed in the region.

Spectator Sports

Baseball The **Seattle Mariners** (tel. 206/628–0888 for tickets) of the American League play in the 60,000-seat indoor Kingdome. Tickets are almost always available. Baseball season runs from April to early October.

Basketball Washington fields a big-league basketball team: the **Seattle SuperSonics** (tel. 206/281–5850) at the Seattle Coliseum. Most universities and colleges also have basketball programs.

Football The **Seattle Seahawks** (tel. 206/628–0888 for tickets) of the National Football League play in the Kingdome during the fall, but games are almost always sold out. Tickets are usually available for the **British Columbia Lions** (tel. 604/280–4400) of the Canadian Football League, who play in the indoor B.C. Place Stadium in Vancouver.

Hockey The **Vancouver Canucks** (tel. 604/254–5141) of the National Hockey League hit the ice at the Pacific Coliseum. Minor-league "junior" hockey has a strong following in Seattle.

Horse Racing Thoroughbred horse racing takes place at **Longacres** (tel. 206/226–3131) in Seattle from April to September and **Exhibition Park** (tel. 604/254–1631) in Vancouver from April to October. Harness racing occurs from April to October at the **Cloverdale Raceway** (tel. 604/576–9141), located south of Vancouver near the U.S. border.

Powerboating Each year, thousands of spectators watch unlimited hydroplanes, or "thunder boats," race on Seattle's Lake Washington in early August as the grand finale of **Seafair** (*see* Festivals and Seasonal events in Before You Go, *above*).

Beaches

The Pacific coasts of Washington and British Columbia have long, sandy beaches that run for miles at a stretch. But the waters are often too cold or treacherous for swimming. Even in summertime, beach goers must be prepared to dress warmly.

The beaches of Washington are more remote from the major centers of population. Seattle, for example, is located on the saltwater Puget Sound but is a two- to three-hour drive from the nearest ocean beaches. Even in summer, the beaches are never crowded.

Most of the west coast of Vancouver Island is totally isolated. Pacific Rim National Park is one of the few places where ocean beaches are accessible. There are some good swimming beaches around the town of Parksville, on the eastern coast of Vancouver Island.

The gravel beaches of Washington's Puget Sound and British Columbia's Inside Passage attract few swimmers or sunbathers, but the beaches are popular for beachcombing and viewing marine life.

Dining

Many Pacific North Coast restaurants serve local specialties such as salmon, crab, oysters, and other seafood delicacies. Seattle's Pike Place Market and Vancouver's Granville Island Market display bountiful supplies of local seafood and produce, and these are good places to scan what you might find on restaurant menus. Ethnic foods are also becoming increasingly popular, especially Asian cuisines such as Japanese, Korean, and Thai.

Portions of the Pacific North Coast are major wine-producing regions. Local wines are often featured in the best restaurants.

Restaurants are divided into the following price categories: Very Expensive, Expensive, Moderate, and Inexpensive. As a general rule, restaurants in metropolitan areas are more expensive than those outside the city. But many city establishments, especially those that feature foreign cuisine, are surprisingly inexpensive. Because of space limitations, it is impossible to include every dining establishment in the following chapters. Therefore, we have listed only those recommended as the best within each price range.

Lodging

Hotels and motels in this guidebook are divided into standard categories based on price: Very Expensive, Expensive, Moderate, and Inexpensive. Although the names of the various hotel and motel categories are standard, the prices listed under each may vary from area to area. This variation is meant to reflect local price standards: For example, a Moderate price in a large urban area might be considered Expensive in a rural region. In all cases, however, price ranges for each category are clearly stated before each listing.

Hotels Most big-city hotels cater primarily to business travelers, with such facilities as restaurants, cocktail lounges, swimming pools, exercise equipment, and meeting rooms. Room rates often reflect the range of amenities offered. Most cities also have cheaper hotels, which are clean and comfortable but have fewer upscale facilities. A new accommodations trend is all-suite hotels, which offer more intimate facilities and are gaining popularity with the business traveler. Examples are **Courtyard By Marriott** (tel. 800/321–2211) and **Embassy Suites Hotels** (tel. 800/362–2779).

Many properties offer special weekend rates, sometimes up to 50% off regular prices. However, these deals are usually not extended during peak summer months, when hotels are normally full.

Vancouver and Seattle have experienced major hotel building booms in the past 10 years. Most of the major chains have properties in one or all of these cities. For more information, contact: **Canadian Pacific** (tel. 800/828–7447), **Doubletree** (tel. 800/528–0444), **Four Seasons** (tel. 800/332–3442), **Hilton** (tel. 800/445–8667), **Holiday Inn** (tel. 800/465–4329), **Hyatt** (tel. 800/233–1234), **Marriott** (tel. 800/228–9290), **Ramada** (tel. 800/228–2828), **Sheraton** (tel. 800/325–3535), **Stouffer** (tel. 800/468–3751), or **Westin** (tel. 800/228–3000).

Motels/Motor Inns The familiar roadside motel of the past is fast disappearing from the landscape. In its place are economical chain-run motor inns, which are strategically located at highway intersections. Some of these establishments offer very basic facilities; others provide restaurants, swimming pools, and other comforts.

Nationally recognized chains include **Best Western** (tel. 800/528–1234), **Days Inn** (tel. 800/325–2525), **La Quinta Inns** (tel. 800/531–5900), **Motel 6** (tel. 505/891–6161), **Quality Inns** (tel. 800/228–5151), **Super 8 Motels** (tel. 800/848–8888), and **Travelodge** (tel. 800/255–3050). **Nendel's** (tel. 800/547–0106), **Red Lion Inns** (tel. 800/547–8010), **Shilo Inns** (tel. 800/222–2244), and **West Coast Hotels** (tel. 800/426–0670) are regional chains.

Inns These establishments generally are located outside cities and have anywhere from 8 to 20 rooms. Lodging is often in an old restored building with some historical or architectural significance. Inns are sometimes confused with bed-and-breakfasts in that they may include breakfast in their basic rate.

Bed-and-Breakfasts Bed-and-breakfasts are private homes that reflect the personalities and tastes of their owners. Generally, B&Bs have 2–10 rooms, some with private baths and others with shared facilities. Breakfast is always included in the price of the room.

B&Bs in North America have flourished in recent years. Some homes advertise to the public, while others maintain a low profile. Most belong to a reservation system through which you can book a room.

Reservation services in the Pacific North Coast include **Best Canadian Bed & Breakfast Network** (1090 W. King Edward Ave., Vancouver, B.C. V6H 1Z4, tel. 604/738–7207) and **Traveller's Bed & Breakfast** (Box 492, Mercer Island, WA 98040, tel. 206/232–2345). You can book a B&B before leaving the United Kingdom through **American Bed & Breakfast, Inter-Bed Network** (31 Ernest Rd., Colchester, Essex CO7 9LQ, tel. 0206/223162).

Resorts The Pacific North Coast has quite a variety of resorts—from rural fishing lodges to luxury destination showpieces.

The Whistler Village resort, north of Vancouver, in British Columbia is best known for its world-class skiing. But Whistler is equally impressive as a year-round destination with golf, tennis, swimming, mountain biking, and horseback riding.

Camping Camping is a popular and inexpensive way to tour the Pacific North Coast. Washington and British Columbia have networks of excellent government-run parks that offer camping and organized activities. A few state and provincial parks will accept advance camping reservations, but most do not. Privately operated campgrounds sometimes have extra amenities such as laundry rooms and swimming pools. For more information, contact the local state or provincial tourism department.

YMCAs/YWCAs YMCAs or YWCAs are usually a good bet for clean, no frills, reliable lodging in larger towns and cities. These buildings are often centrally located, and their rates are significantly lower than those at city hotels. Nonmembers are welcome, but they may pay slightly more than members. A few very large Ys have accommodations for couples, but usually sleeping arrangements are segregated.

Home Exchange Exchanging your home or apartment with a counterpart overseas is a surprisingly low-cost way to enjoy a vacation abroad—especially a long one. Several organizations publish lists of available homes: **Home Base Holidays** (7 Park Ave., London N13 5PG, tel. 071/886–8752), **Home Exchange Ltd.** (8 Hillside High St., Farningham, Kent DA4 0DD, tel. 0322/864527), **International Home Exchange Service** (Box 3975, San Francisco, CA 94119, tel. 415/435–3497), **Loan-a-Home** (2 Park La., Mount Vernon, NY 10552), **Vacation Exchange Club Inc.** (12006 111th Ave., Unit 12, Youngstown, AZ 85363, tel. 602/972–2186).

Credit Cards

The following credit card abbreviations have been used in this book: AE, American Express; D, Discover; DC, Diners Club; MC, MasterCard; and V, Visa.

2 Portraits of Seattle and Vancouver

In the Footsteps of the First Settlers

By Glenn W. Sheehan

A principal investigator at SJS Archaeological Services, Inc., in Bridgeport, PA, Glenn W. Sheehan has worked extensively in the Pacific Northwest and Arctic regions.

There's a sort of primeval mystery about the majestic landscapes of the Pacific Northwest Coast, something elemental and ancient that can give you a strange sense of being dislocated in time. Drive along the coastal roads of Washington's Olympic Peninsula, for example, and you'll pass magnificent rain forest, pounding surf, and partially submerged chunks of headland stranded at sea. Every bridge you cross takes you over an ancient fishing stream where prehistoric Indians harvested salmon. The oldest trees along the road bear scars where these Indians pulled off bark strips dozens of feet long, which they used for clothing, construction work, and rope making. Stop to look out over the water, and you feel the presence of ancient whale hunters scanning the horizon for spouts among the waves.

It isn't just a question of landscape, either. Elders in the Eskimo (Inuit is the preferred term in Canada) and Indian communities along the coast still pass on stories told to them by their ancestors, stories that can sometimes be traced as far back as 1,000 years, and their tribal art is a living expression of cultures whose origins are lost in the mists of prehistory.

Despite a lack of hard evidence, many archaeologists believe the first people to inhabit the New World arrived by way of the Pacific North Coast. Unlike Columbus and the seafaring Vikings, Polynesians, Chinese, and Japanese, all of whom crossed oceans to arrive at different points in North and South America, it is believed that the first Americans came on foot. If these pioneers had boats at all, they were small ones, not designed for long-distance travel across oceans. They came via Alaska and traveled through Canada into the western United States.

Although these assertions sound feasible, there aren't any known archaeological sites to support them. The oldest documented sites in the New World are believed to be 20,000–13,000 years old; the oldest known sites in the Pacific Northwest are Indian settlements that fall at the younger end of this range, at about 13,000 years old. Why then is the Pacific Northwest Coast believed to be the point of entry for the earliest settlers? Because it's the only place where people could have walked into the New World or used their small boats to travel along the coast without excessive danger. The last Ice Age tied up so much water that ocean levels probably dropped by hundreds of feet around the world. On certain winter days today, a person can walk between Alaska and the Soviet Union on ice when the oceans freeze over. But during the Ice Age the oceans were so reduced that the seabed was temporarily exposed as dry land, supporting vegetation and game, with fish in the rivers and sea mammals on the coast. So much ground was exposed, in fact, that the Old World and the New were connected by dry land. And though their languages and blood types differ, evidence strongly suggests that both the Eskimos and Indians have their roots somewhere in Asia. As one Eskimo friend of mine once said, "You know, those Chinese look an awful lot like us. They must be descended from Eskimos."

Why then aren't there any sites to prove this migration theory? All human activity may have been confined to lower ground levels now hidden under the ocean, reason the archaeologists. Or people may have traveled in small numbers, so their remains aren't easily detected. Or we may have already found these sites without recognizing them as such. Even though the two American continents were not inhabited with people at the outset, they did have abundant herds of large game, animals that had no fear of humans. Hunters with such easy prey wouldn't stay in one place for long; as they killed off their local supply of meat, or as the animals learned how to avoid people, the hunters moved on. So it is possible that the settlers arrived in the Pacific Northwest, lived a nomadic life there for a while, and then roamed on to other parts of North America and into South America.

The first Americans came to a land we wouldn't recognize today. Most of Canada, Alaska, and the northern United States were still under ice. Arctic weather and the forests, animals, and plants that are found in today's far north were prevalent halfway down the lower 48 states. Then the weather changed: The ice sheets melted and the ice receded north. The animal and plant distributions we see today started to become established about 10,000 years ago. Rivers and streams that were previously frozen started to run fast and clear at low temperatures. Conditions for pioneering salmon became so ideal that by 5,000 or so years ago, there were huge runs extending hundreds of miles inland.

For hunters it was a revolutionary time. Herds of large animals started to diminish or disappear, and the big-game hunters were increasingly confronted with more work and less to show for their efforts. Many hunters in the Pacific Northwest Coast, particularly those in Washington, British Columbia, and southeastern Alaska, turned to fishing instead. Their nomadic life following the herds became a more settled one as they switched to fishing. And as they started to settle down, they were able to accumulate more material things.

The first Americans moved north to south, from Alaska to Canada and then to the lower 48 states and finally into Central America and South America. The more recent inhabitants who made their living from salmon fishing, however, headed in the opposite direction, from the lower Pacific Northwest up into Canada and Alaska. The art and culture of these people spread and flourished in the Pacific Northwest and continued to do so in the centuries preceding their contact with European explorers. Archaeological sites of these fishing peoples date back 2,500 years and more.

Native Americans often moved when they felt their villages had grown too big. According to stories told by Indian elders, entire clans would depart and make new settlements along the Pacific Coast. Battles between Indian tribes, and warfare between the Eskimos and Indians, also prompted the relocation of some villages. And eventually, as the native and Euro-American economies became entwined, some Indians and Eskimos abandoned their villages. Many of these villages can still be seen today: Houses may have fallen, totem poles may have been reduced by museum acquisitions, and the forest is once again dense, but the villages are there. Not only can archaeologists find and excavate the abandoned sites of these people, they also can talk to their descendants. When an archaeologist is puzzled by an object he digs out of the ground, he can consult the elders of various Indian and Eskimo groups, who can often identify it and describe its use. And when the elders can't identify an object, they can often point researchers in the right direction.

During this prehistoric fishing era, the most prosperous natives were those of Washington, British Columbia, and southern Alaska. They had the good life, and they flaunted it. Their art was larger than life, while their potlatches (celebratory feasts) gave new meaning to the words conspicuous consumption. The success of the fishing peoples led to imitation. The natives of Kodiak Island were Eskimo, for example, and their ancestors came to the New World to fish and hunt sea mammals along the coast, rather than hunt the big land-bound game as the Indians' ancestors did. Surprising enough, however, the Kodiak people achieved a society in many ways remarkably similar to that of Indian tribes living to the east and south. Their art, archaeology, and legends demonstrate the connections.

Indian groups were open to the ways of others too. In the far north of Alaska, where trees don't grow and fish runs can be counted in dozens instead of millions, Eskimo hunters had great success in capturing large whales. Indian groups of the lower Pacific Northwest did the same, using many of the whale-hunting techniques and rituals employed by people as far away as Point Barrow on the Arctic Coast.

Although the native groups along the Pacific Northwest Coast were lucky enough to avoid outright war with the European and American settlers, they did suffer some adversity. The natives of Kodiak, for example, were viciously attacked by Russians, and many natives eventually lost land in Canada and the United States. All the natives suffered when commercial fishing and river dams reduced salmon runs, and again when Yankee whalers destroyed whales in huge numbers. Despite these setbacks, however, both the Indians and Eskimos have retained much of their culture and way of life into the present.

One of the best-known archaeological sites of these settlers is Ozette, located on the Makah Reservation in Washington's Olympic Peninsula. The finds of the site can be viewed by the public, and visitors can request permission to visit the site itself. Call the Makah Reservation (tel. 206/645–2711) for information. The village of Ozette was partially covered by a mud slide several hundred years ago. This apparent catastrophe ironically turned out to preserve the village, however, for the wet mud provided an anaerobic environment hostile to most decay-causing organisms. As a result, the mud-covered section of Ozette was preserved in its entirety, a kind of New World Pompeii.

Archaeologists usually excavate with masons' trowels because they generally dig up stone and ceramics, objects that a skillfully handled trowel won't harm. But at Ozette in the 1970s, there was a delightful obstacle to overcome. Basketry, cordage, clothing, and all kinds of soft materials had been preserved, but since they were preserved wet, they were particularly soft, and the trowels cut through them like mud. Even experienced excavators couldn't feel the damage they were doing to the objects.

A whole new excavation approach was undertaken, called "wet site" archaeology. Using water hoses to excavate the village, the archaeologists discovered that mud and debris could be washed away, leaving artifacts intact. During the handlers' first clumsy attempts at hosing down the mud, artifacts could be seen tumbling downhill with the water, but after some trial and error, the workers were able to keep even small finds in place.

One of the most exciting aspects of the Ozette excavation was the support archaeologists received from Indians living in the region. The Makah tribe encouraged archaeologists to excavate Ozette and assisted in the fieldwork; tribal members provided logistical support and helped interpret finds. And the tribe even built a museum based on the artifacts on its grounds at Neah Bay.

The Indians also helped prepare artifacts for public display, which turned out to be quite a challenge. Generally, archaeological finds of stone and ceramic pieces are preserved simply by being cleaned first in water and then glued together. But Ozette produced all kinds of perishable artifacts, objects that quickly started to deteriorate once they were removed from their muddy entombment. So the

Makah Tribe provided laboratory space and helped the archaeologists preserve and stabilize the finds.'

These descendants of the ancient Indians went one step further and created a living experiment on the site. The Makah people worked outside to build a plank house, like those in Ozette, and then attempted to use the interior in the same ways their ancestors did. Life in the house was set up based upon the directions of tribal elders, historic accounts, and archaeological interpretations. In the end, the house looked as if one good mud slide would turn it into another ruined Ozette home. After this experimental period, the tribe dismantled the house and rebuilt it inside the Makah museum.

A large dugout canoe was also built for the museum. The art of making canoes had almost died out, but it was revived to capture an important part of life in Ozette. Young and old worked together to build the boat and to pass on these ancient skills.

Other archaeological sites in the area require a bit more effort to explore. From southern Alaska to Oregon, you can find hundreds of petroglyphs (rock carvings) and pictographs (rock paintings). Only a handful of them can be dated, however, so they can't be attributed to any particular group of people. Some are easily accessible, and seen by the public every day. Others are so hidden you can only find them if you happen to stumble upon them. Still other carvings are positioned at the tidal zone and consequently are under water at high tide. One worthwhile guide to the many accessible rock carvings is Beth and Ray Hill's *Indian Petroglyphs of the Pacific Northwest*.

Prehistoric Indians also carved petroglyphs on land, although mostly facing the ocean, or else overlooking a river or waterway. Pictographs, on the other hand, can be seen throughout the Northwest Coast. Some of these detailed rocks have been jackhammered from their embedded frames and carted away; others have eroded, and still others lie beneath reservoirs. But the vast majority are right where they were created, and with permission from native or nonnative landowners, or government agencies, visitors can examine them. More than 500 sites are known. One protected site open to the public is Petroglyph Park in the town of Nanaimo, on Vancouver Island. Petroglyphs at Wrangell, Alaska, are also open to the public.

The ancient craft of carving giant totem poles out of trees has survived as a living art form, with plenty of demand for new poles. Carvers today often work in public throughout the Pacific Northwest, at museums or on the grounds of institutions that have commissioned their artwork. Young workers aspire to apprentice with master carvers, and gift shops all over the region offer miniature reproductions.

The totem pole is the best-known example of current Northwest Coast tribal art, but masks, tools, and a variety of paintings and prints also continue the artistic tradition of the area. Artwork can be purchased at local galleries, many of which are located on Indian lands and are run by Indians. The choices are broader and the prices lower here than they are in the native art galleries of New York and California. The Dukuah Gallery (1971 Peninsula Rd., Ocluelet, B.C., V0R 3A0, tel. 604/726–7223) is run by native Lillian Mac and her husband, Bert Mac, the hereditary Chief of the Toquant tribe. Native artists visit and work in the gallery year-round.

The British Columbia Provincial Museum in Victoria, with its unique collection of prehistoric fish bones, is an outstanding research center, with representation from all five species of salmon and almost every other fish that might have been harvested by prehistoric natives. Each fish skeleton has been mounted on wires, with all the bones together in proper anatomical order. While this is a scientific collection, it verges on being a work of art in itself, with skeletal fish elongating and compressing into fantastic shapes.

In Vancouver, at the University of British Columbia's Museum of Anthropology, there's an excellent archaeological collection that's very accessible to the public. Visitors can open any of the Plexiglass-covered drawers to examine even the most delicate artifacts. Other artifacts can be seen at the Thomas Burke Memorial Washington State Museum at the University of Washington in Seattle, and at the Alaska State Museum in Juneau, where they also have a first-rate collection of historic baleen (fibrous plates that hang from the roof of the whale's mouth) baskets. Only native hunters and artisans are legally permitted to own unprocessed baleen.

Any overview of Northwest Coast archaeology inevitably leaves out more than it includes. Paleo-Indian sites, Russian fur-hunting activities, cave sites in Washington's channeled scablands, mastodons and mammoths, and cairns dug up 100 years ago can all be found along the Pacific Northwest Coast. And if you visit the area searching for a glimpse of the past, native people will share their stories, researchers may invite you to observe their work, artisans will explain their ancient crafts, and the museums will let you view even the most fragile artifacts. For here, one thing remains constant: the people's eagerness to document and understand the past.

3 Seattle

Introduction

*By Adam Woog
and Loralee
Wenger*

*Adam Woog is a
Seattle-based
freelance writer
whose works have
appeared in the*
Village Voice,
Seattle Times, *and*
Japan Times.
*Loralee Wenger is
the former travel
editor for* Pacific
Northwest
*magazine and a
freelance writer
whose articles
have appeared in
the* San Francisco
Examiner,
Washington Post,
Parade *magazine,
and* Glamour
magazine.

Seattle is defined by water. There's no use denying the city's damp weather, or the fact that its skies are cloudy for much of the year. People in Seattle don't tan—goes the joke—they rust. Vendors at the city's waterfront Public Market sell T-shirts that read "Seattle Rain Festival: January through December."

But Seattle is also defined by a different sort of water. A variety of rivers, lakes, and canals bisect steep hills, creating a series of distinctive areas along the water's edge that provide for a variety of activities. Funky fishing boats and floating homes, swank yacht clubs and waterfront restaurants, exist side by side.

But a city is defined by people as well as by its layout, and the people of Seattle—some half million within the city proper, another 2 million in the surrounding Puget Sound region—are a diversified bunch. Seattle has long had an active Asian and Asian-American population, as well as being home to well-established communities of Scandinavians, Afro-Americans, Jews, Native Americans, Hispanics, and other ethnic groups.

True, it's impossible to accurately generalize about such a varied group. Still, the prototypical Seattleite was pithily summed up by a *New Yorker* cartoon several years ago in which one arch-eyebrowed East Coast matron says to another, "They're backpacky, but nice." And it's true, nearly everyone in Seattle shares a love for the outdoors.

Aided by the proximity of high mountains (the Cascades to the east, the Olympics to the west) and water (both salt water and fresh water are everywhere), Seattle's vigorous outdoor sports are perennial favorites. The city's extensive park system (designed by Frederick Law Olmsted, creator of New York City's Central Park) and miles of secluded walking and bicycling paths add to one's appreciation of Seattle's surroundings.

On the other hand, the climate tends to foster an easygoing, indoor lifestyle, too. Overcast days and long winter nights help make Seattle a haven for moviegoers and book readers—the city is often used by Hollywood as a testing ground for new films and, according to independent bookstore sales and per-capita book purchases, the city ranks in the highest category.

Shedding its sleepy-town image, Seattle is one of the fastest-growing cities in the United States. For years, giant aerospace manufacturer Boeing was the only major factor in the area's economy besides lumber and fishing—the staples of the Northwest Coast. But as the 1962 World's Fair (and its enduring symbol, the Space Needle) signaled a change from small town to medium-size city, so the 1990s Goodwill Games announced the city's new role as a respected international hub. Seattle is now a major seaport and a vital link in Pacific Rim trade, and the evidence of internationalism is everywhere, from the discreet Japanese script identifying downtown department stores (i.e., "Nordstrom" written as "Katakana") to the multilingual recorded messages at Seattle-Tacoma International Airport.

The town that Sir Thomas Beacham once described as a "cultural wasteland" now has all the trappings of a full-blown big city, with ad agencies and artists' co-ops, symphonies and bal-

let companies. A variety of magazines compete with the two
daily newspapers. There's an innovative new convention center, a covered dome for professional sports, a world-renowned
theater scene, an excellent opera company, and a strong music
world.

As the city grows, though, it is also beginning to display big-
city problems. Increases in crime, drug abuse, homelessness,
and poverty are coupled with a decline in the quality of the public schools. Construction of new skyscrapers has disrupted
downtown life for years. Suburban growth, meanwhile, is ram-
pant; nearby Bellevue, the largest suburb, has swollen in just a
few years from a quiet farming community to the second-lar-
gest city in the state. Further, the area is plagued with one of
the worst traffic problems in the country. But Seattleites are a
strong political group with a great love for their city and a com-
mitment to maintaining its reputation as one of the most liveable in the country.

Essential Information

Arriving and Departing by Plane

Seattle-Tacoma International Airport is 20 miles from downtown Seattle, and is served by Air BC (tel. 206/467–7928), Air
Canada (tel. 206/467–7928), Alaska (tel. 206/433–3100), American (tel. 800/433–7300), America West (tel. 206/763–0737),
British Airways (tel. 800/247–9297), Canadian (tel. 800/426–
7000), Coastal (tel. 206/433–6343), Continental (tel. 206/624–
1740), Delta (tel. 206/433–4711), Harbor (tel. 800/521–3450),
Hawaiian (tel. 800/367–5320), Horizon (tel. 800/547–9308), Japan (tel. 800/525–3663), Northwest (tel. 206/433–3500), Pan
American (tel. 800/221–1111), TWA (tel. 206/447–9400), Thai
(tel. 206/467–0600), United (tel. 206/441–3700), United Express (tel. 206/441–3700), and USAir (tel. 206/587–6229).

**Between the
Airport and
Center City
By Bus**
Gray Line Airport Express (tel. 206/626–6088) operates buses
from major downtown hotels from 6:10 AM to 11:45, with depar-
tures every 20–30 minutes, depending on hotel. Fare: $7 one-way,
and $12 round-trip.

Shuttle Express (tel. 206/622–1424) offers service to and from
the airport. Fares are $14 for singles one-way or $21 for two
one-way tickets.

By Taxi Taxis to the airport take 30–45 minutes; the fare is about $25.

Arriving and Departing by Car, Bus, and Train

By Car I–5 enters Seattle from the north and south, I–90 from the
east.

Washington law requires all passengers to be buckled into seat
belts. Children under age 5 should use car seats. Cars are
allowed to turn right at a red light after stopping to check for
oncoming traffic.

By Bus Seattle is served by **Greyhound** (8th Ave. and Stewart St., tel.
206/624–3456), a nationwide bus line.

By Train **Amtrak** (303 S. Jackson St., tel. 800/USA–RAIL) provides rail
transportation from Seattle.

Getting Around Seattle

By Car Many downtown streets are one-way, so a map with arrows is especially helpful. Main thoroughfares into downtown are Aurora Avenue (the part through downtown is called the Alaskan Way Viaduct) and I–5.

By Bus **Metropolitan Transit** (821 2nd Ave., tel. 206/553–3000) provides a free-ride service in the downtown-waterfront area. Fares to other destinations range from 55¢ to $1.25, depending on the zone and time of day.

By Ferry The **Washington State Ferry System** (tel. 206/464–6400 or 206/464–2000, ext. 5500) is the largest in the world. Ferries leave from downtown Seattle for Winslow (Bainbridge Island) and Bremerton (Kitsap Peninsula) several times daily. Foot-passenger ferries travel to Vashon Island and Southworth (Kitsap Peninsula). Car and passenger ferries leave from Fauntleroy, in West Seattle, to Vashon Island and Southworth; from Edmonds, north of Seattle, to Kingston; and from Mukilteo, further north, to Clinton (Whidbey Island). In Anacortes, about 90 minutes north of Seattle, ferries depart for the San Juan Islands and for Vancouver Island, British Columbia. Fares range from as low as $1.10 for children 5–11 and senior citizens traveling the Mukilteo to Clinton route, to $31.25 for a car and driver going one way from Anacortes to Sydney.

Victoria Clipper I and **II** (tel. 206/448–5000), passenger catamarans, leave from Pier 69. They make the trip to Victoria in 2½ hours and depart four times daily in the summer; two times daily in spring and fall, and once daily in winter. Fares are $79 round-trip. Reservations are necessary.

By Monorail The **Monorail** (tel. 206/684–7200), built for the 1962 World's Fair, runs direct from Westlake Center to the Seattle Center every 15 minutes. Hours are Sunday–Thursday 9–9 and Friday and Saturday 9 AM–midnight. Fare is 60¢ each way; free for children under 6.

By Trolley **Waterfront trolleys** (tel. 206/553–3000) run from Pier 70 into Pioneer Square. Fares (55¢ nonpeak and 75¢ for travel during peak hours) are the same as bus fares.

By Taxi The taxi fare is $1.20 at the flag drop and $1.40 per mile. Major companies are **Farwest** (tel. 206/622–1717) and **Yellow Cab** (tel. 206/622–6500).

Important Addresses and Numbers

Tourist Information The **Seattle/King County Convention and Visitors Bureau** (800 Convention Pl., tel. 206/461–5840), at the I–5 end of Pike Street, can provide you with maps and information about lodging, restaurants, and attractions throughout the city.

Emergencies For **police, ambulance,** or **other emergencies,** dial 911.

Hospitals Area hospitals with emergency rooms include **Harborview Medical Center** (325 9th Ave., tel. 206/223–3074) and **Virginia Mason Hospital** (925 Seneca St., tel. 206/583–6433).

Pharmacies **Fred Meyer** (417 Broadway Ave. E, tel. 206/323–6586) is open until 10 PM.

Guided Tours

Orientation Several guided tours of Seattle's waterfront and nearby areas are available, primarily during summer months. From Pier 55, **Seattle Harbor Tours** offers one-hour tours exploring Elliott Bay and the Port of Seattle. The vessel is the *Goodtime III*, part of the biggest charter fleet in Seattle. Sailings vary according to season, with up to six daily during peak months. *Pier 55, Suite 201, 98101, tel. 206/623–1445. Cost: $8.50 adults, $7.50 senior citizens, $6 youths 12–17, $4 children 5–12.*

Major Northwest Tours offers a 2¼-hour tour from Pier 56 of the harbor and the Hiram Chittendan Locks, with a return by bus. *1415 Western Ave., Suite 503, Seattle 98101, tel. 206/292–0595. Tours depart noon and 3. Cost: $17 adults, $9 children.*

Gray Line offers guided bus tours of the city and environs, ranging in scope from a daily 2½-hour spin to a six-hour "Grand City Tour." The company also offers various specialized tours, including the Boeing 747-767 plants, Mt. Rainier, dinner cruises, and Seattle's waterways by boat. *All departures from the downtown Sheraton, 1400 6th Ave., tel. 206/626–5208. Free transfer service from major downtown hotels. Reservations required.*

Special-Interest From Pier 56, **Tillicum Village Tours** sails across Puget Sound to Blake Island, south of Bainbridge Island, for a four-hour examination of traditional Native American life. A dinner including steamed clams and salmon is served, and presentations are given of dances, wood carving, and other aspects of West Coast Indian culture. *Pier 56, tel. 206/443–1244. Tour schedule varies during the year, with up to 3 tours leaving daily during peak months. Cost: $35 adults, $32 senior citizens, $24 youths 13–19, $14 children 6–12, $7 children 3–5; children under 3 free.*

The **Spirit of Puget Sound** runs dinner cruises in Elliot Bay evenings from 7–10 on a sleek, 175-foot yacht. The cruise includes beef, salmon, and chicken buffet dinner; a 30-minute Broadway revue; and 1 hour of dancing to a five-piece band. Moonlight cocktail cruises set sail at 11:30 and return at 2 AM, and feature a nightclub atmosphere. *2819 Elliot Ave., Suite 204, Seattle 98121, tel. 206/443–1439. Cost for dinner cruise ranges from $36.70–$40.80, depending on weekends or weeknight travel; for moonlight cruises, $14 per person. Call for schedules.*

Gray Line (*see* above).

Seattle's Chinatown, now known as the International District, reflecting its multicultural flavor, is one of the largest Asian-American enclaves in North America. **Chinatown Discovery Tours** offers groups (and individuals on a space-available basis) a three-hour tour of the area that includes such sights as a fortune cookie factory, a Chinese market, and an herb dispensary. Tours end with a traditional dim sum or dinner banquet. *Box 3406, 98114, tel. 206/236–0657. Cost varies depending on tour. Tours offered Tues.–Sat., several times during the day and evening.*

One of the most beloved of Seattle's tours is the **Underground Tour,** begun in 1965 by feisty entrepreneur/historian Bill Speidel as an effort to help preserve the then-derelict Pioneer Square area. This 90-minute walking tour explores (with tongue-in-cheek narration) the rough-and-tumble history of early Seattle; the Great Fire of 1889, which destroyed most of downtown; and the fascinating below-ground sections of Pioneer Square that have been abandoned (and built on top of) since 1907. This tour, however, is not wheelchair- or stroller-accessible, as six flights of stairs are involved. *Departure from Doc Maynard's Public House, 610 1st Ave., tel. for reservations, 206/682–4646; tel. for schedules, 206/682–1511. Cost: $4.75 adults, $3.50 senior citizens and youths 13–17 or with valid student ID, $2.25 children 6–12, children under 6 free. Reservations recommended. Tours run daily except Easter, Thanksgiving, Christmas Eve, Christmas Day, and New Year's Day. Tour schedule varies with season, with up to 7 tours daily in summer.*

Self-Guided Also worth exploring are the unusual self-guided tours found in "Steps to Enjoying Seattle's Public Art," an illustrated brochure published by the Seattle Arts Commission. It describes walks and drives to see more than 1,000 innovative works of **art in public places.** Among these treasures are brass dance-steps inlaid on the sidewalks of Broadway, whirligigs festooning a neighborhood power substation, an "ark" of animals at Woodland Park Zoo, murals on downtown high rises, and a "sound garden" of acoustical sculptures in a lakeside park. "Steps to Enjoying Seattle's Public Art" is free from the Seattle Arts Commission (305 Harrison St., 98109, tel. 206/684–7171).

Ballooning **Balloon Depot** (16138 N.E. 87th St., Redmond 98052, tel. 206/881–9699) offers 90-minute balloon flights for $99–$125 per person, with a half-price discount for children under age 11 who are accompanied by an adult. **Lighter Than Air Adventures** (21808 N.E. 175th St., Woodinville 98072, tel. 206/788–2454) has evening flights lasting 30 minutes–one hour for $125 per person, as well as morning flights lasting one–two hours and featuring a champagne brunch for $145 per person. The **Great Northwest Aerial Navigation Company** (7616 79th Ave. SE, Mercer Island 98040, tel. 206/232–2023) specializes in longer flights and gourmet picnics, lasting about four hours, surveying the Snohomish Valley north and east of Seattle. Morning and evening picnic flights, $145 on weekends, $130 weekdays; flights only, $105.

Highlights for First-time Visitors

Kingdome (*see* Exploring Seattle, below).
Pioneer Square (*see* Exploring Seattle, below).
Seattle Center (*see* Exploring Seattle, below).
Space Needle (*see* Exploring Seattle, below).

Exploring Seattle

Numbers in the margin correspond to points of interest on the Downtown Seattle map.

Downtown Downtown Seattle is bounded by the Kingdome to the south, the Seattle Center to the north, I–5 to the east, and the waterfront to the west. You can reach most points of interest by foot, bus, or the monorail. Bear in mind that Seattle is a city of hills, so comfortable walking shoes are a must.

❶ Start at the **Seattle Visitor Information Center** to pick up maps, brochures, and listings of events. *666 Stewart St., tel. 206/461–*

Aquarium, **5**
Historical Marker, **7**
Omnidome Film
Experience, **6**
Pike Place Market, **4**
Pioneer Square, **8**
Seattle Art Museum, **3**
Seattle Visitor
Information Center, **1**
Westlake Center, **2**

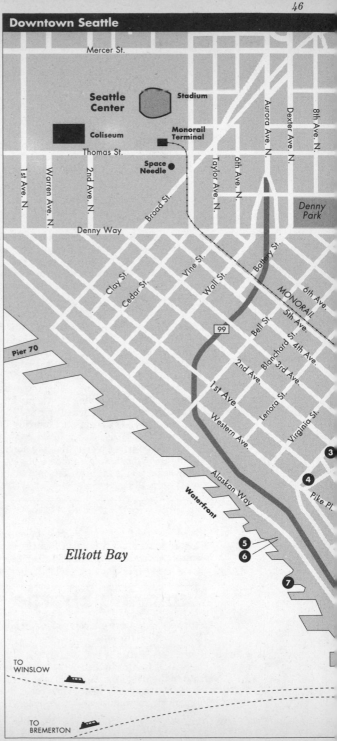

Downtown Seattle

5840. Open weekdays 8:30–5. Other location at the Seattle Center, adjacent to the Space Needle, tel. 206/000–0000. Open Memorial Day–Labor Day.

From the Information Center, you can proceed either north or south. If you choose the latter, take Westlake Avenue to **②** **Westlake Center** (*see* Shopping, below), a complex completed in 1989, in spite of the controversy surrounding its construction. The conflict occurred between city residents—some of whom objected to the 27-story office tower and three-story shopping structure with enclosed walkways—and favored, instead, the large grassy park without commercial buildings. In any case, the center is a major terminus for buses and the monorail, which goes north to Seattle center. *1601 5th Ave., tel. 206/467–1600. Open weekdays 9:30–9.*

③ Make your way from 5th Avenue west to 2nd Avenue. The doors to the new **Seattle Art Museum** will open in the winter of 1991, and the five-story building, designed by post-modern theorist Robert Venturi, is a work of art in itself. The building features a limestone exterior with large-scale vertical fluting, accented by terra-cotta, cut granite, and marble. The museum displays an extensive collection of Asian, Native American, African, Oceanic, and pre-Columbian art, a café, and gift shop. *1320 2nd Ave., tel. 206/625–8900. Admission: $2 adults, $1 senior citizens and students, children under 6 free; free admission on Thurs. and Sun.; free tours Tues.–Sun. at 2, Thurs. at 7. Open Tues.–Sat. 10–5, Thurs. 10–9, Sun. noon–5. Closed Mon., Thanksgiving, Christmas, and New Year's Day.*

④ Go west one block to 1st Avenue and one block north to the **Pike Place Market,** a Seattle institution. It began in 1907 when the city issued permits to farmers allowing them to sell produce from their wagons parked at Pike Place. Later, the city built stalls that were allotted to the farmers on a daily basis. At one time the market was a madhouse of vendors hawking their produce, haggling over prices; some of the fishmongers still carry on this kind of frenzied banter, but chances are you won't get them to waver on their prices. Urban renewal almost killed the market, but just as planners were about to do away with it, city voters led by the late architect Victor Steinbreuck (for whom the park near the market was named) rallied and voted it to be a historical asset. Many of the buildings have been restored, and the project is now connected by stairs and elevator to the waterfront. You can still find fresh seafood (which can be packed in dry ice for your flight home), produce, cheese, Northwest wines, bulk spices, tea, coffee, and arts and crafts sold here. *1st Ave. at Pike St., tel. 206/682–7453. Open Mon.–Sat. 9–6, Sun. 11–5.*

From the market, take the stairs or elevator down to the waterfront. In the early days, the waterfront was the center of activity in Seattle; today it stretches some 19 blocks, from Pier 70 and Myrtle Edwards Park in the north, where there is a bicycle and jogging trail, down to Pier 51 in Pioneer Square.

Pier 70, to the south of the park, is a large warehouse converted to shops, galleries, restaurants, and bars.

⑤ At the base of the Pike Street Hillclimb at Pier 59 is the **Seattle Aquarium,** showcasing Northwest marine life. Sea otters and seals swim and dive in their pools, and the "State of the Sound" exhibit shows aquatic life and the ecology of Puget Sound. *Pier 59, tel. 206/386–4320. Admission: $5.75 adults, $3.50 youths and senior citizens, $2.50 children 6–12, children under 6 free. Open daily 10–7.*

⑥ Next to the aquarium is the **Omnidome Film Experience,** which includes subjects such as the eruption of Mt. St. Helens and a study of sharks and whales. *Pier 59, tel. 206/622–1868. Admission: $5.95 adults, $4.95 youths 13–18 and senior citizens, $3.95 children 6–12, children under 6 free; combination tickets for the Omnidome and aquarium: $9.95 adults, $6.75 youths 13–18 and senior citizens, $5.10 children 6–12. Open daily 10–5.*

⑦ The **historical marker** indicating the landing of the ship *Portland,* on July 17, 1897, is at Pier 58. The ship brought gold and news of the Klondike gold rush; shops at this pier continue to commemorate the event with gold-rush theme merchandise.

From Pier 51 at the foot of Yesler Way, walk a couple of blocks east to **Pioneer Park,** where an ornate iron and glass pergola stands. This was the site of Henry Yesler's (one of Seattle's first businesspeople) pier and sawmill and Seattle's original business district. In 1889, a fire destroyed many of the wood-frame **⑧** buildings in the area now known as **Pioneer Square,** but the industrious residents and businesspeople rebuilt them with brick and mortar.

The term Skid Row originated here, when timber was logged off the hill and sent to the sawmill. The skid road was made of small logs laid crossways and greased so the freshly cut timber could slide down to the mill. With the Klondike gold rush, this area became populated with saloons and brothels; businesses gradually moved north, and the old pioneering area deteriorated. Eventually, drunks and bums hung out on Skid Road, and the term changed to Skid Row. Today, Pioneer Square encompasses about 18 blocks and includes restaurants, bars, shops, and the city's largest concentration of art galleries. In Pioneer Square is the **Klondike Gold Rush National Historical Park** and interpretive center. The center provides insight on the story of Seattle's role in the 1897–98 gold rush through film presentations, permanent exhibits, and gold-panning demonstrations. *117 S. Main St., tel. 206/442–7220. Admission free. Open daily 9–5, except major holidays.*

Numbers in the margin correspond to points of interest on the Metropolitan Seattle map.

⑨ Walk a half block east on Main Street, and two blocks south on Occidental Avenue to the **Kingdome,** Seattle's covered stadium where the Seattle Seahawks NFL team and the Seattle Mariners baseball team play. The 650-feet-diameter stadium was built in 1976 and has the world's largest self-supporting roof, which sits 250 feet high. If you're interested in the inner workings, take the one-hour guided tour. *201 S. King St., tel. 206/296–3111 for information. Admission: $3 adults, $1.50 children and senior citizens.*

⑩ To the east is a 40-square-block area known as the **International District** (the ID). Inhabited by about one-third Chinese and one-third Filipino, other residents come from all over Asia. The ID began as a haven for Chinese workers after they finished the

Boeing Field, **21**

Henry Art Gallery, **18**

International District, **10**

Kingdome, **9**

Museum of History and Industry, **19**

Nippon Kan Theater, **11**

Seattle Center, **13**

Space Needle, **14**

Thomas Burke Memorial Washington State Museum, **17**

University of Washington, **16**

Washington Park Arboretum, **20**

Wing Luke Museum, **12**

Woodland Park Zoo, **15**

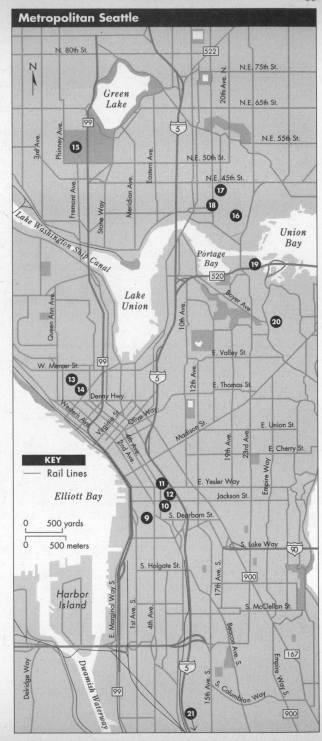

Metropolitan Seattle

Transcontinental Railroad. The community has remained intact, despite the anti-Chinese riots in Seattle during the 1880s and the World War II Japanese-American internment. The district, which includes many Chinese, Japanese, and Korean restaurants, also houses herbalists, massage parlors, acupuncturists, and about 30 private clubs for gambling and socializing. The most notorious club is the **Wah Mee Club,** on Canton Avenue, where a multiple murder linked to gangs and gambling occurred in 1983. **Uwajimaya** (519 6th Ave. S, tel. 206/624–6248), one of the—if not *the*—largest Japanese stores on the West Coast, is in this district as well. Here you will find china, gifts, fabrics, housewares, and a complete supermarket with an array of Asian foods.

Time Out If you're feeling a need to rest your feet a bit by now, stop in at **Okazuya,** the Asian snack bar (tel. 206/624–6248) in Uwajimaya. You can get noodle dishes, sushi, tempura, humbow, and other Asian dishes for carryout or to eat in.

From Uwajimaya, continue north on 6th Street to Washington Street. In summer, as you walk up the hill, you can see the many gardens tended by residents of the ID.

⓫ Historically, the **Nippon Kan Theater** (628 S. Washington St., tel. 206/467–6807) was the focal point for Japanese-American activities, including kabuki theater. Renovated and reopened in 1981 as a national historic site, it presents many Asian-interest productions, including the Japanese Performing Arts series, which runs from October through May.

⓬ The final stop on the southbound Downtown Seattle tour will be at the **Wing Luke Museum,** named for the first Asian person to be elected to a Seattle city office, where exhibits emphasize Oriental history and culture. An acupuncture exhibit demonstrates how needles are inserted into parts of the body to release blocked energy and promote healing. Other elements of the permanent collection includes costumes, fabrics, crafts, basketry, and Chinese traditional medicines. *407 7th Ave. S, tel. 206/623–5124. Admission: $2.50 adults, $1 senior citizens and students, 50¢ children. Open Tues.–Fri. 11–4:30, weekends noon–4; closed Mon.*

North of Downtown To explore outside the downtown area, take the 4th Avenue bus to Westlake Center, where you can pick up the Monorail to ⓭ **Seattle Center,** a 74-acre complex built for the 1962 Seattle World's Fair. It includes an amusement park, the very popular Space Needle with restaurant and observation deck, theaters, ⓮ the Coliseum, exhibition halls, museums, and shops. The **Space Needle,** a Seattle landmark easily recognized from almost anywhere in the downtown area, looks much like something from the "Jetsons" cartoon show. The glass elevator to the observation deck offers an impressive view of the city.

Time Out The **Space Needle Lounge** (tel. 206/443–2100), on the observation deck (one floor above the Space Needle Restaurant), offers fabulous views of Elliot Bay and Queen Anne Hill. The black-and-grey exterior decor emphasizes the 1960s style of the Needle. Ask the bartender for the special "Spirit of the Needle" cocktail or choose from the full bar.

From downtown or from the Seattle Center, take Highway 99 (Aurora Ave. N) north across the Aurora Bridge to the 50th Street exit; follow signs to the **Woodland Park Zoo,** where many of the animals are free to roam their section of the total of 92 acres. The African savannah and the new elephant house are popular features. Wheelchairs and strollers can be rented. *N. 59th St. and Fremont Ave., tel. 206/684–4800. Admission: $4.50 adults, $2.25 children 6–17 and senior citizens, children under 5 free. Open summer, daily 9:30–6; winter, daily 10–4.*

From the Woodland Park Zoo, take the 50th Street exit to 15th Avenue NE, the head south to 45th Street. Turn east for a few blocks to the entrance of the 33,500-student **University of Washington.** The U-Dub, as locals call it, was founded in 1861. On the northwestern corner of the beautifully landscaped campus is the **Thomas Burke Memorial Washington State Museum,** Washington's natural history and anthropological museum. The museum has been renovated recently and features exhibits on cultures of the Pacific region and the state's 35 Native American tribes. *17th Ave. NE and N.E. 45th St., tel. 206/543–5590. Admission free; special exhibit fees vary. Open Mon.–Wed. and Fri.–Sun. 10–5, Thurs. 10–8.*

Going south, on the west side of the campus is the **Henry Art Gallery,** which displays paintings from the 19th and 20th centuries, textiles, and traveling exhibits. *15th Ave. NE and N.E. 41st St., tel. 206/543–2280. Admission: $3 adults, $1.50 students and senior citizens; free Thurs. Open Tues.–Fri. 10–5, Thurs. 10–9, weekends 11–5; closed Mon.*

Close to the university's Husky Stadium, off Montlake and Lake Washington boulevards, is the **Museum of History and Industry.** An 1880s-era room and a Seattle time-line depict the city's earlier days. Other rotating exhibits from the permanent collection and traveling exhibits are displayed. *2700 24th Ave. E, tel. 206/324–1125. Admission: $3 adults, $1.50 children 6–12, children under 6 free. Open daily 10–5.*

At the museum pick up a brochure of self-guided walking tours of the nearby **Washington Park Arboretum.** The arboretum's Rhododendron Glen and Azalea Way are in full bloom from March through June. During the rest of the year, other plants and wildlife flourish. A new visitor center at the north end of the park is open to instruct you on the species of flora and fauna you'll see here. *2300 Arboretum Dr. E, tel. 206/325–4510. Admission free. Park open daily 7 AM–sunset; visitor center open daily 10–4.*

If you have your own plane, land at **Boeing Field** to see the **Museum of Flight.** (You can also get there by metro bus #174 that follows Second Avenue from downtown Seattle.) The **Red Barn,** the original Boeing airplane factory, houses an exhibit on the history of aviation. The **Great Gallery,** a dramatic structure designed by Seattle architect Ibsen Nelson, contains more than 20 airplanes—suspended from the ceiling and on the ground—dating back to the Wright brothers. For a complete lesson, take the free hour-long Boeing tour. *9404 E. Marginal Way S, tel. 206/764–5720. Admission: $5 adults, $3 children 6–16, children under 6 free. Open Mon.–Wed. and Fri.–Sun. 10–5, Thurs. 10–9; closed Christmas.*

Seattle for Free

Rainier Brewery, located 2 miles south of the Kingdome on I–5, offers 30-minute tours of the premises that conclude with free samples for adults of the locally made beer. Daily tours are followed by a tasting. If you don't want to drive, take the #130 bus from downtown. *3100 Airport Way S, tel. 206/622–2600. Tours weekdays 1–6. No children under 3.*

Gallery Walk (begin at any gallery in Pioneer Square, tel. 206/587–0260), an open house hosted by Seattle's art galleries, explores new local exhibits the first Thursday of every month, starting at 5.

Thomas Burke Memorial Washington State Museum (*see* Exploring Seattle, above).

The **Charles and Emma Frye Art Museum** features a large collection of Munich School and American School paintings. *704 Terry Ave., tel. 206/622–9250. Open Mon.–Sat. 10–5, Sun. noon–5.*

The **Elliott Bay Book Company** (101 S. Main St., tel. 206/624–6600) hosts lectures and readings by authors of local and international acclaim. Most are free, but phone ahead to be sure.

Recreational Equipment, Inc. (REI, tel. 206/323–8333), the largest consumer co-op in the United States, hosts free programs on travel, adventure, and outdoor activities at Seattle (1525 11th Ave.), Bellevue (15400 N.E. 20th St.), and Federal Way (2565 Gateway Center Blvd. S) locations, starting at 7 PM every Thursday, and at Lynnwood (4200 194th St. SW) at 7 PM on Tuesdays.

Seattle's summer concerts, the **Out To Lunch Series** (tel. 206/623–0340), runs from mid-June to early September every weekday at noon in various parks, plazas, and atriums in downtown. Concerts feature local and national musicians and dancers. Call ahead for schedule and location.

What to See and Do with Children

Burke-Gilman Trail (*see* Sports and Fitness, below) offers good bike trails for children.

Burke Thomas Memorial Washington State Museum (*see* Exploring Seattle, above).

Elliott Bay Book Company (*see* Seattle for Free, above) hosts a children's story hour at 11 AM the first Saturday of the month.

Green Lake (*see* Sports and Fitness, below).

Museum of Flight (*see* Exploring Seattle, above).

Myrtle Edwards Park (*see* Exploring Seattle, above).

Seattle Aquarium (*see* Exploring Seattle, above).

Seattle Children's Museum is a colorful, spacious facility at the Seattle Center's Center House. An infant-toddler area features a giant, soft ferryboat for climbing and sliding. A bubble area helps children learn about shapes and gravity. The pretend neighborhood lets children play in a post office, café, fire station, grocery store, and more. Intergenerational programs, special exhibits, and workshops are offered. *Fountain level of Seattle Center House, 305 Harrison St., tel. 206/441-1768. Admission: $3, children under 1 free. Open Tues.-Sun. 10-5.*

Seattle Children's Theater is nationally recognized for its artistic excellence. Five plays per year, performed at the PONCHO Theatre, are presented by professional actors and are appropriate for children ages five and older and their families. *N. 50th St. and Freemont Ave. N, at south entrance to the Woodland Park Zoo, tel. 206/633-4567. Admission: $14 adults, $8.25 senior citizens, students, and children. Call for the performance schedule.*

Off the Beaten Track

Touring **brew pubs**—drinking establishments attached to actual breweries—is a congenial and educational alternative to usual city attractions. Seattle, as well as a good portion of the Pacific Northwest, has become a hotbed for microbrews (high-quality beers made for local distribution). Note that all brew pubs below serve a variety of food and nonalcoholic beverages. If live music is performed, a cover charge may be required; otherwise admission is free.

The **Pacific Northwest Brewing Co.**, located in the heart of Pioneer Square, offers six mild beers that reflect the taste of its British owner. The elegantly decorated interior—smooth high-tech design, blended with antiques and brewing equipment in full view—fits not only the personality of Richard Wrigley, the proprietor, but also the downtown location. *322 Occidental Ave. S, tel. 206/621-7002. Open Tues.-Sat. 11:30 AM-midnight.*

Near the north end of the Fremont Bridge, just 8 miles from downtown, is the **Trolleyman,** birthplace of the much-loved Ballard Bitter and Red Hook Ale. The premises mixes Northwest style—whitewashed walls and a nonsmoking policy—with a cozy British pub atmosphere that includes a fireplace and ample armchairs. *3400 Phinney Ave. N, tel. 206/548-8000. Open weekdays 8:30 AM-11 PM, Sat. 11-11, Sun. noon-6. Tours given weekdays at 3, weekends at 1:30, 2:30, 3:30, and 4:30.*

Catering to the nearby university crowd, the **Big Time Brewery** resembles a typical college pub, with a moose head on the walls and co-ed decor. Pale ale, amber, and porter are always on tap; specialty brews change monthly. *4133 University Way NE, tel. 206/545-4509. Open daily 11:30 AM-1 AM.*

Noggins, in the downtown Westlake Mall, offers at least five distinctive beers at a given time. *Westlake Mall, 400 Pine St., tel. 206/682-BREW. Open Mon.-Thurs. 9 AM-11 PM, Fri. and Sat. 9 AM-midnight, Sun. 11-9.*

Technically not a brew pub, **Cooper's Northwest Alehouse,** located north of the University District, nonetheless deserves mention as the mecca of Northwest microbreweries. Twenty-one of its 22 brews are specialties from all over the West Coast, and the staff is awesomely knowledgeable about their subtle distinctions between the brews. If you don't come for the drink, come for the dart tournaments that are played on a regular ba-

sis. *8065 Lake City Way NE, tel. 206/522-2923. Open weekdays*
3 PM-2 AM, Sat. 1 PM-2 AM, Sun. 1 PM-midnight.

Perhaps the best way to tour the pubs without worrying about
who's driving is to take a four-hour tour offered by **Northwest
Brewery & Pub Tours** (4224 1st Ave. NE, tel. 206/547-1186).
The $26 fee includes free tastings and van transportation on
weekend afternoons and Monday evenings. Reservations are
required.

If your preference is grapes, visit **Ste. Michelle Winery,** one of
the oldest wineries in the state. It's located 15 miles northeast
of Seattle, nestled on 87 wooded acres that were once part of
the estate of lumberman Fred Stimson. Some of the original
1912 buildings are still on the property, including the family
home—the manor house—which is on the National Register of
Historic Places. Trout ponds, a carriage house, a caretaker's
cottage, and formal gardens are part of the original estate. The
landscaping, created by New York's Olmsted family (designers
of New York City's Central Park), has been restored, and the
gardens feature hundreds of trees, shrubs, and plants. Visitors
are invited to picnic and explore the grounds. Delicatessen
items, wines, and wine-related gifts are available at the winery shop. In the summer, the company hosts a series of nationally recognized performers and arts events in the
amphitheater. *14111 N.E. 145th St., Woodinville, tel. 206/488-
1133. From downtown Seattle take I-90 east, then go north on
I-405. Take Exit 23 east (S.R. 522) to the Woodinville exit.
Complimentary wine tastings and cellar tours are available
daily 10-4:30, except for holidays.*

Another option if you're looking to go off the beaten track is to
visit the Hiram M. Chittenden Locks, more commonly called
the **Ballard Locks,** part of the 8-mile Lake Washington Ship Canal linking Lakes Washington and Union with the salt water of
Shilshole Bay and Puget Sound. Completed in 1917, the locks
currently service some 100,000 boats yearly by raising and low-
ering water levels anywhere from 6 to 26 feet.

The locks themselves are fascinating to watch as a variety of
commercial fishing boats and pleasure craft go through them,
but there are several other sights nearby that are well worth
seeing. The **Fish Ladder** has 21 levels that allow fish to swim
upstream on a gradual incline. A series of lighted windows lets
visitors watch several varieties of salmon and trout—an esti-
mated half-million fish yearly—as they migrate upstream.
(This, by the way, is where various attempts are being carried
out to prevent sea lions, including the world-famous Herschel,
from depleting the salmon population.)

On the north side of the locks is a fine 7-acre **ornamental garden**
of native and exotic plants, shrubs, and trees. Also on the north
side is a staffed visitor center with displays on the history and
operation of the locks, and several fanciful sculptures by local
artists. Along the south side is a lovely 1,200-foot promenade
with a footbridge, fishing pier, and observation deck. *North
entrance, 3015 N.W. 54th St., west of the Ballard Bridge. Locks
tel. 206/783-7001; visitor center tel. 206/783-7059. Visitor center open daily 10-7; closed in winter, Tues., Wed.; locks open
year-round, except for maintenance.*

Two legendary performers—rock guitarist Jimi Hendrix and
kung-fu movie star Bruce Lee—are buried in the Seattle area;

their graves are popular sites for fans wishing to pay respects. In addition, there is a memorial to Hendrix, a Seattle native, overlooking the African Savannah exhibit at Woodland Park Zoo; appropriately enough, it's a very big rock.

Jimi Hendrix's grave site is at the Greenwood Cemetery, in Renton. *From Seattle, take I–5 south to the Renton exit, then I–405 past Southcenter to Exit 4B. Bear right under the freeway, take a right along Sunset Blvd. 1 block and right again up 3rd St. Continue 1 mi and go right at the 3rd light; the cemetery is on the corner of 3rd and Monroe Sts., tel. 206/255–1511. Open daily until dusk. Inquire at the office; a counselor will direct you to the site.*

Bruce Lee's grave site is at the Lakeview Cemetery on the north slope of Capitol Hill. *1554 15th Ave. E, directly north of Volunteer Park, tel. 206/322–1582. Open weekdays 9–4:30. Inquire at the office for a map.*

Shopping

Shopping Districts

Westlake Center (1601 5th Ave., tel. 206/467–1600) lies in the middle of downtown Seattle. The new three-story steel-and-glass building contains 80 upscale shops, as well as covered walkways to Seattle's three major department stores, **Nordstrom's, Frederick & Nelson,** and **The Bon.**

Pike Place Market (*see* Exploring Seattle, above).

The **University District** (University Ave., north and south of 45th St., tel. 206/527–2567) has an eclectic mixture of such student-oriented imports as ethnic jewelry and South American sweaters; a few upscale shops; and the city's largest concentration of bookstores.

Seattle's **Fremont area** (N. 35th St. and Fremont Ave. N, north of the ship canal and the Fremont Bridge), a remnant from hippie days, offers products of a different variety—namely funky and used. There's the **Daily Planet** (3416 Fremont Ave. N, tel. 206/633–0895), and **Guess Where** (615 N. 35th St., tel. 206/547–3793) for vintage clothing. At **Armadillo & Co.** (3510 Fremont Pl. N, tel. 206/633–4241) you'll find jewelry, T-shirts, and other armadillo-theme accessories and gifts. The **Frank & Dunya Gallery** (3418 Fremont Ave. N, tel. 206/547–6760) features unique art pieces, from furniture to jewelry. You'll also find **Dusty Strings** (3406 Fremont Ave. N, tel. 206/634–1656) a hammered dulcimer shop.

Capitol Hill's **Broadway Avenue** features clothing stores, high-design housewares shops, espresso bars, and restaurants. An unusual boutique is the **Bead Works** (233 Broadway Ave. E, tel. 206/323–4998).

Northgate Mall, located 10 miles north of downtown, encompasses 118 shops including **Nordstrom's, The Bon, Lamonts,** and **J.C. Penney.** *I–5 and Northgate Way, tel. 206/362–4777. Open Mon.–Sat. 9:30–9:30, Sun. 11–6.*

Southcenter Mall contains 140 shops, which are anchored by major department stores. *I–5 and I–405 in Tukwila, tel. 206/ 246–7400. Open Mon.–Sat. 9:30–9:30, Sun. 11–6.*

Bellevue Square, an upscale shopping center about 8 miles east of Seattle, houses more than 200 shops and includes a children's play area, the Bellevue Art Museum, and covered parking. *N.E. 8th St. and Bellevue Way, tel. 206/454-8096. Open Mon.-Sat. 9:30-9:30, Sun. 11-6.*

Specialty Stores

Antiques   **Antique Importers** (640 Alaskan Way, tel. 206/628-8905) carries mostly English oak antiques.

Art Dealers   **Michael Pierce Gallery** (600 Pine St., tel. 206/447-9166) specializes in limited-edition prints and paintings on paper.

Art Glass   **The Glass House** (311 Occidental Ave. S, tel. 206/682-9939), Seattle's only working glass studio, features one of the largest displays of glass in the city.

Chocolates   **Cafe Dilettante** (416 Broadway Ave. E, tel. 206/329-6463) is well-known for its mouth-watering dark chocolates. Recipes come via Julius Rudolf Franzen, who obtained them from the kitchen of the imperial court of Russia when he was commissioned by Czar Nicholas II as master pastry chef. Later, he was master chocolatier to Franz Joseph I, emperor of Austria.

Crafts   **Pike Place Market** (*see* Exploring Seattle, above).
Flying Shuttle Ltd. (607 1st Ave., tel. 206/343-9762) displays handcrafted jewelry, whimsical folk art, handknits, and handwoven garments.

Jewelry   **Fireworks Gallery** (210 1st Ave. S, tel. 206/682-8707; 400 Pine St., tel. 206/682-6462) features whimsical earrings and pins. **Fourth & Pike Building** houses many retail/wholesale jewelers, including **Turgeon-Raine Jewelers** (9th floor, tel. 206/447-9488), an exceptional store with a sophisticated but friendly staff.

Leather and Luggage   **Bergman Luggage Co.** (1930 3rd Ave., tel. 206/448-3000) features luggage in a variety of prices and materials.

Men's Apparel   **Jeffrey-Michael** (1318 4th Ave., tel. 206/625-9891) provides a fine line of traditional, business, and casual men's clothing. **Mario's** (1513 6th Ave., tel. 206/223-1461) offers a wide selection of contemporary men's wear.

Outdoor Wear and Equipment   **REI** (1525 11th Ave., tel. 206/323-8333) sells clothing as well as outdoor equipment including water bottles, tents, bikes, and freeze-dried food in a creaky, funky building on Capitol Hill. **Eddie Bauer** (5th Ave. and Union St., tel. 206/622-2766) features sports and outdoor apparel.

Toys   **Magic Mouse Toys** (603 1st Ave., tel. 206/682-8097) carries two floors of toys, from small windups to giant stuffed animals. **Great Windup** (Pike Place Market, tel. 206/621-9370) carries all sorts of windup action toys.

Wine   **Delaurenti Wine Shop** (1435 1st Ave., tel. 206/340-1498) has a knowledgeable staff and a large selection of Northwest Italian wines. **Pike & Western Wine Merchants** (Pike Pl. and Virginia St., tel. 206/441-1307 or 206/441-1308) carries a wide selection of Northwest wines from small wineries.

Women's Apparel   **Boutique Europa** (1015 1st Ave., tel. 206/624-5582) features sophisticated clothing from Europe.

Littler's (Rainier Sq., tel. 206/223–1331) offers classic fashions
for women.
Local Brilliance (1535 1st Ave., tel. 206/343–5864) showcases
fashions from local designers.

Sports and Fitness

Participant Sports

"The best things in life are free" is a homily that holds true, at
least in part, when it comes to keeping fit in this most health-
oriented of cities. Walking, bicycling, hiking, and jogging require little money; pay-as-you-go alternatives such as golf, kayak, sailboat, or sailboard rentals require only marginally more.

Bicycling   Although much of Seattle is so hilly that recreational bicycling
is strenuous, many residents nonetheless commute by bike.
The trail circling **Green Lake** and the **Burke-Gilman Trail** are
popular among recreational bicyclists, although at Green Lake
the crowds of joggers and walkers tend to impede fast travel.
The Burke-Gilman Trail is a city-maintained trail extending for
12.1 miles along Seattle's waterfront from Lake Washington
nearly to Salmon Bay along an abandoned railroad line; it is a
much less congested path. **Myrtle Edwards Park,** north of Pier
70, has a two-lane path for jogging and bicycling. For general
information about Seattle's parks and trails, call the Seattle
Parks Department (tel. 206/684–4075).

A number of shops around Seattle rent mountain bikes as well
as standard touring or racing bikes and equipment. Among
them are **Greg's Greenlake Cycle** (7007 Woodlawn Ave. NE, tel.
206/523–1822) and **Mountain Bike Specialists** (5625 University
Way NE, tel. 206/527–4310).

Fishing   There are plenty of good spots for fishing on **Lake Washington,**
Green Lake, and **Lake Union,** and there are several fishing piers
along the **Elliott Bay** waterfront. A number of companies operating from **Shilshole Bay** also offer charter trips for catching
salmon, rock cod, flounder, and sea bass. A couple of the many
Seattle-based charter companies are **Ballard Salmon Charter**
(tel. 206/789–6202) and **Seattle Salmon and Bottom Fishing**
(tel. 206/292–0595).

Golf   There are almost 50 public golf courses in the Seattle area.
Among the most popular municipally run courses are **Jackson**
Park (1000 N.E. 135th St., tel. 206/363–4747) and **Jefferson**
Park (4101 Beacon Ave. S, tel. 206/762–4513). For more infor-
mation, contact the Seattle Parks and Recreation Department
(tel. 206/684–4075).

Jogging, Skating,   **Green Lake** is far and away Seattle's most popular spot for jog-
Walking   ging and the 3-mile circumference of this picturesque lake is
custom-made for it. Walking, bicycling, roller skating, fishing,
and lounging on the grass and feeding the plentiful waterfowl
are also popular pastimes here. In summer, a large children's
wading pool on the northeast side of the lake is a popular gathering spot. Several outlets clustered along the east side of the
lake offer skate and cycle rentals.

Other good jogging locales are along the **Burke-Gilman Trail,**
around the reservoir at **Volunteer Park,** and at **Myrtle Edwards**
Park, north of the waterfront.

Skiing Snoqualmie Pass in the Cascade Mountains, about an hour's drive east of Seattle on I–90, has a number of fine resorts offering both day and night downhill skiing. Among them: **Alpental, Ski Acres, Snoqualmie Summit** (for all areas: 3010 77th St. SE, Mercer Island 98040, tel. 206/232–8182). All of these areas rent equipment and have full restaurant/lodge facilities.

For ski reports for these areas and the more distant White Pass, Crystal Mountain, and Stevens Pass, call 206/634–0200 or 206/634–2754. For recorded messages about road conditions in the passes, call 206/455–7900.

Tennis There are public tennis courts in many parks around the Seattle area. For information, contact the King County Parks and Recreation Department (tel. 206/296–4258).

Water Sports It stands to reason that sailboating and powerboating are popu-
Boating lar in Seattle. **Sailboat Rentals & Yachts** (2046 Westlake Ave. N, tel. 206/281–9176), on the west side of Lake Union, rents sailboats, with or without skippers, 14–38 feet in length, by the hour or the day. **Wind Works Rentals** (7001 Seaview Ave. NW, tel. 206/784–9386), on Shilshole Bay, rents sailboats ranging from 25 to 40 feet on the more challenging waters of Puget Sound, with or without skippers and by the half-day, day, or week. **Seacrest Boat House** (1660 Harbor Ave. SW, tel. 206/ 932–1050), in West Seattle, rents 18-foot aluminum fishing boats, with or without motors, by the hour or the day.

Kayaking Kayaking—around both the inner waterways (Lake Union, Lake Washington, the Ship Canal) and open water (Elliott Bay)—is a terrific and easy way to get an unusual view of Seattle's busy waterfront. **The Northwest Outdoor Center** (2100 Westlake Ave. N, tel. 206/281–9694), on the west side of Lake Union, rents one- or two-person kayaks and equipment by the hour or week and provides both basic and advanced instruction. Canoes and rowing shells are also available.

Sailboarding Lake Union and Green Lake are Seattle's prime sailboarding spots. Sailboards can be rented year-round at the **Bavarian Surf Shop** (711 N. Northlake Way, tel. 206/545–9463), on Lake Union. Lessons are available.

Spectator Sports

Baseball The **Seattle Mariners,** an American-league team, play April through early October at the Kingdome (201 S. King St., tel. 206/628–3555).

Basketball The **Seattle SuperSonics,** an NBA team, play October through April at the Seattle Center Coliseum (1st Ave. N, tel. 206/281– 5850).

Boat Racing The **unlimited hydroplane** (tel. 206/628–0888) races cap Seattle's Seafair festivities, from mid-July through the first Sunday in August. The races are held on Lake Washington near Seward Park, and tickets cost $10–$20. Weekly **sailing regattas** are held in the summer on Lakes Union and Washington. Call the Seattle Yacht Club (tel. 206/325–1000) for schedules.

Football Seattle's NFL team, the **Seahawks,** play August through December in the Kingdome (201 S. King St., tel. 206/827–9777).

Dining

By John Doerper

Food editor of
Washington
magazine, John
Doerper is a local
food critic and
travel writer whose
pieces have
appeared in Travel
& Leisure and
Pacific Northwest
Magazine.

Highly recommended restaurants are indicated by a star ★.

Category	Cost*
Very Expensive	over $35
Expensive	$25–$35
Moderate	$15–$25
Inexpensive	under $15

*per person, excluding drinks, service, and sales tax (about
7.9%, varies slightly by community)

**American/
Continental
★**

Canlis. This sumptuous restaurant is almost more of a Seattle
institution than a place of fine dining, dating from a time when
steak served by kimono-clad waitresses was the pinnacle of
high living in the city by the sound. Little has changed here
since the '50s. The restaurant is still very expensive, very good
at what it does, and very popular, and the view across Lake Union is as good as ever (though curtained off by a forest of recently built high rises on the far shore). Besides the famous steaks
there are equally famous oysters from Quilcene Bay and fresh
fish in season, cooked to a turn. *2576 Aurora Ave. N, tel. 206/
283–3313. Reservations advised. Jacket required. AE, DC,
MC, V. Closed lunch and Sun. Very Expensive.*

Landau's. Conceived by Hong Kong transplants David and
Mary Jane Landau, this elegant dining spot has established itself as the East Side's top restaurant. The interior is a harmony
of pastel-color walls, polished granite, Oriental artworks, huge
flower arrangements, and plush carpeting. The menu, like the
Hong Kong original, consists mostly of Continental dishes,
with a creative sprinkling of Chinese, Indian, and East/West
dishes. Vegetables, seafood, veal, pork, and even steaks are
prepared with uncommon flair. Try the cream of mushroom
soup (made from scratch), the homemade pâté, or the crab
cannelloni. *500 108th Ave. NE, tel. 206/646–6644. Reservations
accepted. Jacket required. AE, DC, MC, V. Closed Sat. lunch
and Sun. Expensive.*

Place Pigalle. Despite its French name, this is a very American
restaurant and a popular place with locals. Large windows look
out over Elliott Bay and, in nice weather, are open to admit the
salt breeze. Bright flower bouquets lighten up the café tables,
and the friendly staff makes you feel right at home in this small,
intimate restaurant located behind a meat market in the Pike
Place Market's main arcade. Seasonal meals feature seafood
and local ingredients. Go for the rich oyster stew, the fresh
Dungeness crab (available only when it is truly fresh), or the
fresh fish of the day baked in hazelnuts. *Pike Place Market, tel.
206/624–1756. Reservations advised. Dress: casual but neat.
MC, V. Closed Sun. Moderate.*

★ **Vic & Mick's Nine-10 Cafe.** Victor Rosellini has done more for
the Seattle dining scene than anyone else in town in his 40-odd
years behind his famous reservation podium. Trained in San
Francisco, he was the first to introduce such amenities as white
tablecloths and wine lists to Seattle. The Nine-10 is his latest
venture (in partnership with fellow restaurateur Mick Mc-
Hugh). In the 1970s McHugh set a new tone for Seattle restau-

rants by introducing clubby atmosphere with lots of dark wood, polished brass, genteel prints, and a saloonlike atmosphere. The Nine-10 fits this mold snugly. The menu is basically Continental with an Italian flair, and a number of well-cooked local foods are thrown in for variety. The recipes have been carried over from two of Victor Rosellini's previous establishments, and Seattleites are lining up to once again taste the famous Four-10 sandwich; the Italian-style sautéed tenderloin tips; the veal scaloppine saltimbocca; the spaghettini with Italian meatballs; and the cappelletti with fresh chopped tomatoes, cream, and pesto. *910 2nd Ave., tel. 206/292–0910. Reservations advised. Dress: casual but neat. AE, DC, MC, V. Closed Sat. lunch and Sun. Moderate.*

Beeliner Diner. A long, narrow storefront, Formica tables, and vinyl settees make for a surprisingly comfortable diner. The food is classic diner fare—a throwback to the 1950s—with thick burgers, french fries, meat loaf, macaroni and cheese, and huge chili dogs. Even though a sign says EAT IT AND BEAT IT, you're encouraged to linger over coffee and pie. *2114 N. 45th St., tel. 206/547–6313. No reservations. Dress: casual. No credit cards. Closed Mon. lunch, Sun. Inexpensive.*

Caveman Kitchen. Despite its out-of-the-way location in suburban Kent, this low-key establishment is Seattle's favorite barbecue joint. It's almost southern in concept, except that the late Dick Donley, who started the place, perfected the cooking of meat over smokey alder or apple wood instead of hickory. His children now run the place and old-timers insist nothing has changed; the ribs, chicken, turkey, salmon, and sausage are as good and moist as ever. Also try the beans, coleslaw, and bread pudding. There's no inside seating, but in nice weather you can sit outside at picnic tables and, if you choose, pick up beer at the store across the street. *807 West Valley Hwy., Kent, tel. 206/854–1210. No reservations. Dress: casual. MC, V. BYOB. Inexpensive.*

Asian
★

Hirshens
Sun Din ner

Wild Ginger. This restaurant's specialty is Pacific Rim cookery—primarily tasty and eclectic Asian fare—including southern Chinese, Vietnamese, Thai, and Korean dishes served in a warm, clubby dining room. The *satay* (chunks of beef, chicken, or vegetables skewered and grilled, and usually served with a spicy peanut sauce) bar, where you can sit to sip local brews and eat tangy, elegantly seasoned skewered seafood or meat until 2 AM, has quickly become a favorite local hangout. In the dining room, daily specials, based on seasonally available products, make meals exciting. No wonder the locals come back again and again. Be sure to start your meal with satay and wandering sage soup, and don't neglect the sweetly flavored duck, a house specialty. *1400 Western Ave., tel. 206/623–4450. Reservations advised. Dress: casual but neat. AE, CB, DC, MC, V. Closed Sun. lunch. Moderate.*

Chinese **Linyen.** This comfortable restaurant comes into its own late at night, when Seattle celebrities mingle here with chefs from Chinatown restaurants. The standard fare is Cantonese, in the new light style, but you're best off to stick to the blackboard specials: clams in black bean sauce, geoduck, spicy chicken, and fish dishes. The dart games in the bar are a popular—and heated—diversion. *424 7th Ave. S, tel. 206/622–8181. Reservations advised. Dress: casual but neat. AE, DC, MC, V. Closed lunch. Moderate.*

Chau's Chinese Restaurant. This small, very plain place on the

Cafe Alexis, **10**
Cafe Sport, **1**
Campagne, **4**
Chau's Chinese, **15**
El Puerco Lloron, **5**
Emmet Watson's
Oyster Bar, **2**
Han II, **17**
Hien Vuong, **16**
Hunt Club, **11**
Kells, **3**
Linyen, **18**
Metropolitan Grill, **13**
Place Pigalle, **8**
Takara, **6**
Three Girls Bakery, **7**
Trattoria Mitchelli, **14**
Vick & Mick's Nine–10
Cafe, **12**
Wild Ginger, **9**

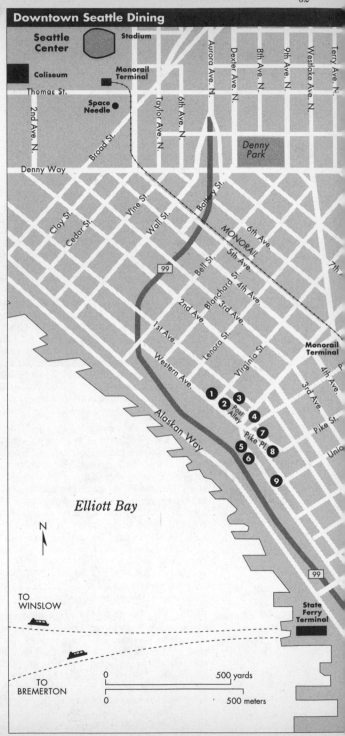

Sandy's street "Village"

Republican St.

Boren Ave. N.

Fairview Ave. N.

Harrison St.

Minor Ave. N.

Pontius Ave. N.

Yale Ave. N.

Seattle Freeway

Melrose Ave. E.

Eastlake Ave. E.

E. Harrison St.

Bellevue Ave. E.

E. Thomas St.

Summit Ave. E.

Belmont Ave. E.

Boylston Ave. E.

Harvard Ave. E.

E. Broadway

10th Ave. E.

Federal Ave. E.

11th Ave. E.

Thomas St.

John St.

Denny Way

E. John St.

E. Denny Way

Boren Ave.

Terry Ave.

9th Ave.

8th Ave.

Ave.

Stewart St.

Howell St.

E. Howell St.

E. Olive Way

Seattle Central Community College

Broadway Playfield

E. Pine St.

E. Pike St.

Broadway

10th Ave.

11th Ave.

Olive Way

7th Ave.

6th Ave.

Pine St.

5th Ave.

E. Union St.

Terry Ave.

Boren Ave.

Minor Ave.

Summit Ave.

Boylston Ave.

Madison St.

Seattle University

9th Ave.

11

University St.

Seneca St.

Spring St.

Madison St.

Marion St.

Columbia St.

8th Ave.

James St.

2nd Ave.

10

12

13

1st Ave.

Post Ave.

14

Western Ave.

Cherry St.

James St.

Yesler Way

5

E. Jefferson St.

Spruce St.

10th Ave.

11th Ave.

Boren Ave.

Yesler Way

Washington St.

Main St.

Jackson St.

4th Ave.

15

16

5th Ave.

King St.

6th Ave.

17

Maynard Ave.

7th Ave.

18

A. Jay's, **32**
Bahn Thai, **30**
Beeliner Diner, **25**
Cafe Juanita, **27**
Canlis, **26**
Caveman Kitchen, **34**
Cucina! Cucina!, **29**
Landau's, **28**
Le Tastevin, **31**
Pacifica, **19**
Ray's Boathouse, **24**
Rover's, **33**
Saleh Al Lago, **20**
Salvatore Ristorante
Italiano, **22**
Santa Fe Cafe, **21, 23**

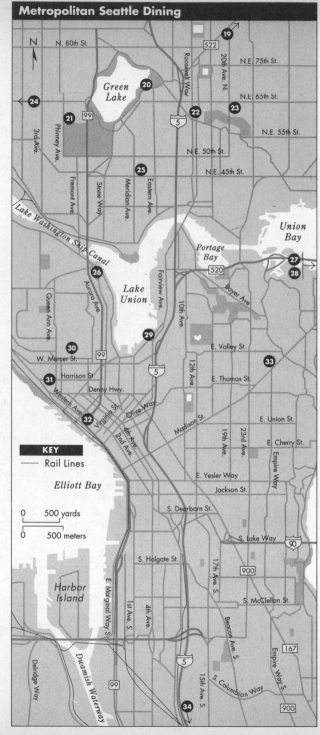

64

Metropolitan Seattle Dining

outer limits of Seattle's Chinatown serves great seafood, such
as steamed oysters in garlic sauce, Dungeness crab with ginger
and onion, and geoduck. Avoid the standard dishes of the Cantonese repertoire that dominate much of the menu, and stick to
the seafood and specials. *310 4th Ave. S, tel. 206/621–0006. Reservations advised. Dress: casual. MC, V. Closed weekend
lunch. Inexpensive.*

Deli **A. Jay's.** This small, simple place proves that homey deli fare
can be very good. For breakfast, try one of the half-dozen
fluffy, overstuffed omelets or a thick, well-seasoned frittata.
Bagels come with plenty of cream cheese and good lox. Coffee
flows freely, and the service is friendly. You can sit and talk
without being rushed. At lunch you'll discover large sandwiches (good pastrami), burgers, and soup. *2619 1st Ave., tel.
206/441–1511. Reservations advised. Dress: casual. AE, MC,
V. Closed nights and weekends. Inexpensive.*

Three Girls Bakery. It's a 13-seat glassed-in lunch counter behind a bakery outlet, serving sandwiches and soups to hungry
folks in a hurry. Go for the chili and a hunk of Sicilian sour-
dough. Another idea is to buy a loaf at the takeout counter, get
smoked salmon at the fish place next door, and head for a picnic
table in Waterfront Park. *Pike Place Market, 1514 Pike Pl.,
tel. 206/622–1045. No reservations. Dress: casual. No credit
cards. No alcohol. Closed nights and Sun. Inexpensive.*

French **Campagne.** Overlooking Pike Place Market and Elliott Bay,
Campagne is intimate and urbane. White walls, picture windows, and colorful modern prints set the up tone; wood floors
with Oriental rugs add a touch of class. The lusty flavors of Pro-
vence pervade the menu in such dishes as chicken stuffed with
goat cheese and fresh herbs, salmon in a cognac and champagne
butter sauce, garlic sausage and duck leg served on red cabbage, and *pan bagna* (ratatouille with goat cheese sandwich).
The chef's interpretation of salade Niçoise comes with local
Blue Lake beans, Niçoise olives, and fresh seared (and thus
very tender) tuna. A lamb salad (thinly sliced lamb served on a
bed of greens with goat cheese) is perfectly seasoned. Occasionally the service can be brusque, but the food more than
makes up for grumpy waiters. *Inn at the Market, 86 Pine St.,
tel. 206/728–2800. Reservations advised. Jacket required. AE,
MC, V. Expensive.*

Le Tastevin. This restaurant may have set a new tone for
Seattle's French restaurants when it opened several years ago.
Instead of dark wood and subdued lighting, you'll find a sunny,
trellised dining room, bright with light wood and green plants,
and racks of wine bottles along the far walls. The windows face
west, toward the Olympic Mountains and colorful sunsets.
Since Le Tastevin can't make up its mind whether it serves classical French or Northwest nouvelle cuisine, you're likely to find
such dishes as salmon, bouillabaisse, or sweetbreads with port
sauce paired with berry soups, fresh halibut with tart fruit
puree, or steamed pink scallops served whole in the shell, like
clams. Cream, the staple of traditional French cookery, is almost absent. For dessert, you should not miss the fresh fruit
ices—made daily from scratch—or the wine sorbets. As an alternative to the expensive regular lunch menu, try the bar
lunch, that's just as good. In the late afternoon, during happy
hour, inexpensive dishes and great snack food are served. The
wine list is vast, spanning many countries and vintages, and
quite reasonably priced. *19 W. Harrison St., tel. 206/283–0991.*

Reservations advised. Jacket required. AE, DC, MC, V. Closed Sat. lunch and Sun. Expensive.

Rover's. This is French cooking at its best, with a daily menu based on what is locally available. Specialties include salmon, pheasant, quail, venison, and rabbit in elegant yet surprisingly light sauces. The enormous pasta dishes are among Seattle's best. Recently, chef/owner Thierry Rautureau has experimented with sea urchin roe and truffles, and walnuts and wild mushrooms. The setting is highly romantic, in a small house with a garden. Herbs and flowers grow in flower beds just outside the windows. Service is excellent—friendly but not obtrusive. *2808 E. Madison St., tel. 206/325-7442. Reservations advised. Dress: casual but neat. AE, MC, V. Closed lunch and Mon. Moderate.*

Irish   Kells. Tucked into an old brick building along the Pike Place Market's most romantic thoroughfare, you'll forget you're in America when you step through the door of this pub. The accoutrements, too, look like they've been brought over from the old country: bar, taps, wood paneling, sporting prints are all very Irish, down to the accents and politics. The food is simple but tasty: Irish stew, leg of lamb, meat pies. Guinness and Harp on tap are very fresh, or try one of the hearty Northwest brews. The place rings with live Irish music Wednesday through Saturday nights. Kells is very friendly and feels an instant home away from home. In summer there's limited outdoor seating in the alley. *Pike Place Market, 1916 Post Alley, tel. 206/728-1916. Reservations advised. Dress: casual but neat. MC, V. Closed Sun. Moderate.*

Italian   Saleh Al Lago. This very fashionable spot with a view of Green
★   Lake and the park serves up some of the best Italian fare in the city. The well-lit dining room with light pinks and pastels invites simple, well-paced evening dining and choices such as the antipasti, fresh pasta, and veal dishes are always excellent. Be sure to try the ravioli *al mondo mio*, the chef's special ravioli (filling and sauce vary), or the *tagliatelle* (flat, ribboned egg pasta) with champagne and caviar. Even deceptively plain fare, like grilled breast of chicken with olive oil and fresh herbs, is superb here, with just the right—very light—touch. *6804 E. Greenlake Way N, tel. 206/522-7943. Reservations advised. Jacket required. AE, MC, V. Closed Sat. lunch and Sun. Expensive.*

Cafe Juanita. This comfortable, casual place—decorated with beige linens and offering wonderful views from the windows—is more than just a restaurant. There's a winery in the basement, and the vintages made there—bottled under owner/chef/winemaker Peter Dow's Cavatappi label—are available upstairs. The veal scaloppine and chicken dishes can be a bit on the rich and buttery side, but there's plenty of inexpensive Italian wine on the lengthy wine list to dilute the cream. *9702 N.E. 120th Pl., Kirkland, tel. 206/823-1505. Reservations advised. Dress: casual but neat. MC, V. Closed lunch. Moderate.*

Cucina! Cucina! This is where Seattle goes for fun and good food. The restaurant and its large deck overlook Lake Union, Seattle's downtown lake, which is large enough to accommodate oceangoing ships. Of the many lakefront restaurants, Cucina has the best view, the most sheltered deck (to guard against cold winds that can spring up even on warm summer afternoons), and the friendliest service. Some of the waiters and waitresses double as fashion models at local studios (which adds glitz and chic to the place). The restaurant itself is simple in design, with concrete tabletops in the bar and colorful surroundings. The food is basic Italian, with a good selection of lightly sauced pasta and seafood dishes and a tempting assortment of one-person pizzas topped with wild mushrooms, smoked chicken, and even salmon. If you're out on the deck, expect seaplanes buzzing above the restaurant as they prepare to land on the lake. *901 Fairview Ave. N, tel. 206/447–2782. Reservations advised. Dress: casual but neat. AE, MC, V. Closed Sun. lunch. Moderate.*

Trattoria Mitchelli. This archetypal Seattle storefront café is usually noisy and crowded, especially in the wee hours of the morning (the place stays open till 4 AM), and has a Bohemian-like atmosphere that's fast-paced and friendly, though you're never rushed. The food is a bargain and comes in plentiful portions: heaping servings of Italian pasta, sandwiches, and antipasti. *84 Yesler Way, tel. 206/623–3885. No reservations. Dress: casual. AE, CB, DC, MC, V. Moderate.*

Salvatore Ristorante Italiano. You have to wait for a table in this small storefront restaurant, but most customers don't consider that an obstacle. Go for one of the four or five specials, which always include individual pizzas, pasta dishes, and meat and fish courses, chalked onto the blackboard above the kitchen window. Chef/owner Salvatore Anania learned the fine art of pizza making in Paris, but his pasta dishes hark straight back to his native Calabria. Be sure to try the *pesce misto*, a delightful seafood stew whose contents are very mutable—and very Italian. The wine list has some locally rare Italian bottlings. *6100 Roosevelt Way NE, tel. 206/527–9301. No reservations. Dress: casual. MC, V. Closed Sat. lunch and Sun. Inexpensive.*

Japanese

Takara. Kuma-san in full action can look like a character from a Japanese wood-block print: the famed swordsman Miyamoto Musashi getting ready to fight heaven and earth. But there's nothing bellicose about this ever-smiling sushi chef—except for his determination to serve only the freshest seafood for sushi and sashimi. It's the freshness of the raw materials and the quality of the knife handling (one is almost tempted to say swordsmanship) that's making Kuma-san the hottest sushi chef in town. He's been known to create a perfect rose from translucent slices of raw tuna, and he can form a phoenix in full flight from a lump of rice (for the body), golden salmon caviar (to simulate the iridescent back feathers), and sparkling *nori* seaweed (for the head, beak, and wings). No wonder Japanese businessmen flock here for lunch. The dining room serves classic Japanese dishes using Northwest ingredients. The salmon teriyaki is superb, and so is the steamed black cod. *Pike Place Market Hillclimb, 1501 Western Ave., tel. 206/682–8609. Reservations advised for dining room, no reservations for sushi bar. Dress: casual but neat. AE, MC, V. Beer and sake. Closed Sun., except May–Labor Day. Moderate.*

Japanese/Korean

Han Il. This upstairs, upscale Korean restaurant overlooks an urban square in Seattle's Asian shopping district. Classic Korean barbecue, prepared on gas burners at your table, comes with a plethora of side dishes and dipping sauces. But the much less expensive luncheon specials are just as good. Barbecued chicken, pork, or beef come to the table with kimchi (the Han Il's version of this Korean cabbage pickle has just the right degree of pungency and is piquant but not overspiced), plus *daikon* radish pickles, a tangy sea vegetable salad, rice, a couple of tempura prawns, and a bottomless pot of tea. *409 Maynard Ave. S, tel. 206/587–0464. Reservations advised. Dress: casual. MC, V. Inexpensive.*

Mexican **El Puerco Lloron.** Don't be put off by the cafeteria line and the studied "sleazy-south-of-the-border" bar look. The fresh, handmade tortillas have great texture, and the fillings are endowed with all the right flavors. The chili relleno is tops. But it almost doesn't matter what you order—tacos, *taquitos*, tamales—they're all good. The salsas are zesty and the beer is cold. *Pike Place Market Hillclimb, 1501 Western Ave., tel. 206/624–0541. No reservations. Dress: casual. AE, MC, V. Inexpensive.*

Northwest **Cafe Alexis.** This is a small intimate, but elegant place that's ★ highlighted by the tapestry wall coverings, teal-colored walls, and wood-burning fireplace. In addition, it offers one of the more imaginative menus in town, with a fare that changes according to the seasons. Expect artistically arranged salads with uncommon ingredients like grilled trout and dressings like avocado-mint crème fraîche with smoked salmon or curried walnuts; steamed clams and mussels in spicy peanut–black bean sauce; king salmon steamed over aromatic herbs and served with a lemon-thyme-ginger butter; and other seasonal fish grilled and seasoned to perfection. The braised veal shank with sun-dried tomatoes, herb *pistou*, and grilled polenta is very tender and flavorful; the roast duck breast with cardamom hazelnut sauce and apple catsup is a fowl delight. *Alexis Hotel, 1007 1st Ave., tel. 206/624–3646. Reservations advised. Jacket required. AE, D, DC, MC, V. Expensive.*

Hunt Club. Owner Barbara Figueroa may be the most accomplished chef in Seattle, a suitable match for this very traditional, almost clubby restaurant with dark wood and plush seats and innovative and exciting food. Besides perfectly prepared lamb with shiitake mushrooms in Madeira sauce, or seasonal king salmon with Pinot noir butter, you may happen upon such surprising fare as green cattail spikes (the texture of asparagus, the flavor of artichokes), *salicornia* (a fleshy herb grown in salt marshes), or just plain corn fritters. There are occasionally odd desserts—jalapeño sorbet, anyone? Ask for local goat cheeses on your cheese platter. *Sorrento Hotel, 900 Madison St., tel. 206/622–6400. Reservations advised. Jacket required. AE, DC, MC, V. Expensive.*

Cafe Sport. This trendy Pike Place Market restaurant—affiliated with the athletic club next door—prepares some of the city's most original and delicious cookery in a modern dining room decorated with muted tones, fresh flowers, and white linens. A few of the best seafood choices include *sake kasu* cod and lingcod in a spicy peanut and coconut sauce. But the fare can be quite eclectic, since the ever-changing menu varies wildly depending on the availability of seasonal products and the whim of the cooks. You might walk in one day and find dishes that would do the finest Italian restaurant proud, from a well-designed antipasto platter to a succulent osso buco with wild mushrooms. Another time, you might think you have accidentally stepped into a Thai café, an American diner (replete with cheeseburger and fries), or perhaps a New England fish house. That sort of eclectic approach is fraught with danger, but at Cafe Sport it works. *2020 Western Ave., tel. 206/443–6000. Reservations advised. Dress: casual but neat. AE, DC, MC, V. Moderate.*

Pacifica. Located in the heart of the Woodinville wine country—25 miles east of Seattle—this airy country place is Washington's first "wine country" restaurant. The lushly green valley grows few grapes, but much wine is made here from grapes brought in from eastern Washington. Seafood dishes and meats are handled with a light touch; the homemade sausages—including pesto chicken sausage and Milwaukee-style beer sausage—alone are worth the trip. Taste wines nearby at the Château Ste. Michelle, French Creek, and Salmon Bay wineries. *14450 Woodinville–Redmond Rd., Woodinville, tel. 206/487–1530. Reservations advised. Dress: casual but neat. AE, MC, V. Closed Mon. Moderate.*

Seafood **Ray's Boathouse.** The view of Puget Sound may be the drawing card here, but the seafood is impeccably fresh and well prepared. Perennial favorites include broiled salmon, sake kasu cod, prawns baked in their shells, and superb (lingcod) fish 'n chips. Ray's has a split personality: a fancy dining room downstairs, a café and bar upstairs. Go for the café, where prices are lower and the food is just as good as in the more formal setting downstairs. In warm weather, sit outside and watch boats float past almost below your table. The gap in the rocky shore is the mouth of Seattle's ship canal, which runs to Lakes Union and Washington. You can't get bored: Pilot boats, tugs, fishing boats, pleasure yachts—a continuous stream of marine vessels flows past. *6049 Seaview Ave. NE, tel. 206/789–3770. Reservations advised for window seats in dining room; no reservations for café. Dress: casual but neat. AE, DC, MC, V. Moderate.*

★ **Emmet Watson's Oyster Bar.** This small oyster bar may be a bit hard to find: It's in the back of the Pike Place Market's Soames-Dunn Building and fronts a small flower-bedecked (from spring through fall) courtyard. The decor is unpretentious, the inside booths are cramped, and a seat at the bar (in rainy weather) or in the courtyard (when the sun shines) is hard to find. But Seattleites know their oysters, and this is the locals' favorite hangout. The place is worth the special effort, for the oysters are very fresh (and come in a great number of varieties) and the beer list is ample (50 or more selections, from local microbrews to fancy imports). Both oysters and beer are very inexpensive. If you don't like oysters, try the salmon soup or the fish-and-chips (large flaky pieces of fish with very little grease). *Pike Place Market, 1916 Pike Pl., tel. 206/448–7721. No reservations. Dress: casual. No credit cards. Closed dinner and Sun. Inexpensive.*

Southwest **Santa Fe Cafe.** In this casual dining room you can enjoy such spicy New Mexican dishes as green-chili burritos made with blue-corn tortillas. Interesting brews on tap help mitigate the heat of such fiery fare as the red-chili burrito (it's so hot, the waiter warns you as you order). Other choices are less *picante*, but still flavorful: the green-chili stew, the blue-corn crepes, the red or green enchiladas. Chili relleno may come in the form of a quiche. The thick, hand-patted flour tortillas are uncommonly flavorful; sauces are made from red and green chilis brought in from New Mexico. The 65th Street location offers a cozier, homey appeal, with its woven rugs and dried flowers, and is popular with graduate students and professors. The Phinney Avenue restaurant is slicker and more chic; skylights fill the place with light that brightens the soft pink-and-mauve color scheme. Visitors from Santa Fe admit that this is about as authentic as it gets. *Two locations: 2255 N.E. 65th St., tel. 206/*

524–7736; 5910 Phinney Ave. N, tel. 206/783–9755. Reservations advised. Dress: casual but neat. MC, V. Closed weekend lunch and Mon. Moderate.

Steaks **Metropolitan Grill.** This favorite lunch spot of the executive crowd serves custom-aged, mesquite-broiled steaks in a classic steakhouse atmosphere. The steaks—the best in Seattle—are huge and come with baked potatoes or pasta. This is not food for timid eaters: Even the veal chop is extra thick, and the hamburger ("Western Ground Sirloin Steak") is so big that one person may have problems finishing it. Among the accompaniments, the onion rings and sautéed mushrooms are tops. Don't be surprised if you hear more Japanese than English as you eat here: The place is so popular with visiting businessmen that there's a menu in Japanese, too. *818 2nd Ave., tel. 206/624–3287. Reservations advised. Dress: casual but neat. AE, CB, DC, MC, V. Closed Sun. lunch. Moderate.*

Thai **Bahn Thai.** Thai cooking is ubiquitous in Seattle—it almost can be considered a mainstream cuisine. Because of the variety of dishes and the quality of the preparations, the Bahn Thai, one of the pioneers of local Thai food, is still one of the best and most popular. Start your meal with a skewer of tangy chicken or pork satay or with the *tod mun goong* (spicy fish cake), and continue with hot-and-sour soup and one of the many prawn or fish dishes. The deep-fried fish with garlic sauce is particularly good—and you can order it very hot. This restaurant promises a relaxed—particularly romantic—atmosphere in the evenings. *409 Roy St., tel. 206/283–0444. Reservations advised. Dress: casual but neat. AE, DC, MC, V. Closed weekend lunch. Inexpensive.*

Vietnamese **Hien Vuong.** Talk about unpretentious: This small café, set in
★ the International District, is about as plain as such places get in Seattle, but the food is superb. Aficionados make special trips for the Cambodian soup and the shrimp rolls. The peanut dipping sauce is more flavorful than usual. Do try the papaya with beef jerky—it's unusual but very enjoyable. The prices are incredibly low, just one reason why this is one of the best lunch places in town. Parking can be a problem here. *502 S. King St., tel. 206/624–2611. No reservations. Dress: casual. No credit cards. No alcohol. Closed Tues. Inexpensive.*

Lodging

There is no shortage of lodging in Seattle. The variety ranges from the elegant deluxe hotels of downtown to the smaller, less expensive hotels in the University District; from the string of budget motels along Aurora Avenue North (Hwy. 99), many of which are legacies of the 1962 World's Fair, to the big new hotels strung along Pacific Highway South (Hwy. 99) that accommodate travelers near Seattle-Tacoma International Airport. Also available are a number of bed-and-breakfast accommodations: For more information, contact the **Washington State Bed-and-Breakfast Guild** (2442 N.W. Market St., Seattle, WA 98107, tel. 509/548–7171) or the **Pacific Bed & Breakfast Agency** (701 N.W. 60th St., Seattle, WA 98107, tel. 206/784–0539).

Highly recommended hotels are indicated by a star ★.

Category	Cost*
Very Expensive	over $150
Expensive	$100–$150
Moderate	$50–$100
Inexpensive	under $50

*per room, double occupancy, not including 14.1% combined
hotel and state sales tax*

Downtown Seattle **Alexis.** The Alexis is an intimate hotel in an artfully restored
Very Expensive historic 1901 building on 1st Avenue near the waterfront, the
★ Public Market, and the new Seattle Art Museum. Guests are
greeted with complimentary sherry at this small, quietly understated elegant hotel. The 54 rooms are decorated in subdued colors, with mauve as a primary color, and some suites
feature Jacuzzis, wood-burning fireplaces, and some marble
fixtures. Unfortunately, there are no views in this simple hotel;
rooms facing the avenue can be noisy. Cafe Alexis, an elegant
dining room in wine and green colors with a marble fireplace,
located on the ground floor of the hotel, features fine Northwest cuisine. Amenities include complimentary Continental
breakfast, shoe shines, morning newspaper, and guest membership at the Seattle Club, the place to be seen working out.
*1007 1st Ave., 98104, tel. 206/624–4844 or 800/426–7033; fax
206/621–9009. 54 rooms. Facilities: restaurant, café/bar, access to health club, steam room. AE, CB, MC, V.*

★ **Four Seasons Olympic Hotel.** The Olympic is Seattle's most elegant hotel. In 1982, Four Seasons restored it to its 1920s gran-
deur, with the public rooms furnished with marble, thick rugs,
wood paneling, armchairs, and potted plants. Palms and skylights in the Garden Court provide a relaxing background for
lunch, afternoon tea, or dancing to the Fred Radke swing band
on the weekends. The Georgian Room, the hotel's premier dining room, exudes Italian Renaissance elegance, while
Shuckers, oyster bar is more casual. The 450 rooms, less luxurious than the public rooms, feature period reproductions.
Amenities include valet parking, 24-hour room service,
stocked bar, chocolates on your pillow, complimentary shoe
shines, and a bathrobe in the room for each guest. Locals drop
in occasionally to pamper themselves with a massage and swim
at the health club. *411 University St., 98101, tel. 206/621–1700
or 800/223–8772; fax 206/682–9633. 450 rooms. Facilities: 3
restaurants, health club, indoor pool. AE, DC, MC, V.*

Stouffer Madison Hotel. This new high-rise hotel, located between downtown and I–5, was built in 1983. Peach and green
are the identifying colors of the Stouffer Madison, and the
rooms are equipped with wood cabinets and marble counter-
tops and have good views of downtown, Elliott Bay, and the
Cascade Mountains. Club Level floors (25 and 26) feature their
own concierge, complimentary Continental breakfast, and a library. The health club includes a 40-foot rooftop pool and a
Jacuzzi. *515 Madison St., 98104, tel. 206/583–0300 or 800/468–
3571; fax 206/622–8635. 554 rooms. Facilities: 2 restaurants,
lounge, indoor pool, Jacuzzi, health club, indoor parking. AE,
D, DC, MC, V.*

Expensive **Edgewater.** The only hotel situated on Elliott Bay, the Edgewater is an institution, known for the now-defunct tradition of
guests' fishing from their waterside windows. In 1988 the new

Alexis, **13**
Best Western,
Greenwood, **28**
Doubletree, **21**
Edgewater, **2**
Four Seasons
Olympic Hotel, **11**
Holiday Inn
Sea-Tac, **24**
Hyatt Bellevue, **27**
Inn at the Market, **5**
Mayflower Park, **6**
Meany Tower, **18**
Pacific Plaza, **14**
Park Inn Club &
Breakfast, **1**
Red Lion Bellevue, **25**
Red Lion/Sea-Tac, **20**
Seattle Airport
Hilton, **22**
Seattle Hilton, **12**
Seattle International
Youth Hostel, **10**
Seattle Marriott, **23**
Seattle Sheraton Hotel
and Towers, **9**
Seattle YMCA, **15**
Sixth Avenue Inn, **4**
Sorrento, **17**
Stouffer Madison, **16**
University Plaza, **19**
Warwick, **3**
WestCoast Camlin, **8**
Westin, **7**
Woodmark, **26**

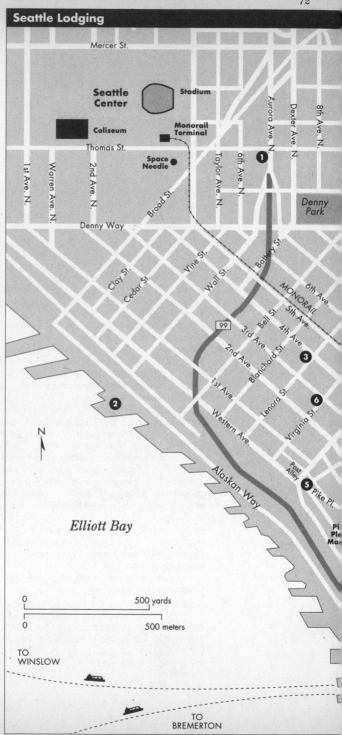

Mercer St.

9th Ave. N.

Westlake Ave. N.

Terry Ave. N.

Boren Ave. N.

Fairview Ave. N.

Republican St.

18 **19**

E. Mercer St.

St.

10th Ave. E.

Federal Ave. E.

Seattle Freeway

Melrose Ave. E.

Bellevue Ave. E.

E. Republican

Belmont Ave. E.

Boylston Ave. E.

Harvard Ave. E.

E. Broadway

Harrison St.

Minor Ave. N.

Pontius Ave. N.

Yale Ave. N.

Eastlake Ave. E.

E. Harrison St.

Summit Ave. E.

Thomas St.

E. Thomas St.

John St.

5

E. John St.

E. Denny Way

Denny Way

Boren Ave

Terry Ave

9th Ave.

8th Ave.

7th Ave

Stewart St.

Howell St.

E. Howell St.

Broadway Playfield

Seattle Central Community College

E. Olive Way

4

7

Olive Way

7th Ave.

8

E. Pine St.

E. Pike St.

Broadway

10th Ave.

Monorail Terminal

Pine St.

6th Ave.

4th Ave.

3rd Ave.

5th Ave.

9

E. Union St.

Boren Ave.

Minor Ave.

Summit Ave.

Boylston Avenue

Seattle University

Pike St.

Union St.

Terry Ave.

9th Ave.

Pike Place Market

10

University St.

11

12

Seneca St.

8th Ave.

17

1st Ave.

2nd Ave.

14

Spring St.

16

15

Madison St.

Marion St.

Columbia St.

Cherry St.

James St.

13

Post Ave.

Boren Ave.

E. Jefferson St.

10th Ave.

99

Western Ave.

5

25 **26** **27** **28**

State Ferry Terminal

20 **24**

Yesler Way

Washington St.

owners banned hotel fishing and remodeled the 250 rooms, and the results are magnificent. The lobby features oak furnishings and comfortable chairs and sofas, with a fireplace and a panoramic bay window from which you can sometimes see sea lions frolicking by. Spacious rooms on the water provide views of ferries, barges, and the Olympic Mountains and are decorated in green-and-blue rustic Northwest plaids and unfinished wood furnishings. *Pier 67, 2411 Alaskan Way, 98121, tel. 206/728–7000 or 800/624–0670; fax 206/441–4119. 250 rooms. Facilities: restaurant, bar, free parking. AE, DC, MC, V.*

Seattle Sheraton Hotel and Towers. The Sheraton is a modern, 840-room hotel catering largely to conventioneers, as it is conveniently located near the Washington State Convention & Trade Center. The lobby features an art-glass collection by Dale Chihuly, a Northwest artist of international repute. The Towers (top five floors) feature larger, more elegant rooms with concierge. Within the complex is a diverse selection of restaurant entertainment options, including Banners, which offers an authentic Japanese breakfast, buffet luncheon, and Continental menu; Gooey's (named after the geoduck, a large, sausagelike northwestern clam that is the subject of many jokes), the bar/disco nighttime hot spot; and Fullers, one of the best restaurants in Seattle, serving nouvelle cuisine using local ingredients. *1400 6th Ave., 98101, tel. 206/621–9000 or 800/325–3535; fax 206/621–8441. 840 rooms. Facilities: 2 restaurants, 2 bars, health club, indoor pool. AE, D, DC, MC, V.*

★ **Sorrento.** This deluxe European-style hotel, originally built in 1909 for the Alaska-Yukon Exposition and since restored to its original elegance, is relatively small and has an intimate, cordial atmosphere. Sitting high on First Hill, it has wonderful views overlooking downtown and the waterfront. The rooms are smaller than in modern hotels, but are quiet and very comfortable; they're decorated in understated, elegant earth tones. The stylish Hunt Club restaurant features exquisite Continental and Northwest dishes by chef Barbara Figueroa, while the dark-paneled Fireside Lounge in the lobby is a warm and inviting locale for sipping coffee, tea, or a cocktail. Other amenities include a complimentary limousine service within the downtown area, concierge, and guest privileges at a nearby athletic club. *900 Madison St., 98104, tel. 206/622–6400; fax 206/625–1059. 76 rooms, 42 suites. Facilities: restaurant, lounge, access to health club. AE, DC, MC.*

Moderate–Expensive
★ **Inn at the Market.** This is a sophisticated but unpretentious hotel adjacent to the Pike Place Public Market. It combines the best aspects of a small, deluxe hotel with the informality of the Pacific Northwest, offering a lively setting that's perfect for travelers who prefer originality and personality over big-hotel amenities. The rooms are spacious and tastefully decorated with comfortable modern furniture and small touches such as fresh flowers and ceramic sculptures. Ask for a room with views of the Market and Elliott Bay. An added plus is a 2,000-square-foot deck, furnished with Adirondack chairs and overlooking the water and the market. There are three restaurants that are not part of the hotel but share the building: Campagne (*see* Dining, above); the Gravity Bar, an ultratrendy hangout with a variety of juices and coffees; and Cafe Dilettante for light meals, fine chocolates and coffees. *86 Pine St., 98109, tel. 206/443–3600; fax 206/448–0631. 65 rooms; nonsmoking rooms*

available. Facilities: 3 restaurants, access to health club and spa, room service, TV. AE, D, DC, MC, V.

Mayflower Park Hotel. This pleasant older hotel, built in 1927, is conveniently connected with Westlake Center and the Monorail terminal to Seattle Center. Brass fixtures and antiques give both the public and private spaces a muted Oriental feel, and the service is similarly unobtrusive and smooth. The rooms are somewhat smaller than in modern hotels, but the Mayflower Park is so sturdily constructed that it is much quieter than many modern downtown hotels. *405 Olive Way, 98101, tel. 206/ 623–8700; fax 206/382–6997. 182 units, including 14 suites; nonsmoking rooms available. Facilities: restaurant, lounge, access to health club. AE, DC, MC, V.*

Seattle Hilton. This Hilton is a favorite for conventions and meetings, particularly because of its central location. Rooms are furnished in the same nondescript, but tasteful style as Hiltons worldwide, with soothing color schemes. One of its two restaurants, the Top of the Hilton, has excellent views of the city and well-prepared variations of salmon steak and other local specialties. An underground passage connects the Hilton with a shopping concourse, Rainier Square, as well as the 5th Avenue Theater and the Washington State Convention Center. *1301 University St., 98101, tel. 206/624–0500, 800/542–7700, or 800/426–0535; fax 206/682–9029. 237 rooms, including 6 suites; nonsmoking rooms available. Facilities: 2 restaurants, lobby, top-floor lounges, gift shop. AE, D, DC, MC, V.*

Warwick Hotel. The Warwick manages to combine its somewhat large size with an intimate European-style charm. Service is friendly and leisurely (but not slow), and the rooms are understated without being bland. All rooms have small balconies and good views of downtown. There is live entertainment nightly in the Liaison restaurant and lounge. *401 Lenora St., 98121, tel. 206/443–4300; fax 206/448–1662. 230 units, including 4 suites; nonsmoking rooms and handicapped rooms available. Facilities: 24-hr courtesy transportation within downtown, pool, Jacuzzi, exercise room, sauna. AE, D, DC, MC, V.*

Westin Hotel. The large high-rise hotel, located just north and east of the Public Market, is easily recognized by its twin-tower cylindrical shape. With this design, all rooms, equipped with balconies, can maximize the terrific views of the waterfront and Lake Union. Inside, the rooms are airy and bright, though furnished in a plain but high-quality style. The informal Market Cafe, the more formal Palm Court, and the famous Trader Vic's, as well as three lounges, are located in-house. *1900 5th Ave., 98101, tel. 206/728–1000 or 800/228–3000; fax 206/728– 2259. 865 rooms, including 47 suites; nonsmoking and handicapped rooms available. Facilities: 3 restaurants, 3 lounges, indoor pool, Jacuzzi, sauna, exercise and weight rooms, voice mail for guests, concierge service. AE, CB, D, DC, MC, V. 50% discounts Fri. and Sat. nights.*

Moderate **Pacific Plaza.** Built in 1929 and refurbished in 1989, this hotel now reflects its original character. The rooms and furnishings, reminiscent of the 1920s and 1930s, are appropriate for singles or couples but are too small to comfortably accommodate a family. Because of its downtown location and modest rates, the Plaza is a fairly good bargain for anyone who is not seeking contemporary luxury. *400 Spring St., 98104, tel. 206/623–3900 or 800/426–1165; fax 206/623–2059. 160 rooms. Facilities: 2* *restaurants, complimentary Continental breakfast. AE, DC, MC, V.*

WestCoast Camlin Hotel. This 1926 Seattle hotel/motor inn was recently remodeled, and the renovation turned out a gracious lobby featuring Oriental carpets, large mirrors, and lots of marble. Located on the edge of the downtown office area, but close to the convention center, the reasonably priced hotel is popular with business travelers. Rooms ending with 10 are best because they feature windows on three sides, and all have working spaces with a chair and table, along with gray-and-maroon cushioned chairs for relaxing. One drawback to staying here, though, is that the heating, air-conditioning, and ventilation system can be noisy. *1619 9th Ave., 98101, tel. 206/682–0100 or 800/426–0670; fax 206/682–7415. Facilities: restaurant, lounge, outdoor pool. AE, D, DC, MC, V.*

Inexpensive **Seattle YMCA.** This accommodation has 198 units and is a member of the American Youth Hostels Association. Rooms are clean and plainly furnished with a bed, phone, desk, and lamp. Rooms cost $25–$50; dorm units, designed to accommodate four people each, cost $14. *909 4th Ave., 98104, tel. 206/382–5000. 198 units. Facilities: pool, health club. No credit cards.*

Youth Hostel: Seattle International. Situated near the Pike Place Market is a bright, clean youth hostel with 126 dormitory-style beds, kitchen, dining room, lounge, and small library for about $10 a night. It's closed between 11 and 4 daily and has a midnight curfew on weeknights. *84 Union St., 98101, tel. 206/622–5443. 126 units. No credit cards.*

Seattle Center **Park Inn Club & Breakfast.** This 1960s-vintage motel, set off
Moderate Aurora Avenue (Hwy. 99), is relatively close to Seattle Center. The decor is typical of its vintage, not fancy but comfortable, and service is friendly and brisk. Continental breakfast, cafeteria, weight room, and play area for children make this lodging a good value. *225 Aurora Ave. N, 98107, tel. 206/728–7666. 160 rooms, nonsmoking rooms available. Facilities: indoor pool, Jacuzzi, parking. AE, MC, V.*

Sixth Avenue Inn. This small but comfortable motor hotel a few blocks north of downtown is a suitable location for families and business travelers. Rooms are pleasant, with standard-issue but well-maintained decor and color schemes; the service is cheerful. This is the hotel of choice for musicians playing at Dimitriou's Jazz Alley, the highly regarded club across the street where jazz buffs may spot a hero or two. *2000 6th Ave., 98121, tel. 206/441–8300; fax 206/441–9903. 166 rooms; nonsmoking rooms available. Facilities: restaurant, lounge. AE, DC, MC, V.*

Inexpensive **Meany Tower Hotel.** Built in 1931 and completely remodeled
★ several times, this is a pleasant hotel just a few blocks from the University of Washington campus. It has managed to retain much of its old-fashioned charm, with a muted-peach color scheme throughout, brass fixtures, and careful, attentive service. The rooms, especially those on the higher floors, have good views of the college grounds and surrounding areas, such as Green Lake and Lake Union. Other amenities include room service and a complimentary morning paper. The Meany Grill on the ground floor serves breakfast, lunch, and dinner; there is a large street-level lounge, as well. *4507 Brooklyn Ave. NE, 98105, tel. 206/634–2000; fax 206/634–2000. 55 rooms;*

nonsmoking rooms available. Facilities: restaurant, lounge. AE, DC, MC, V.

University Plaza Hotel. This is a full-service motor hotel, just on the other side of I–5 from the University of Washington campus, thus it is popular with families and others having business in the area. The mock-Tudor decor gives its lobby and other public areas a slightly outdated feel, but the service is cheerful and the rooms are spacious and pleasantly decorated in teak furniture, with pale pinks and grays being the predominant colors. The rooms on the freeway side can be noisy. *400 N.E. 45th St., 98105, tel. 206/634–0100; fax 206/633–2743. 135 rooms; nonsmoking rooms available. Facilities: restaurant, lounge, outside heated pool, beauty parlor, fitness room. AE, D, DC, MC, V.*

Seattle-Tacoma Airport
Expensive

Red Lion/Sea-Tac. The Red Lion is a popular, hospitable 850-room, full-service convention hotel. Built about 1970, it was recently remodeled in mauve, teal, and gray. Rooms are spacious and bright, with large panoramic balconies; the corner "King Rooms" feature wrap-around balconies and have the best views. Furnishings include chests of drawers, comfortable chairs, a dining table, and desk; this is the perfect accommodation for the business traveler who plans on doing some work between meetings. *18740 Pacific Hwy. S, 98168, tel. 206/246–8600; fax 206/242–9727. 850 rooms. Facilities: restaurant, coffee shop, 2 lounges, 24-hr workout facility with outdoor pool. AE, D, DC, MC, V.*

Moderate–Expensive

Doubletree Inn and **Doubletree Suites.** These two hotels, situated across the street from each other, are adjacent to Southcenter Shopping Mall and convenient to the myriad of business-park offices there. Rooms at the Inn are smaller and less lavish, but perfectly fine and are at least $25 less than rooms at the Suites. Suites, decorated in neutrals, mauves, and pinks, feature a queen-size sofa, table and chairs, and a wet bar in the living room. Vanity area includes a full-size closet with mirrored doors. The room rate includes complimentary buffet breakfast for up to four people per room and two drinks in the bar nightly. *Doubletree Inn, 205 Strander Blvd., Tukwila 98188, tel. 206/246–8220. 200 rooms. Facilities: dining room, coffee shop, lounge, outdoor pool. Doubletree Suites, 16500 Southcenter Pkwy., Tukwila 98188, tel. 206/575–8220; fax 206/575–4743. 221 suites. Facilities: restaurant, lounge, health club, indoor pool, Jacuzzi, sauna, 2 racquetball courts. Doubletree Inn: Moderate; Doubletree Suites: Moderate–Expensive. AE, D, DC, MC, V (for both).*

Seattle Airport Hilton. This relatively small hotel (for the Hilton chain) has an intimate, original feel accentuated by its oak furnishings and cozy fireplace in the lobby, and paintings with Northwest scenery decorating the lobby. The large rooms are presently undergoing a renovation that will make them brighter and livelier with shades of peach and blue. This is also conveniently located: only a half-hour drive from downtown, and a 10-minute drive from Southcenter shopping mall. *17620 Pacific Hwy. S, 98188, tel. 206/244–4800; fax 206/439–7439. 173 rooms. Facilities: restaurant, sports bar, health facilities, outdoor pool, complimentary shuttle to airport. AE, D, DC, MC, V.*

★ **Seattle Marriott.** A surprisingly luxurious and substantial hotel for being in a non-downtown location, this Marriott, built in 1981, features a five-story-high, 20,000-square-foot tropical atrium that's complete with waterfall, dining area, indoor pool, and lounge. The newly renovated rooms are decorated in greens and mauve with dark wood and brass furnishings. Gambits, an in-house jazz club, books nationally known acts that play. *3201 S. 176th St., 98188, tel. 206/241–2000, international reservations tel. 800/228–9290; fax 206/248–0789. 459 rooms; nonsmoking rooms available. Facilities: restaurant, jazz club, 2 whirlpools, health club, games room, airport shuttle, concierge service. AE, D, DC, MC, V. Special rates available to AAA and AARP members; package rates available for weekends.*

Moderate **Holiday Inn Sea-Tac.** This 260-room hotel, built in 1970, has recently been remodeled with an atrium lobby, and a more private garden room, convenient for meeting people. The Top of the Inn revolving-view restaurant features singing waiters. *17338 Pacific Hwy. S, 98188, tel. 206/248–1000 or 800/HOLIDAY; fax 206/242–7089. 260 rooms. Facilities: restaurant, coffee shop, lounge, health club, indoor pool, Jacuzzi. AE, DC, MC, V.*

Bellevue/Kirkland **Red Lion Bellevue.** This 10-story hotel was built in 1982 with a
Expensive large airy atrium full of trees, shrubs, and flowering plants. The property also has a formal dining room, a lounge with two dance floors and 350 oversize rooms, many decorated in mauve and sea-foam green. Rooms have either king- or queen-size beds and two-room suites feature wet bars and spas or Jacuzzis. *300 112th Ave. SE, Bellevue 98004, tel. 206/455–1300 or 800/274–1415; fax 206/454–0466. 350 rooms. Facilities: 2 restaurants, lounge, health club, outdoor pool. AE, D, DC, MC, V.*

★ **Woodmark Hotel.** This new hotel, built in 1989, is the only one situated on the shores of Lake Washington; downtown Kirkland is only a few steps away from the hotel. Its 100 contemporary-style rooms face the water, courtyard, or street and are tastefully furnished in European-style luxury, with earth tones, heavy comforters, and numerous amenities such as terry-cloth bathrobes and fragrant soaps. Comfortable chairs surround the fireplace in the large, open lobby, and a circular staircase descends past a huge bay window and vast view of Lake Washington to the lounge. *1200 Carillon Point, Kirkland 98033, tel. 206/822–3700 or 800/822–3700; fax 206/822–3699. 100 rooms. Facilities: restaurant, access to health club. AE, MC, V.*

Moderate–Expensive **Hyatt Bellevue.** This is a deluxe new high-rise complex in the heart of downtown Bellevue, within a few blocks of Bellevue Square and other fine shopping. The exterior looks like any other sleek high rise, but the interior has such oriental touches as antique Japanese *tansu* (wood chests of drawers) and huge displays of fresh flowers. The rooms are decorated in similarly understated ways, with dark wood and earth tones predominating, and the service is impeccable. Some rooms have been specially designed for Japanese travelers, and come complete with slippers and Japanese meals; others are deluxe suites with two bedrooms, bar facilities, and meeting rooms with desks and full-length tables. The Eques restaurant serves excellent and reasonably priced breakfast, lunch, and dinner; an English-style pub serves a variety of drinks as well as lunch and dinner. *900 Bellevue Way NE, 98004, tel. 206/462–2626; fax 206/646–7567. 382 units, including 30 suites and deluxe suites; nonsmoking rooms available. Facilities: restaurant, pub, 24-*

hr room service, access to health club and pool. *AE, D, DC, MC, V.*

Moderate **Best Western Greenwood Hotel.** This hotel/motor inn features 176 rooms, 16 of which are town-house suites, suitable for two-four people, with sleeping lofts and wood-burning fireplaces. Rooms are clean; those in the corporate wing face the courtyard and are larger and more quiet than the others. These rooms provide thick terry robes for guest use. The hotel is about eight blocks or a 20-minute walk from Bellevue Square. A complimentary appetizer buffet, offered in the lounge weekdays between 5 PM and 7 PM, is substantial and includes seafood and roast beef, and sometimes is built around a theme, such as Mexican or Scandinavian cuisine. *625 116th Ave. NE, Bellevue 98004, tel. 206/455–9444 or 800/445–9444; fax 206/455–2154. 176 rooms. Facilities: restaurant, coffee shop, lounge, outdoor pool. AE, D, DC, MC, V.*

The Arts and Nightlife

The Arts

In recent years Seattle has gained a world-class reputation as a theater town, and it also has a strong music and dance scene for local, national, and international artists. A good handle on what's happening in town can be found in any of several periodicals. Both the *Seattle Times* and *Post-Intelligencer* have pull-out sections on Friday detailing most of the coming week's events. *Seattle Weekly,* which hits most newsstands on Wednesday, has even more detailed coverage and arts reviews. *The Rocket,* a lively free monthly, covers music news, reviews, and concert information, with an emphasis on rock and roll.

Ticketmaster (tel. 206/628–0888) provides (for an added fee) tickets to most productions in the Seattle area through charge-by-phone. **Ticket/Ticket** (401 Broadway E, tel. 206/324–2744) or **Pike Place Market Information Booth** (1st Ave. and Pike St., tel. 206/682–7453 ext. 26) sell half-price tickets for most events on the day of the performance.

Part of the legacy left by the 1962 World's Fair is a series of performance halls at **Seattle Center** (305 Harrison St., tel. 206/684–8582). Seattle also boasts two fine examples of the classic (and beautifully renovated) early 20th-century music hall—the **Fifth Avenue** (1308 5th Ave., tel. 206/625–1900) and the **Paramount** (907 Pine St., tel. 206/682–1414). Other prominent venues are the **Moore Theater** (1932 2nd Ave., tel. 206/443–1744), the small but acoustically outstanding **Broadway Performance Hall** (1625 Broadway, tel. 206/323–2623) at Seattle Central Community College, and **Kane** and **Meany halls** on the University of Washington campus (tel. 206/543–4880).

The **Cornish College of the Arts** (710 E. Roy St., tel. 206/323–1400) is an internationally recognized school that also serves as home to a number of distinguished professional performing groups. These groups stage productions September–May, ranging from dance and jazz to art lectures and multimedia performances. Of particular note are the Professional Acting Conservatory and the renowned Cornish New Performance Group, which often premieres important new pieces of music.

Theater The **Seattle Repertory Theater** (Bagley Wright Theater at Seattle Center, 155 Mercer St., tel. 206/443–2222) presents a variety of high-quality programming, from classics to new plays. During its October–May season, six mainstage productions and three smaller shows (in the adjoining PONCHO Forum) are presented.

The **New City Arts Center** (1634 11th Ave., tel. 206/323–6800) is home to a wide range of experimental performances, produced by a resident company as well as in conjunction with major national and international artists. Its annual output includes six plays, a director's festival and a playwright's festival, three dance concerts, a monthly film showing, and a lively, late-night monthly cabaret.

The **Empty Space Theater** (107 Occidental Ave. S, tel. 206/467–6000) has a strong reputation for introducing Seattle to new playwrights. The season generally runs October–July, with five or six mainstage productions plus several smaller shows throughout the season.

The **Fifth Avenue Musical Theater Company** (Fifth Avenue Theater, 1308 5th Ave., tel. 206/625–1468) is a resident professional troupe that mounts four lavish musicals between October and May each year, with each run lasting about two weeks. (During the rest of the year, this chinoiserie-style historical landmark, carefully restored to its original 1926 condition, hosts a variety of other traveling musical as well as theatrical performances.)

The **Intiman Theater** (Playhouse at Seattle Center, 2nd and Mercer Sts., tel. 206/624–4541) presents the great plays with enduring themes of world drama in an intimate, high-quality setting. The season generally runs May–November.

The **Evergreen Theater Company** (305 Harrison St., tel. 206/443–1490) offers non-Equity but professional musical theater in an intimate setting. (None of its 158 seats is more than 25 feet from the stage.) It stages five productions a season, September–May.

The **Group Theater** (3940 Brooklyn Ave. NE, tel. 206/543–4327) is a multicultural troupe that prides itself on presenting socially provocative works—old and new—by artists of varied cultures and colors. The season runs September–June, and the Group also mounts a special summertime playwrights' festival. Of the regular season's six productions, one is always the popular *Voices of Christmas*, a study of the holidays with consideration to cultural differences and ethnic and emotional barriers.

A Contemporary Theater (100 W. Roy St., tel. 206/285–5110) specializes in developing works by emerging playwrights, including at least one world premiere every year. The season runs May–November, and every December ACT mounts a popular production of Dickens's *A Christmas Carol*.

The **Bathhouse Theater** (7312 W. Greenlake Dr. N, tel. 206/524–9108) produces six productions on a year-round schedule, specializing in innovative updates on classics. In addition, it mounts numerous free public shows in various Seattle parks.

The **Village Theater** (120 Front St. N, Issaquah, tel. 206/392–2202) produces high-quality family musicals, comedies, and dramas September–May in Issaquah, a town east of Seattle.

Dance **Pacific Northwest Ballet** (Opera House at Seattle Center, tel. 206/547–5920) is a resident company and school that presents 60–70 performances annually. Its Christmastime production of *The Nutcracker*, with choreography by Kent Stowell and sets by Maurice Sendak, has become a beloved Seattle tradition.

Allegro Dance Company (Broadway Performance Hall, 1625 Broadway, tel. 206/32–DANCE) presents the best in local and regional choreography, with some productions that include other elements of the performing arts. It schedules about 10 concerts a year between September and June.

Meany Hall for the Performing Arts (University of Washington campus, tel. 206/543–4880) presents important national and international companies, September–May, with an emphasis on modern and jazz dance.

On the Boards (Washington Performance Hall, 153 14th Ave., tel. 206/325–7901) presents and produces a wide variety of contemporary performances, including not only dance but also theater music, and multimedia events by local, national, and international artists. Although the main subscription series runs October–May, OTB events happen nearly every weekend year-round.

Music **Civic Light Opera** (11051 34th Ave. NE, tel. 206/363–2809) is a non-Equity, semipro company that offers three or four high-quality productions per season of large-scale American musical theater. The season runs roughly October–May.

Seattle Symphony (Opera House at Seattle Center and other locations, tel. 206/443–4747) presents some 120 concerts September–June in Seattle and around the world and—under the musical direction of Gerard Schwartz—continues to uphold its long tradition of excellence.

Northwest Chamber Orchestra (tel. 206/343–0445) is the Northwest's only professional chamber music orchestra. At the Moore Theater, the Nippon Kan, and other venues, it presents a full spectrum of music, from Baroque to modern. The season, generally September–May, includes a Bach festival every fall, a spring subscription series, and special holiday performances in December.

A number of other organizations sponsor classical series throughout the year. An integral part of Seattle's strong early music scene is the **Early Music Guild** (tel. 206/325–7066), which presents regional, national, and international artists in various intimate settings during a season running roughly September–May. The 100-year-old **Ladies Musical Club** (tel. 206/328–7153), composed of professional or retired musicians, sponsors four or five important recitals each year by internationally-known artists.

For live rock concerts, the **Moore Theater** (1932 2nd Ave., tel. 206/443–1744) and the **Paramount** (907 Pine St.; for tickets and information, Ticketmaster, tel. 206/628–0888) are elegant former movie/music halls that now host visiting and national rock acts.

Opera **Seattle Opera** (Opera House at Seattle Center, Mercer St. at 3rd Ave., tel. 206/443–4711) is a world-class opera company, generally considered to be one of the top organizations in

America. During the August-May season, it presents six performances of six productions.

Nightlife

For a city of relatively small size, Seattle has a remarkably strong and diverse music scene. On any given night, you can hear high-quality live sounds at a variety of venues. There's a particularly strong blues circuit, a lively folk/bluegrass/Celtic scene, and a steady diet of good local jazz provided by the many internationally known teachers and students at the Cornish School. The two areas with the highest concentration of clubs are Pioneer Square and Ballard; the clubs and taverns in both areas often place an emphasis on high-quality blues and R&B.

Bars and Nightclubs Bars with waterfront views are plentiful in Seattle. Among the best: on the Ship Canal, **Hiram's at the Locks** (5300 34th Ave. NW, tel. 206/784–1733); on Lake Union, the **Lakeside** (2501 N. Northlake Way, tel. 206/634–0823) and **Arnie's** (1900 N. Northlake Way, tel. 206/547–3242); and on Shilshole Bay, **Ray's Boathouse** (6049 Seaview Ave. NW, tel. 206/789–3770) and **Anthony's Home Port** (6135 Seaview Ave. NW, tel. 206/783–0780).

Panoramic views of the city can be found at the **Mirabeau** (1001 4th St., tel. 206/624–4550), on the 46th floor of the Seafirst Building, and at the **Space Needle** (Seattle Center, tel. 206/443–2100), where the revolving restaurant provides a 360-degree view over the course of an hour.

Other fine places for a drink downtown are the **Garden Court** (411 University St., tel. 206/621–1700) at the Four Seasons Olympic, a rather formal and elegant locale; the **J&M Cafe** (201 1st Ave. S, tel. 206/624–1670), a lively and casual Pioneer Square joint; and, near the Kingdome, **F.X. McRory's** (419 Occidental Ave. S, tel. 206/623–4800), famous for its huge selection of single-malt whiskies and equally huge singing bartender.

Folk Clubs **Backstage** (2208 N.W. Market St., tel. 206/781–2805) is an often-packed basement venue in Ballard that has a lively mix of national and local acts with the emphasis on world music, offbeat rock, and new folk.
Kells (1916 Post Alley, tel. 206/728–1916), a snug Irish-style pub, is located near the Public Market and plays live Celtic music Wednesday–Saturday starting at 9 PM.
Murphy's Pub (2110 45th St. NE, tel. 206/634–2110) features open-mike Wednesdays, with Irish and other folk music on Friday and Saturday in this cozy neighborhood bar.
New Melody Tavern (5213 Ballard Ave. NW, tel. 206/782–3480), a lively and casual Ballard bar, is the mecca of serious Seattle folkies. Irish, bluegrass, and other music is played nightly.

Blues/R&B Clubs The **Ballard Firehouse** (5429 Russell St. NW, tel. 206/784–3516) is the music mecca in the heart of Ballard, with an emphasis on local and national blues acts.
Chicago's (315 1st Ave. N, tel. 206/282–7791) features Chicago-style pizza and other kinds of good, reasonably priced Italian food in this restaurant just west of the Seattle Center. Live blues is played on weekends.
Doc Maynard's (610 1st Ave., tel. 206/682–4649) is another

R&B-oriented tavern with a small and always jam-packed dance floor.

Larry's (209 1st Ave. S, tel. 206/624–7665) features live R&B and blues nightly in an unpretentious, friendly, and usually jam-packed tavern/restaurant in Pioneer Square.

Old Timer's Cafe (620 1st Ave., tel. 206/623–9800) is a popular Pioneer Square restaurant and bar with live music—mostly R&B—nightly.

Owl Cafe & Tavern (5140 Ballard Ave. NW, tel. 206/784–3640) is a casual and popular tavern near the Ballard waterfront, with good food, live R&B nearly every night, and a spacious dance floor.

The **Scarlet Tree** (6521 Roosevelt Way NE, tel. 206/523–7153), a neighborhood institution, is a restaurant and bar just north of the University District. Great burgers and live R&B are offered nightly.

Jazz Clubs   **Dimitriou's Jazz Alley** (2037 6th Ave., tel. 206/441–9729) is a downtown club with nationally known, consistently high-quality performers every night but Sunday. Excellent dinners are served before the first shows.

Gambits (3201 S. 176th St., tel. 206/241–2000), in the Marriott Hotel near Seattle-Tacoma airport, is an attractive lounge that features nationally known jazz acts on a regular basis.

Latona Tavern (6423 Latona Ave. NE, tel. 206/525–2238) is a funky, friendly, often jazz-oriented, neighborhood bar at the south end of Green Lake with a variety of local musicians nightly.

Lofurno's (2060 15th Ave., tel. 206/283–7980), located south of the Ballard Bridge, offers reasonably priced Italian food and jazz nightly.

New Orleans Creole Restaurant (114 1st Ave. S, tel. 206/622–2563) is a popular Pioneer Square restaurant with good food and live jazz nightly—mostly top local performers but occasionally national acts as well.

Rock Clubs   **Central Tavern** (207 1st Ave. S, tel. 206/622–0209) is a crowded Pioneer Square tavern with an ever-changing roster of local and national rock acts.

OK Hotel (212 Alaskan Way, tel. 206/621–7903), a small venue near Pioneer Square, is dedicated to national and local rock and experimental music.

Parker's (17001 Aurora Ave. N, tel. 206/542–9491) was a venerable North Seattle teen palace of the '50s and '60s but has since become a more sophisticated dinner-and-show venue for a variety of rock artists, often nationally known acts.

Squid Row Tavern (518 E. Pine St., tel. 206/322–2031), an avant-garde and very casual tavern on Capitol Hill, features ultranew rock and occasional poetry readings.

The **Square on Yesler** (111 Yesler St., tel. 206/447–1514) has high-quality live rock and R&B Thursday through Saturday.

Vogue (2018 1st Ave., tel. 206/443–0673), a club in Belltown, the artist's community just north of the Public Market, presents a variety of au courant local and national rock.

Comedy Clubs   **Comedy Underground** (2225 Main St., tel. 206/628–0303), a Pioneer Square club (literally underground, beneath Swannie's), presents stand-up comedy nightly, with Monday and Tuesday reserved as open-mike nights; the other nights are mixtures of nationally known and local comics.

Giggles (5220 Roosevelt Way NE, tel. 206/526–JOKE), in the

University District, presents the best of local and nationally known comedians six nights a week, with late shows on weekend nights.

Dance Clubs In Pioneer Square, there are several popular, chic clubs featuring recorded dance music, including the **Celebrity** (313 2nd Ave. S, tel. 206/467–1111), the **Hollywood Underground** (323 2nd Ave. S, tel. 206/628–8964), and the **Borderline** (608 1st Ave., tel. 206/624–3316).

In the downtown area, **Fitzgerald's on Fifth** (1900 5th Ave., tel. 206/728–1000) and **Pier 70** (2815 Alaskan Way at Broad St., tel. 206/624–8090) are dance clubs that feature Top-40 music nightly.

Ballroom Dancing The U.S. Amateur Ballroom Dancing Association's local chapter (tel. 206/822–6686) sponsors regular classes and dances throughout the year. These are either at the **Avalon Ballroom** (1017 Stewart St.) or **Carpenter's Hall** (2512 2nd Ave.). The **Washington Dance Club** (1017 Stewart St., tel. 206/628–8939) sponsors Friday-night workshops on various styles, and the **All-City Dance Club** (2245 N.W. 57th St., tel. 206/747–2707) hosts regular Saturday-night get-togethers.

Excursions from Seattle

The heavily developed I–5 corridor runs through Seattle, north to Vancouver, British Columbia, or south to Portland, Oregon. But venturing off this ribbon of highway—either toward the mountains in the east or the water to the west—will quickly bring the traveler to some relatively isolated areas. Five of the many excellent trips that can be taken from Seattle are to Winslow on Bainbridge Island, a short but delightful ferry ride from downtown across Puget Sound; the scenic Snoqualmie Falls, where snowcapped mountains meet lush farmland; Whidbey Island and the San Juan Islands, with scenic beaches, rolling countryside, and good fishing; or Leavenworth, a mock Bavarian village high in the Cascade Mountains.

Winslow

On a nice day, there's no better way to escape Seattle than on board a Washington State Ferry for a trip across Puget Sound. It's a great way to watch seagulls, sailboats, and massive container vessels in the sound—not to mention the surrounding scenery, which takes in the San Juan Islands, the Kitsap Peninsula and Olympic Mountains, Mt. Rainier, the Cascade Mountains, and the Seattle skyline. Even when the weather isn't all that terrific, travelers can stay snug inside the ferry, have a snack, and listen to the folk musicians who entertain the cross-sound commuters. Winslow combines a small-town atmosphere with scenic country surroundings.

Tourist Information **Bainbridge Island Chamber of Commerce** (166 Winslow Way, tel. 206/842–3700) has free maps that detail shops, restaurants, and sights.

Getting There **By Ferry** Although there are several ferries that leave from the Seattle area (*see* Getting Around Seattle, above), probably the best one for a single-day excursion is the ferry to **Winslow,** on Bainbridge Island. The advantages of walking on board are obvious; it's cheap (only $3.30 for a round-trip ticket) and hassle-free (no long waits in lines of frustrated drivers during peak commute hours or on weekends).

The Winslow ferry leaves from Seattle's busy downtown terminal at Colman Dock (Pier 52, south of the Public Market and just north of Pioneer Square), and the trip takes about a half-hour each way.

A word on ferries in general: The Washington State Ferry System, the biggest in the United States, includes vessels ranging from the 40-car *Hiyu* to jumbo ferries capable of carrying more than 200 cars and 2,000 passengers each. They connect points all around Puget Sound and the San Juan Islands. There is no smoking allowed in public areas.

If you do take your car, there are several points to note: Passengers and bicycles always load first unless otherwise instructed. Prior to boarding, lower antennas. Only parking lights should be used at night, and it is considered bad form to start your engine before the ferry docks.

Sunny weekends are heavy traffic times all around the San Juans, and weekdays at commuting times for ferries headed into or out of Seattle are also crowded. Peak times on the Seattle runs are sunny weekends, eastbound in the morning and Sunday nights, as well as westbound Saturday morning and weekday afternoons. Since no reservations are accepted on Washington State Ferries (except for the Sidney–Anacortes run during summer), arriving at least a half-hour before a scheduled departure is always advised. *Colman Dock, Pier 52, tel. 206/464–6400, 206/464–2000 (press #5500 for schedules), or 800/543–3779, in WA. 800/542–7052; for information concerning Winslow, 206/464–6990. Cost: Winslow ferry auto and driver: $6.65; passenger (in car or as walk-on) $3.30; senior citizens and disabled persons half-fare; children under 5 free; no extra charge for bicycles. Special rates for mobile homes and other oversize vehicles. Schedules vary according to season and time of day, but generally ferries leave daily every 30–40 min, early morning–2 AM.*

Once you reach the Winslow terminal, walk north up a short hill on Olympic Drive to Winslow Way; about ¼ mile farther north on Olympic is the **Bainbridge Island Vineyard and Winery** (682 S.R. 305, tel. 206/842–9463), which is open for tastings and tours Wednesday–Sunday noon–5.

If you turn west on Winslow Way, you'll find yourself in town, with several square blocks of interesting antiques shops, clothing stores, Scandinavian gift shops, galleries, restaurants, and other services. Shopping in Winslow is a refreshing change from the bustle of most big towns: There are usually only a few customers, and shopkeepers tend to carry on protracted, friendly conversations with natives and visitors alike.

Snoqualmie Falls

Driving east out of Seattle, you'll travel through bucolic farmland with snowcapped mountains in the background. Spring and summer snowmelt turns the Snoqualmie River into a thundering torrent as it cascades through a 268-foot rock gorge (100 feet higher than Niagara Falls) to a 65-foot-deep pool below.

Tourist
Information

For information on Snoqualmie call the **Seattle/King County Visitors Bureau** (800 Convention Pl., tel. 206/461–5840).

Getting There
By Car

Snoqualmie, Exit 27 off I-90, is about 30 miles east of Seattle.

Snoqualmie is the site of the first major electric plant in the Northwest to use falling water as a power source, and the world's first completely underground electric generating facility. The power plant, started in 1889, is a National Historic Civil Engineering Landmark; plant No. 2 was added just downstream from the falls in 1910 and expanded in 1957. Electricity from the two power plants provides enough power to serve 16,000 homes.

A 2-acre park, including an observation platform 300 feet above the Snoqualmie River, offers a view of the falls and surrounding area. Hike the **River Trail,** a 3-mile round-trip route through trees and open slopes, ending with a view from the base of the falls. (Note: Be prepared for an uphill workout on the return to the trailhead.)

Steam locomotives power vintage trains on **Puget Sound** and **Snoqualmie Valley Railway.** The 75-minute trip travels through woods and farmland, stopping briefly at Snoqualmie Falls. Railroad artifacts and memorabilia are displayed at both the Snoqualmie Depot (Hwy. 202, in downtown Snoqualmie) and Railroad Park Depot in downtown Northbend. For children, a special Santa train runs the first two weekends in December and a spook train runs the last two weekends in Oct.; tickets for all special trips must be prepurchased. *Box 459, Snoqualmie, tel. 206/888–3030. Admission: $6 adults, $5 senior citizens, $4 children. Trains operate Sept., May, and June, weekends; Oct. and Apr., Sun.; July–Aug., Fri.–Sun. Call for departure times.*

Snoqualmie Falls Forest Theater produces three plays a summer (the Passion Play, a melodrama, and a well-known classic performed by acting students and community theater performers) in the 250-seat outdoor amphitheater near Fall City, usually on Friday and Saturday nights and Sunday afternoons. *From I–90 take Exit 22 and go 4 mi; take a right on David Powell Rd., follow signs, continue through gate to parking area. 36800 S.E. David Powell Rd., tel. 206/222–7044. Admission: $8.50; for another $9 per person, you can enjoy a salmon or steak barbecue after the matinee and before the evening performances. Reservations required for dinner.*

Snoqualmie Pass is the site of three ski areas—Alpental, Ski Acres, and Snoqualmie Summitt for downhill and cross-country skiing in winter and spring, and for hiking in the summer (*see* Sports and Fitness, above).

The **Snoqualmie Winery** (1000 Winery Rd., tel. 206/888–4000) offers daily tours, tastings, and great views.

Dining
★

The Herbfarm. If there is such a thing as Northwest Cuisine, then The Herbfarm must rank as its temple. But the attraction here surpasses the fine, fresh food: This restaurant offers intimate, elegant dining among wildflower bouquets, Victorian-style prints, and a friendly staff. Try such delicacies as goat's milk cheese and parsley biscuits, green pickled walnuts in the husk, fresh salmon with a sauce of fresh garden herbs, and sorbet of rose geranium and lemon verbena. There's only one drawback: The Herbfarm is commonly booked up months ahead of time, which means you should plan a meal long before you're getting to Seattle. Is all that effort worth it? Yes. Only wine is served. *From I-90, Exit 22, go 3 mi. 32804 Issaquah-Fall City Rd., Fall City, tel. 206/784-2222. Some 75% of the 24 seats for each lunch or special dinner are reserved on Apr. 10 starting at 9 AM. The other 6 seats can be reserved by phoning at 1 PM the Fri. before you wish to go. Allow 2 hours for lunch ($39.50 per person) and the garden tour. 8 twilight dinners, including five fine wines, are scheduled in the summer ($82-$89 per person). Dress: casual but neat. Restaurant closed Mon.-Thurs.; closed dinner; closed Jan.-early Apr. MC, V. Expensive.*

Dining and Lodging **Salish.** This lodge at the top of the falls has been rebuilt and is operated by the Oregon-based Salishan Lodge. Eight of the 91 rooms look out over the falls, and others have a view upriver. Rooms have an airy feeling with wood furniture and window seats or balconies. You can sit in the whirlpool bath and open a window to view the fire in the flagstone fireplace. The Salish restaurant, which serves three meals daily, also has a wide-spread reputation for its Sunday brunch that includes course upon course of eggs, bacon, fish, fresh fruit, pancakes, and its renowned oatmeal. *37807 Snoqualmie-Fall City Rd., Fall City 37807, tel. 206/888-2556. 91 rooms. Facilities: 2 restaurants, lounge, health club, country store. Reservation for restaurant necessary. Dress for restaurant: casual; jacket and tie recommended for dinner. AE, DC, MC, V. Expensive.*

Puget Sound and the San Juan Islands

Whidbey Island and the San Juan Islands are the jewels of Puget Sound. Because the islands are reachable only by ferry or airplane, with the exception of Whidbey, which can be reached via a bridge from the north end of the island (90 minutes from Seattle), the islands beckon to souls longing for a quiet change of pace, whether it be kayaking in a cove, walking a deserted beach, or nestling by the fire in an old farmhouse.

Unfortunately, solitude can be a precious commodity in summer when the islands, particularly the San Juans, are overrun with tourists. On weekends and even some weekdays, expect to wait at least three hours in line once you arrive at the ferry terminal. You will face the same challenge or worse if you return Sunday afternoon or evening.

Island residents enjoy their peace and quiet; while some of them rely on tourism, many do not, and they would just as soon not have their country roads and villages jammed with "summer people." So it should come as no surprise that tourism and development are hotly contested issues on the islands.

One way to avoid crowds and the possibility of a cantankerous island resident is to plan a trip in the spring, fall, or winter. Reservations are a must any time in the summer and are advised for weekends in the off-season, too. Because Whidbey Island is more accessible to the mainland, its sandy beaches, villages, and viewpoints make it a perfect day-trip destination.

Tourist Information For information concerning Puget Sound and its islands, contact the **San Juan Tourism Cooperative** (Box 65, Lopez 98261, tel. 206/468-3663).

Getting There
By Plane Coastal Airways (tel. 800/547–5022) and Chart Air (tel. 800/237–1101) fly to the San Juan Islands from Seattle-Tacoma International; Harbor Airlines (tel. 800/521–3450) flies to Whidbey Island from the airport, as well.

Lake Union Air (tel. 206/284–0300 or 800/826–1890) and Kenmore Air (tel. 206/486–8400, 800/832–9696 in WA, or 800/423–5526 outside WA) fly float planes from Lake Union in Seattle to the San Juan Islands and can arrange charter flights to Whidbey Island.

By Car To reach the San Juan Islands, drive north on I–5 to La Conner; go west on 536 to 20W and follow signs to Anacortes; pick up the Washington State Ferry (see below).

Whidbey Island can be reached via the Mukilteo-to-Clinton ferry, or you can drive from Seattle along I–5, heading west on Hwy. 20; cross the dramatic Deception Pass via the bridge at the north end of the island.

By Ferry The Washington State Ferry System (tel. 206/464–6400 or 800/542–9052) provides car and passenger service from Mukilteo to Clinton (Whidbey Island). From Anacortes, about 90 miles north of Seattle, ferries depart for the San Juan Islands.

A.I.T. Waterways (tel. 206/671–1137) takes passengers from Bellingham, Orcas, and Friday Harbor.

Calm Sea Charters (tel. 206/385–5288) runs a passenger service from Port Townsend and Friday Harbor.

Guided Tours Discovery Washington (Box 14493, Seattle 98114, tel. 206/838–6043) runs tours of Puget Sound, and customizes itineraries.

Grey Line Water Sightseeing (500 Wall St., Suite 31, Seattle 98121, tel. 206/441–1887) operates three-and-a-half-hour nature cruises through the San Juan Islands.

The Mosquito Fleet (Box 196, Langley, WA 98260, tel. 206/321–0506 or 800/235–0506; fax 206/321–4122) offers several cruises of Whidbey Island and Deception Pass from mid-May–October.

The Rosario Princess (#5 Harbor Esplanade, Bellingham 98225, tel. 206/734–8866) conducts whale-watching, nature, and island cruises on an 83-foot tour boat.

Western Prince Cruises (tel. 206/378–5315) charters boats for half days during the summer; in the spring and fall bird-watching and scuba diving tours are offered. Cruises depart from Friday Harbor.

Bear in mind that Whidbey, a 50-mile island, is mostly rural with undulating hills, gentle beaches, and little coves.

Numbers in the margin correspond to points of interest on the Puget Sound map.

This tour begins at the southern tip of Whidbey, before progressing to Lopez, Orcas, and San Juan Islands. Naturally, on an island such as Whidbey, wildlife is plentiful, and it's not unusual to see eagles, great blue herons, and oyster catchers, as well as Orcas, gray whales, dolphins, and otters. Perhaps the best view of the sea creatures can be had from Langley, the quaint town that sits atop a 50-foot-high bluff overlooking the southeastern shore. In the heart of town, particularly along

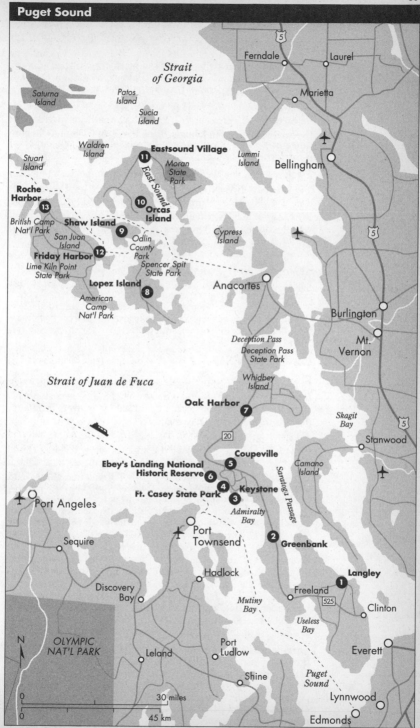

Puget Sound

Strait of Georgia

Saturna Island

Patos Island

Sucia Island

Waldren Island

Stuart Island

Ferndale

Laurel

Marietta

Lummi Island

Bellingham

Eastsound Village

11

Moran State Park

Roche Harbor

13

British Camp Nat'l Park

10

Orcas Island

East Sound

Cypress Island

Shaw Island

9

San Juan Island

Odlin County Park

Spencer Spit State Park

Friday Harbor

12

Lime Kiln Point State Park

Lopez Island

8

American Camp Nat'l Park

Anacortes

Burlington

Mt. Vernon

Deception Pass

Deception Pass State Park

Strait of Juan de Fuca

Whidbey Island

Skagit Bay

Stanwood

Oak Harbor

7

20

Coupeville

5

Camano Island

Ebey's Landing National Historic Reserve

6

4

Keystone

Ft. Casey State Park

3

Admiralty Bay

Saratoga Passage

Port Angeles

Sequire

2

Greenbank

Port Townsend

1

Langley

Hadlock

Freeland

525

Clinton

Discovery Bay

Mutiny Bay

Useless Bay

Everett

N

OLYMPIC NAT'L PARK

Leland

Port Ludlow

Shine

Puget Sound

Lynnwood

Edmonds

0

30 miles

0

45 km

First Street, there are boutiques that sell art, glass, antiques, jewelry, and clothing.

About halfway up this long, skinny island is Whidbey's town of **Greenbank,** home to the historically recognized **Loganberry Farm.** The 125-acre site is now the place of production for the state's newest spirit, Whidbey's Liqueur. *657 Wonn Rd., tel. 206/678-7700. Admission free. Tours offered daily 10–4.*

While in Greenbank, you may want to see the 53-acre **Meerkerk Rhododendron Gardens,** with 1,500 native and hybrid species of rhododendrons, numerous walking trails, and ponds. The best time for viewing the flowers in full bloom is in April and May. *Resort Rd., Greenbank, tel. 206/321-6682. Admission free.*

❸ Farther north you'll come to **Keystone,** an important town because it is the port of call for the ferry bound for Port Townsend on the Olympic Peninsula.

❹ **Ft. Casey State Park** (tel. 206/678-4519), just north of Keystone, is one of three forts built in 1890 to protect Puget Sound. Today it offers a small interpretive center, camping, picnic sites, fishing, and a boat launch.

❺ About two-thirds of the way up this long island is **Coupeville,** home of many restored Victorian houses and one of the largest National Historic Districts in the state. The town was founded in 1852 by Captain Thomas Coupe; his house, built in 1853, is one of the state's oldest. The town is also the site of the new **Island County Historical Museum** (908 N.W. Alexander St., tel. 206/678-3310).

❻ **Ebey's Landing National Historic Reserve** (tel. 206/678-4636), west of Coupeville, is a 22-acre area including Keystone, Coupeville, and Penn Cove. Established by Congress in 1980, the reserve is the first and largest of its kind. It is dotted with some 91 nationally registered historical structures, farmland, parks, and trails.

❼ About 11 miles farther north is **Oak Harbor,** which derived its name from the Garry oaks in the area. It was settled by Dutch and Irish immigrants in the mid-1800s, and several Dutch windmills are still in existence. Unfortunately, the island's largest city has not maintained the sleepy fishing-village pace that much of the rest of the island follows. Instead, Oak Harbor has the look of suburban sprawl, with strips of fast-food restaurants and service stations. Just north of Oak Harbor is **Whidbey Island Naval Air Station** (tel. 206/257-2286), at which group tours can be arranged. At **Deception Pass State Park,** 3 miles from the naval base, take some time to notice the spectacular view and stroll among the madrona trees with their reddish-brown peeling bark. While walking across the bridge, you won't be able to miss seeing the dramatic gorge below, well-known for its tidal currents. The Deception Pass bridge links Whidbey to Fidalgo Island and the mainland. From here it's just a short distance to Anacortes and ferries to the San Juans.

There are 172 named islands in the San Juan archipelago, although at low tide the islands total 743 and at high tide, 428. Sixty are populated, and 10 are state marine parks. Ferries stop at Lopez, Shaw, Orcas, and San Juan; other islands, many privately owned, must be reached by private plane or boat. In any case, the San Juans are a gold mine for naturalists, because they are home to more than 80 orcas, a few minke whales, seals, dolphins, otters, and more than 60 active pairs of breeding bald eagles.

8 The first ferry stop is **Lopez Island,** with old orchards, weathered barns, and pastures of sheep and cows. Because of the relatively flat terrain, this island is a favorite for bicyclists. Two popular parks to note are **Odlin County Park** and **Spencer Spit State Park.**

9 At the next stop, **Shaw Island,** Franciscan nuns wear their traditional habits while running the ferry dock. You may notice that few people get off here; the island is mostly residential, and tourists rarely stop.

10 **Orcas,** the next in line, is a large, mountainous, horseshoe-shape island. Roads sweep down through wide valleys and rise to marvelous hilltop views. A number of little shops featuring the island's cottage industries—jewelry, weaving, pottery—

11 are in **Eastsound Village,** the island's business and social center situated in the middle of the horseshoe. Walk along Prune Alley, where you'll find a handful of small shops and restaurants.

On the other side of the horseshoe from the ferry landing, following aptly named Horseshoe Highway, is **Moran State Park** (Star Rte., Box 22, Eastsound 98245, tel. 206/376-2326). The ranger station will supply information, but applications for camping permits within the park for Memorial Day through Labor Day must be received by mail, at least two weeks prior to requested date. From the summit you of the 2,400-foot **Mt. Constitution** can have panoramic views of the San Juans, the Cascades, the Olympics, and Vancouver Island.

12 The last ferry stop in the San Juans is at **Friday Harbor** on San Juan Island, with a colorful, active waterfront that always conveys a holiday feeling. Although Friday Harbor—the island's county seat—is the largest town, it is also the most convenient destination for visitors traveling on foot. The shops here cater to tourists, offering clever crafts, gifts, and whimsical toys. A short walk from the ferry dock, the **San Juan Historical Museum** displays a number of farm implements used by early settlers. *405 Price St., tel. 206/378-3949. Admission free. Open June–Aug., Wed.–Sat. 1–4:30.*

Standing at the ferry dock, you'll recognize the **Whale Museum** by the mural of the whale painted on the wall. To reach the entrance, walk up Spring Street and turn right on First Street. This modest museum doesn't attempt to woo you with expensive exhibits; models of whales, whale skeletons, baleen, recordings of whale sounds, and videos of whales are the attractions. The museum also offers workshops on marine mammals and San Juan ecology. *62 1st St. N, tel. 206/378-4710. Admission: $2.50 adults, $2 senior citizens, $1 children 3–12. Open June–Sept., daily 10–5; Oct.–May, daily 11–4.*

For an opportunity to see whales cavorting in the water, go to **Lime Kiln Point State Park,** just 6 miles from Friday Harbor. This viewpoint is America's first official whale-watching park, situated on San Juan's west side. The best seasons to visit are late spring, summer, and fall. *6158 Lighthouse Rd., tel. 206/ 378-2044. Admission free. Open daily 6:30 AM–10 PM. Day-use only; no camping facilities.*

The **San Juan Island National Historic Park** is a unique attraction, with two camps that attest to the island's benign history.

For a number of years both the Americans and British occupied San Juan Island. In 1859, a Yank killed a Brit's pig, thus setting off tempers (on both sides) that had been ready to explode. Both nations sent armed forces to the island, but no gunfire was exchanged in the Pig War, which lasted from 1859 to 1872. The proof of this scuffle is the existence of the **British Camp**, with a blockhouse, commissary, and barracks, and of the armaments that remain from the American Camp. The Visitor Center headquarters is at **San Juan Island Chamber of Commerce Office** (125 Spring St., tel. 206/378–2240). Phone ahead to check when the center is open and in June through August to find out about guided hikes and historical re-enactments of life in an 1860s-era military camp.

❸ Roche Harbor, at the northern end of San Juan, is an elegant site with well-manicured lawns, rose gardens, cobblestone waterfront, hanging flower baskets on the docks, the Hotel de Haro, and its restaurant and lounge.

Shopping
Lopez Island The **Chimera Gallery** (Lopez Village, tel. 206/468–3265) is a local artists' cooperative.

Grayling Gallery (Hummel Lake Rd., tel. 206/468–2779) features the work of a sculptor and a painter who live and work on the premises.

Orcas Island **Darvill's Rare Print Shop** (Eastsound, tel. 206/376–2351) specializes in antique and contemporary prints.

San Juan Island **Ravenhouse Art** (1 Spring St. W, Friday Harbor, tel. 206/378–2777) features watercolors, oil paintings, jewelry, and pottery.

Cabezon Gallery (60 1st St. W, tel. 206/378–3116) features works of local artists.

Waterworks Gallery (315 Argyle St., Friday Harbor, tel. 206/378–3060) emphasizes marine art.

Whidbey Island On Whidbey Island, **Langley's First Street** offers a number of unique items. You can meet the artist and shop owner, Gwenn Knight, at **The Glass Knight** (214 1st St., Langley, tel. 206/321–6283), where her glass art and jewelry is for sale.

Annie Steffen's (101 1st St., tel. 206/321–6535) specializes in hand-painted, handwoven, and hand-knit apparel and jewelry.

The **Childers/Proctor Gallery** (302 1st St., Langley, tel. 206/321–2978) exhibits and sells paintings, jewelry, pottery, and sculpture.

Sports and
Outdoor Activities
Bicycling *Orcas Island:* **Key Moped Rental** (Box 279, Eastsound, tel. 206/376–2474) rents mopeds during the summer.

Wildlife Cycles (Box 1048, Eastsound, tel. 206/376–4708) has bikes for rent at various roadside stands during the summer.

San Juan Island: **San Juan Island Bicycles** (380 Argyle St., Friday Harbor, tel. 206/378–4941) has a reputation for good service as well as equipment.

Susie's Mopeds (Box 1972, Friday Harbor, tel. 206/378–5244) offers mopeds for rent.

Whidbey Island: **The Pedaler** (5603½ S. Bayview Rd., tel. 206/321–5040) has bikes to rent.

Fishing *San Juan Islands:* You can fish year-round for bass and trout at **Hummel Lake** on Lopez Island, and at **Egg** and **Sportsman lakes** on San Juan Island. On Orcas, there are three lakes at **Moran State Park** that are open to fishing from late April through October.

You can go saltwater fishing through **Buffalo Works** (tel. 206/378-4612), **Captain Clyde's Charters** (tel. 206/378-5661), **Custom Designed Charters** (tel. 206/376-5105), and **King Salmon Charters** (tel. 206/468-2314).

Whidbey Island: You can catch salmon, perch, cod, and bottomfish from the Langley dock. Supplies are available from the **Langley Marina** (202 Wharf St., tel. 206/321-1771).

Water Sports   On the **San Juan Islands:**

Lopez Island: **Islander Lopez Resort** (tel. 206/468-6121) and **Islands Marine Center** (tel. 206/468-3377) have most standard marina amenities.

Orcas Island: **Deer Harbor Resort & Marina** (tel. 206/376-4420), **Lieber Haven Marina Resort** (tel. 206/376-4420), and **West Sound Marina** (tel. 206/376-2314) offer standard marina facilities and more. **Russell's Landing/Orcas Store** (tel. 206/376-4389) has gas, diesel, tackle, and groceries at the ferry landing. For small boat and motor rentals, sales, and service, try **Eastsound Marine** (tel. 206/376-4420).

San Juan Island: **Port of Friday Harbor** (tel. 206/378-2688), **San Juan Marina** (tel. 206/378-2841), and **Roche Harbor Resort** (tel. 206/378-2155) have standard marina facilities; Port of Friday Harbor and Roche Harbor are also U.S. Customs Ports of Entry.

On **Whidbey Island:**

Langley's small boat harbor (tel. 206/321-6765) offers moorage for 35 boats, utilities, and a 160-foot fishing pier, all protected by a 400-foot timber-pile breakwater.

Marine State Parks (tel. 206/753-2027) are accessible by private boat only. No moorage or camping reservations are available, and fees are charged at some parks from May through Labor Day. Fresh water, where available, is limited. Island parks are **Blind, Clark, Doe, James, Matia, Patos, Posey, Stuart, Sucia,** and **Turn.** All have a few campsites; there are no docks at Blind, Clark, Patos, Posey, or Turn islands.

Skippered sailing charters are available through **Amante Sail Tours** (tel. 206/376-4231), **Custom Designed Charters** (tel. 206/376-2927), **Harmony Sailing Charters** (tel. 206/468-3310), **Kismet Sailing Charters** (tel. 206/468-2435), **Nor'wester Sailing Charters** (tel. 206/378-5478), and **Wind N' Sails** (tel. 206/378-5343).

Bare-boat sailing charters are available through **McKinney Marine Inc.** (tel. 206/468-2130), **Snug Harbor Marina** (tel. 206/378-4762), and **Wind N' Sails** (tel. 206/378-5343).

If you are kayaking on your own, beware of ever-changing conditions, ferry and shipping landings, and strong tides and currents. Go ashore only on known public property. Day trips and longer expeditions are available from **Shearwater Sea Kayak Tours** (tel. 206/376-4699), **Doe Bay Resort** (tel. 206/376-2291), **Black Fish Paddlers** (tel. 206/376-4041), **San Juan Kayak Expeditions** (tel. 206/378-4436), and **Seaquest** (tel. 206/378-5767).

Beaches *Orcas Island:* The best beaches on this island include the low bank beach at **Odlin County Park** (Rte. 2, Box 3216, tel. 206/468–2496) and a mile of waterfront at **Spencer Spit State Park** (Rte. 2, Box 3600, tel. 206/468–2251).

San Juan Island: You'll find 10 acres of beachfront at the **San Juan County Park** (380 Westside Rd. N, Friday Harbor, tel. 206/378–2992).

Whidbey Island: Beaches are best on Whidbey Island's west side, where the sand stretches out to the sea and you have a view of the shipping lanes and the Olympic Mountains. **Maxwelton Beach** (Maxwelton Beach Rd.), popular with the locals, is on the west side of the island. **Possession Point** (west on Coltas Bay Rd.) includes a park, a beach, and a boat launch. **Forts Casey** and **Ebey** offer more hiking trails and bluff outlooks than wide, sandy beaches. **West Beach,** north of the forts, is a stormy beach with lots of driftwood.

Dining *Rates correspond to Seattle Dining chart.*

Orcas Island **Christina's.** Here you will find an elegant atmosphere whether you dine inside, on the enclosed porch, or on the rooftop terrace with views of East Sound. The emphasis is on fresh, local seafood, with some of the best salmon entrées in the Northwest. Other specialties include grilled breast of chicken with an eggplant and pepper stuffing and mouthwatering desserts. *North Beach Rd. and Horseshoe Hwy., tel. 206/376–4904. Reservations suggested. Dress: neat but casual. AE, DC, MC, V. Moderate–Expensive.*

Bilbo's Festivo. This house with a courtyard features stucco walls, Mexican tiles, wood benches, and weavings from New Mexico. The menu features Bilbo's renditions of burritos, enchiladas, and other Mexican favorites. With a typical entrée being orange-sauce marinated chicken grilled over mesquite and served with fresh asparagus, potatoes, and salad. Sunday brunch, featuring pan dulce—a Mexican sweet bread and omelets with tortillas—is also served. *Northbeach Rd. and A St., Eastsound, tel. 206/376–4728. No reservations. Dress: casual. AE, MC, V. Closed Mon.; lunch Tues.–Wed. Inexpensive–Moderate.*

San Juan Island **Duck Soup Inn.** This Mediterranean-inspired kitchen emphasizes fresh local fish such as squid sautéed in butter and olive oil and served in a fresh tomato sauce, Wescott Bay oysters from across the island, and mussels in a tomato-wine sauce. There is a good list of Northwest, California, and European wines. *3090 Roche Harbor Rd., tel. 206/378–4878. Reservations suggested. Dress: casual. No credit cards; checks accepted. Closed winter; rest of year, closed dinner Mon.–Tues. Expensive.*

Springtree Eating Establishment and Farm. Meals are prepared from organically grown produce on the farm, and entrées include such items as cod with a fresh citrus and garden mint sauce, seafood chowder, and meal-size salads. Lots of plants and chintz fabrics decorate the interior, and patio dining is available, too, but the service is mediocre at best. *Spring St., tel. 206/378–4848. Reservations suggested. Dress: casual. MC, V. Moderate.*

Whidbey Island **Garibyan Brothers Café Langley.** Terra-cotta tile floors, antique oak tables, Italian music, and the aromas of garlic, basil, and oregano are the backdrop to your lunch or dinner. Greek salads, vegetarian eggplant, fresh mussels, lamb loin chops, moussaka, and lamb shish kebabs are just some of the menu selections. *113 1st St., Langley, tel. 206/221–3090. Reservations suggested. Dress: neat but casual. MC, V. Moderate.*

Star Bistro. This black, white, and red bistro, atop the Star Store, serves up Caesar salads, shrimp-and-scallop linguine, and gourmet burgers. *201½ 1st St., Langley, tel. 206/221–2627. No reservations. Dress: casual. AE, MC, V. Moderate.*

Dog House Backdoor Restaurant. This somewhat run-down waterfront grub house serves large, juicy burgers, offers a great view of Saratoga Passage, and provides a pool table. *230 1st St., Langley, tel. 206/321–9996. No reservations. Dress: casual. No credit cards. Inexpensive.*

Lodging *Rates correspond to Seattle Lodging chart.*

Lopez Island **Edenwild.** The imposing gray Victorian-style farmhouse, surrounded by rose gardens, looks as if it's a restored island building, but actually it was newly opened in 1990. Rooms feature whitewashed oak floors, a muted gray interior, and white painted woodwork, along with botanical prints, lace curtains from Scotland, leaded glass windows, and some antiques. A three-course breakfast is served in the dining room. *Box 271, Lopez Island, WA 98261, tel. 206/468–3238. 7 double rooms with baths. Facilities: bicycle rentals, kennel in garage. MC, V. Expensive.*

Mackaye Harbor Inn. At the south end of Lopez Island, across the road from MacKaye Harbor, is this inn, a two-story frame Victorian-style home. The 1920s sea captain's house with ½ mile of beach features rooms with golden oak and brass details and wicker furniture; three guestrooms have views of the harbor. Owners Robin, who is Swedish, and Mike Bergstrom take turns cooking breakfast, which often includes Scandinavian specialties. Mike also provides guided kayak tours. *Box 1940, Lopez Island, WA 98261, tel. 206/468–2253. 5 rooms. Facilities: kayak tours, bikes, rowboat. MC, V. Moderate.*

Orcas Island **Rosario Spa & Resort.** Originally built by shipbuilding magnate Robert Moran (who was told he had six months to live), this Mediterranean-style mansion cost $1.5 million in 1905, and includes six tons of copper for the roof. The interior of the mansion, now the dining room and spa, is of fine teak and mahogany. Moran lived another 30 years, and now the mansion is on the National Register of Historic Places. Fire codes prohibit rental of guest rooms in the old structure, so villas and hotel units were added after Rosario was converted to a resort in 1960. These guest rooms are not spectacular like the mansion, but they do have decent views and most have decks or patios. *Horseshoe Hwy., Eastsound 98245, tel. 206/376–2222. 179 rooms. Facilities: dining room, indoor pool, 2 outdoor pools, health spa, sauna, whirlpool, games room, tennis courts, marina with boat rentals, fishing, hiking. AE, DC, MC, V. Expensive.*

Orcas Hotel. Sitting on the hill overlooking the Orcas Island ferry landing is this three-story, red-roofed Victorian hotel with a wrap-around porch and white picket fence. Dating to 1900, when construction first began, the lodging is on the National Register of Historic Places. The dining room, open to the public, overlooks the ferry landing and gardens, and the parlor is decorated in Victorian antiques. Guest rooms feature wicker, brass, antique furnishings, and feather beds, and some units have small sun decks. Breakfast is in the dining room and guests order off the menu, which includes French toast, omelets, and other egg dishes. *Box 155, Orcas, WA 98280, tel. 206/376–4300; fax 206/376–4399. 12 rooms. Facilities: restaurant, lounge. AE, DC, MC, V. Moderate–Expensive.*

Turtleback Farm. Just 15 minutes from the Orcas Island ferry landing is this forest-green with white trim inn, set on 80 acres of meadow, forest, and farmland in the shadow of Turtleback Mountain. The inside is spacious and airy with an absence of frills. Guest rooms have cozy chairs, good beds with woolen comforters made from the fleece of resident sheep, some antiques, cream colored muslin curtains, and views of meadows and forest. Breakfast, cooked by Susan Fletcher and served by her husband, Bill, can be taken in the dining room or on the deck overlooking the valley. *R.R. 1, Box 650, Eastsound, WA 98245, tel. 206/376–3914. 7 rooms. No facilities. MC, V. Moderate–Expensive.*

Doe Bay Village Resort. This is a rustic place that is actually an International Youth Hostel, personal-growth center, and retreat. The resort feels faintly countercultural: leftover from its earlier days as an artists colony. Units vary from dormitory rooms to cottages, some with sleeping quarters only and access to shower house and community kitchen; other units feature kitchens and baths. The peaceful, scenic grounds are great for walks or sitting and reading. *S.R. 86, Olga 98279, tel. 206/376–2291. 100 units. Facilities: natural-food café, general store, guided kayak trips, hot tub, massage therapist. AE, MC, V. Inexpensive–Moderate.*

San Juan Islands **Roche Harbor Resort.** Choice of cottage, condominium, or rooms in the 1886 restored Hotel de Haro are the options here. It's better to look at the old hotel than to actually stay in that part of the resort, since guest rooms are fairly shabby or, at best, rustic. *Box 1, Friday Harbor 98250, tel. 206/378–2155. 60 rooms. Facilities: restaurant, swimming pool, tennis court, boat moorage for 200 yachts, complete boating facilities, 4,000-ft airstrip. MC, V. Moderate–Expensive.*

Blair House. Just 4 blocks uphill from the ferry landing in Friday Harbor on more than an acre of landscaped grounds is Blair House. The two-story gray Victorian house with dormer windows and a wide wraparound porch, now furnished with wicker chairs and table, was built in 1909 and has been enlarged several times. Rooms are decorated around farm animal themes with country-print wallpapers, color-coordinated linens and ivory comforters on the beds. Guests can eat breakfast in the large dining room, on the front porch, or alongside the outdoor pool. *345 Blair Ave., Friday Harbor, WA 98250, tel. 206/378–5907. 7 rooms, 1 cottage. Facilities: cable TV, outdoor pool, hot tub. AE, MC, V. Moderate.*

Hillside House. Less than a mile outside of Friday Harbor, this contemporary house sits on a hill, providing stunning views of the harbor and Mt. Baker. The home features a large living room, kitchen, and deck with views of the harbor and Mt. Baker. All of the comfortable guest rooms have sophisticated decor. Queen-size beds, oak chests, and one- or two-person window seats are in all rooms. The Robinsons, who own the inn, encourage guests to use the recycled books in the hallway—take one or leave one—and provide badminton, horseshoes, and a cable swing (a present from guests with fond memories of their stay) in the yard. Breakfast includes entrées made from resident hens' eggs, island jams, and fresh berries. *365 Carter*

Ave., Friday Harbor, WA, tel. 206/378–4730. 6 rooms. Facilities: access to health club in town. MC, V. Moderate.

San Juan Inn. This restored 1873 inn is comfortable but modestly furnished and within walking distance of the ferry terminal. Rooms, which are all on the second floor, are small but include brass, iron, or wicker beds, and some antiques. Breakfast of muffins, coffee, and juice is served each morning in a parlor overlooking the harbor. *50 Spring St., Box 776, Friday Harbor 98250, tel. 206/378–2070. 10 rooms. No facilities. MC, V. Moderate.*

Whidbey Island **Cliff House.** This luxury house, situated in near Freeland, sleeps one-two couples in a secluded setting overlooking Admiralty inlet. The three-story house, one side nearly all glass, affords romantic views to the couple enjoying the elegant bedroom loft. Rain and occasionally snow whisk through the open-air atrium in the middle of the house. Guests are pampered with fresh flowers, a huge stone fireplace, and miles of driftwood beach. *5440 Windmill Rd., Freeland 98249, tel. 206/321–1566. 1 room. Facilities: fireplace, spa, art collection. No credit cards. Expensive.*

Guest House Cottages. This B&B, just outside Greenbank, includes a luxurious log lodge for one couple, four private cottages, and a three-room suite in a farmhouse located on 25 acres of forest and pastureland. The accommodations are cozy, with fireplaces, stained-glass pieces, and country antique furnishings. *835 E. Christianson Rd., Greenbank 98253, tel. 206/678–3115. 6 units. Facilities: fireplaces, microwaves, some kitchens, swimming pool, exercise room, spa. Expensive.*

Dining and Lodging **Deer Harbor Inn.** The original log lodge—situated on a knoll overlooking Deer Harbor—was the first resort built on the island (1915) and is now the dining room of the inn. A newer log cabin features eight spacious, airy rooms with peeled log furniture; views; balconies; and breakfast delivered to your door in a picnic baskets. Although large, the dining room, which specializes in fresh seafood, feels cozy, with its natural wood and floral prints, and has an adjoining deck for outdoor dining. *Box 142, Eastsound 98243, tel. 206/376–4110. 8 units. No facilities. Reservations in restaurant suggested. Dress: casual. AE, MC, V. Moderate.*

Whidbey Island **Inn at Langley.** This concrete and wood Frank Lloyd Wright-inspired structure perches on the side of a bluff descending to the beach. Guest rooms feature Asian-style decor using neutrals, wood and glass, and spectacular views of Saratoga Passage and the Cascade Mountains. Entering the inn's Country Kitchen restaurant is like walking into someone's living room—no maître d' or coatroom. A huge fireplace rises before you, and then you notice tables for two unobtrusively lining the walls. On the other side of the fireplace is the "great table," which seats 10. Dinner may include locally gathered mussels in a black bean sauce, breast of duck in a loganberry sauce, or rich Columbia River salmon. Appetizers, side dishes, salad greens so fresh they have never touched a refrigerator, and desserts such as a bowl of island-grown strawberries with cream round out the satisfying entrées. Continental breakfast is served Monday–Wednesday, 8–10, for guests of the inn. Dinner starts promptly at 7, with a glass of sherry and a tour of the wine cellar. *400 1st St., Langley, tel. 206/221–3033. 24 rooms. Facili-*

ties: restaurant. Reservations in restaurant necessary. Jacket
and tie suggested. MC, V. Expensive.

Captain Whidbey Inn. There are a wide variety of accommodations offered by this inn, including the original madrona log inn
(listed on the National Register of Historic Places), cottages, a
duplex, and houses with views of Penn Cove. Inn rooms are rustic, though they feature a few antiques, but do have feather
beds and shared baths. Lagoon rooms are large and have private baths. Cottages and the duplex have one or two bedrooms,
sitting rooms, some kitchens, fireplaces, and private baths.
The dining room, serving breakfast, lunch, and dinner, is cozy
with dark paneling, soft lighting, and several tables overlooking Penn Cove. *2072 W. Captain Whidbey Inn Rd., Coupeville
98239, tel. 206/678–4097. 33 units. Facilities: bicycles and row-
boats available. Reservations for restaurant suggested. Dress:
neat but casual. MC, V. Moderate.*

The Arts   On the San Juan Islands, check performance schedules at the
Orcas Performing Arts Center (Box 567, Eastsound 98245, tel.
206/376–ARTS) and the **San Juan Community Theatre** (100 2nd
Ave., Friday Harbor 98250, tel. 206/378–3210.)

Leavenworth

On the way to Leavenworth, traveling northeast from Seattle
along I–5 and U.S. 2, visitors will pass through the densely
forested mountain country along the Skykomish River. At the
summit, in the Stevens Pass/Leavenworth area, the main attractions are the towering Cascades. (Leavenworth itself has
an elevation of 1,170 feet; the surrounding mountains rise to
8,000 feet.) Some of the best skiing, hiking, rock climbing, rafting, canoeing, and snowshoeing in the Northwest starts at
Leavenworth, and the town itself is well worth exploring.

In the early ’60s, Leavenworth was a moribund village that had
once been a center for mining and railroading. Civic leaders
seeking ways to revitalize the area decided to capitalize on the
town’s spectacular alpine setting; the result is a charming (and
only sometimes overly cute) center for both winter and summer
sports. Shopkeepers and hostelers, maintaining the town’s
buildings in gingerbread Tyrolean style and sponsoring events
modeled after those found in a typical Bavarian village, keep a
European spirit of simple elegance alive in a setting that is never short of spectacular.

The many specialty shops, restaurants, and hotels almost all
subscribe to the Bavarian theme. There are restaurants specializing in Bavarian food; candy shops with gourmet Swiss-
style chocolate; shops featuring music boxes, nutcrackers, and
other Bavarian specialties; and charming European-style pension hotels. (There’s even a laundromat called Die Washerie.)
Throughout the year the village engages in festivities that reflect the alpine theme.

Tourist   **Leavenworth Chamber of Commerce** (703 U.S. 2, 98826, tel.
Information   509/548–5807).

Getting There   Small airports in Wenatchee, Cashmere, and Lake Wenatchee
By Plane   serve the Leavenworth area.

By Car   Leavenworth is about 120 miles from Seattle, north on I–5 to
Everett and east on U.S. 2. To return, take the long scenic loop
by continuing on U.S. 2 past Leavenworth, then south on High-

way 97 to Cle Elum, and back to Seattle on I–90 across Snoqualmie Pass.

By Bus   Greyhound (tel. 509/548–7414) serves Leavenworth with two westbound and two eastbound buses daily, year-round. The bus stop is at the Kountry Kitchen restaurant on U.S. 2 at the east end of town.

Sports and Outdoor Activities   Leavenworth's setting in the mountains can be appreciated from a car, of course, but the main attraction here is a variety of vigorous outdoor sports in the backcountry.

Cross-Country and Downhill Skiing   The beginning and advanced skier will find more than 20 miles of maintained cross-country ski trails in the Leavenworth area. Meanwhile, Stevens Pass has downhill slopes and lifts for every level of skier. Several shops in Leavenworth rent and sell ski equipment. For more information, contact the **Leavenworth Winter Sports Club** (Box 573, 98826, tel. 509/548–5115).

Golf   Those hankering for more placid sports can try the **Leavenworth Golf Club** (Box 247, 98826, tel. 509/548–7267), an 18-hole, par-71 course with a pro shop and clubhouse.

Hiking and Rock Climbing   Leavenworth also offers hiking trails that take in some of the most breathtaking vistas in the entire Cascades. There are more than 320 miles of scenic trails in the Leavenworth Ranger District alone, including **Hatchery Creek, Icicle Ridge, the Enchantments, Tumwater Canyon, Fourth of July Creek, Snow Lake, Stuart Lake,** and **Chatter Creek.** Contact the **Leavenworth Ranger District** (600 Sherburne St., 98826, tel. 509/782–1513) for more details, or consult one of the many fine books detailing backcountry hikes in the Northwest. Rock climbing is also popular because of the solid granite cliffs in the area.

Horseback Riding   The hourly and daily horseback rides and pack trips at **Eagle Creek Ranch** (7951 Eagle Creek Rd., Leavenworth 98826, tel. 509/548–7798) may also be appealing to the less rugged.

White-Water Rafting   Rafting is a popular sport during March–July, with the prime high-country runoff in May and June. The **Wenatchee River,** which runs through Leavenworth, is generally considered the best white-water river in the state—a Class 3 (out of six on a scale of difficulty) on the International Canoeing Association scale. Depending on the season and location, anything from a relatively calm scenic float to an invigorating white-water shoot is possible on the Wenatchee or on one of several other nearby rivers. Some rafting outfitters and guides in the Leavenworth area are **Northern Wilderness River Riders** (10645 Hwy. 209, Leavenworth 98826, tel. 509/548–4583), **Wenatchee Whitewater and Scenic Float Trips** (Box 12, Cashmere 98815, tel. 509/782–2254), and **Leavenworth Outfitters** (21588 S.R. 207, Leavenworth 98826, tel. 509/763–3733).

Dining   *Rates correspond to Seattle Dining chart.*

Cougar Inn. This stylish family restaurant is about 25 miles outside Leavenworth on the shores of Lake Wenatchee. Locals often come by boat and tie up at the restaurant's dock. The atmosphere is very pleasant, with lots of natural wood, airy rooms, great views of the lake and, in summer, a big outside deck. The hearty American-style Sunday brunch is especially popular, but breakfast, lunch, and dinner are also served daily. The menu, featuring burgers, steaks, and prime rib, is rather unadventurous, but the food is well-prepared and the service friendly. *23379 S.R. 207, Lake Wenatchee, tel. 509/763–3354. Reservations advised, especially for Sun. brunch. Dress: casual. AE, MC, V. Moderate.*

Reiner's Gasthaus. Authentic central European cuisine with a Hungarian/Austrian accent is presented in this small, cheerful restaurant. The decor is heavy on the pine furnishings and thick drapes, with lots of vintage photos and other knickknacks on the walls to look at, and the service is bustling and friendly. Music is performed on weekend evenings: Usually a jolly accordion player is featured. Specialties include pork schnitzel and Hungarian goulash; these and all the reasonably priced and well-prepared dinners include hearty soups and salads. *829 Front St. (upstairs), tel. 509/548–5111. No reservations. Dress: casual. MC, V. Moderate.*

Baren Haus. Good, unpretentious food is served in a big, high-ceiling beer-hall-style room. It can get crowded and noisy in this spacious place that's decorated with blue tablecloths and large booths. House specialties include German-style sandwiches (such as bratwurst on grilled whole-wheat bread, with sauerkraut and hearty mustards) and pizzas. *208 9th St., tel. 509/548–4535. Reservations accepted, except during festival time. Dress: casual. MC, V. Inexpensive.*

Danish Bakery. Tasty homemade pastries, good strong espresso drinks, and a self-serve coffee bar are the attractions in this small, pleasant shop. The decor is tastefully done with dark woods and mural paintings, and the service is fast and friendly. This is a perfect place to escape the crowds on the sidewalks. *731 Front St., tel. 509/548–7514. No reservations. Dress: casual. No credit cards. Inexpensive.*

Lodging The number of hotels, motels, B&Bs, and long-term-rental cabins in Leavenworth has increased in recent years as the area has become more popular among hikers and skiers. **Bavarian Bedfinders** (905 Commercial St., Suite 1, tel. 800/323–2920) matches travelers with more than 100 facilities such as condominiums, private cabins, and small lodges, in Leavenworth and around the state, and it also books dinner reservations, snowmobile tours, sleigh rides, and more. Their services are free to guests.

Rates correspond to the Seattle Lodging chart.

Der Ritterhof. This is a relatively new and large hotel on the highway to Leavenworth from Seattle. Its 51 units, decorated in fairly standard-issue motel style, include suites that sleep six comfortably; some units have small kitchenettes. Amenities include a recreation area, barbecue pit, and volleyball and badminton courts on the lawn. The service is friendly and efficient. *190 Hwy. 2, 98826, tel. 509/548–5845 or 800/255–5845. 51 rooms. Facilities: outdoor heated pool, hot tubs. AE, MC, V. Moderate–Expensive.*

Pension Anna. This small, family-run Austrian-style pension in the middle of the village has a farmhouse atmosphere. Although it's newly built, it has a distinctly old-fashioned feel; rooms and suites are decorated with sturdy, pine antique furniture, with such added touches as fresh flowers and comforters on the beds. Two of the suites have whirlpool baths, and all except the ground-level rooms have small balconies. The two largest suites have fireplaces and handsome four-poster beds. A hearty European-style breakfast (cold cuts, meats, cheeses, soft-boiled eggs), inclusive in the room price, is served in a breakfast room decorated in traditional European style with crisp linens, pine decor, dark green curtains, and (of course) a cuckoo clock. The staircases to the upper floors are quite steep. *926 Commercial St., 98826, tel. 509/548–6273. 11 units. Facilities: TV. Moderate–Expensive.*

Evergreen Motel. Popular with hikers and skiers, the pleasant Evergreen was built in the 1930s and still has a lot of the charm of the old-fashioned roadside inn it once was. Some of its two-bedroom suites have fireplaces and/or kitchens (though no utensils), while some have multiple beds and can sleep up to six comfortably. Thus, although there are only 26 units, the motel's capacity is about 80 guests. Complimentary Continental breakfast is offered by a very friendly staff and the motel is one block from downtown. *1117 Front St., 98826, tel. 509/548–5515 or 800/327–7212. 26 rooms. AE, D, DC, MC, V. Moderate.*

Edelweiss Hotel. This is an unpretentious hotel above the restaurant of the same name. Small rooms, plainly furnished and with either shared or private baths, are available. This is not the place to spend a romantic weekend, but if you're on a budget and simply need a place to lay your head, the Edelweiss's price ($15 for a single room, no view or TV) is hard to beat in this hotel-hungry town. The service is genial but sometimes harried, and the staircase is steep. *843 Front St., 98826, tel. 509/548–7015. 14 units. MC, V. Inexpensive.*

4 Vancouver

Introduction

By Terri Wershler

Terri Wershler, publisher of Brighouse Press, a regional book publisher, is also the author of The Vancouver Guide.

Vancouver is a young city, even by North American standards. While three to four hundred years of settlement may make cities like Québec and Halifax historically interesting to travelers, Vancouver's youthful vigor attracts visitors with powerful elements not yet ground down by time. Vancouver is a mere 105 years old; it was not yet a town in 1870, when British Columbia became part of the Canadian confederation.

Vancouver's history, such as it is, remains visible to the naked eye. Eras are stacked east to west along the waterfront like some horizontal, century-old archaeological dig—from cobbled, late-Victorian Gastown to shiny postmodern glass cathedrals of commerce grazing the sunset.

The Chinese were among the first to recognize the possibilities of Vancouver's setting. They came to British Columbia during the 1850s seeking the gold that inspired them to name the province *Gum-shan,* or Gold Mountain. They built the Canadian Pacific Railway that gave Vancouver's original townsite a purpose—one beyond the natural splendor that Royal Navy Capt. George Vancouver admired during his lunchtime cruise around its harbor on June 13, 1792. The transcontinental railway, along with its Great White Fleet of clipper ships, gave Vancouver a full week's edge over the California ports in shipping tea to New York at the dawn of the 20th century.

Vancouver's natural charms are less scattered than in other cities. On clear days, the mountains appear close enough to touch. Two thousand-acre wilderness parks lie within the city limits. The saltwater of the Pacific and fresh water direct from the Rocky Mountain Trench form the city's northern and southern boundaries.

Bring a healthy sense of reverence when you visit: Vancouver is a spiritual place. For its original inhabitants, the Coast Salish peoples, it was the sacred spot where the mythical Thunderbird and Killer Whale flung wind and rain all about the heavens during their epic battles—how else to explain the coast's occasional climatic fits of temper? Devotees of a later religious tradition might worship in the sepulchre of Stanley Park or in the polished, incense-filled quiet of St. James Anglican Church, designed by English architect Sir Adrian Gilbert Scott and perhaps Vancouver's finest building.

Vancouver has a level of nightlife possible only in a place where the finer things in life have never been driven out to the suburbs and where sidewalks have never rolled up at 5 pm. There is no shortage of excellent hotels and restaurants here either. But you can find good theater, accommodations, and dining almost anywhere these days. Vancouver's *real* culture is in its tall fir trees practically downtown and its towering rock spires close by, the ocean at your doorstep and people from every corner of the earth all around you.

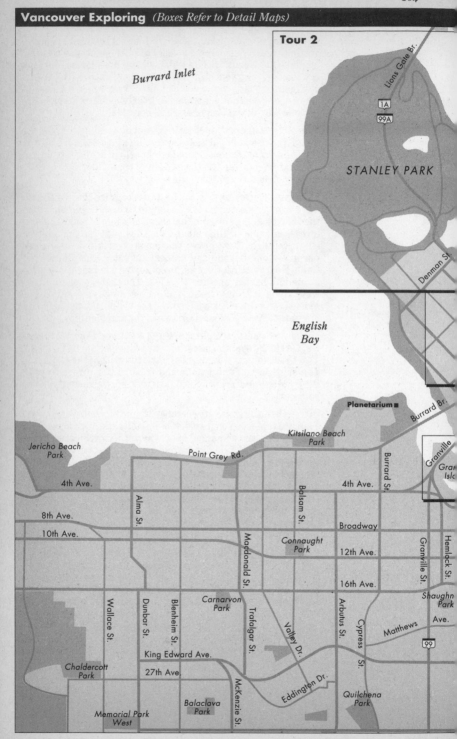

Tour 2

Burrard Inlet

Lions Gate Br.

1A
99A

STANLEY PARK

Denman St.

English Bay

Planetarium ■

Burrard Br.

Kitsilano Beach Park

Granville

Gran
Isl

Point Grey Rd.

Jericho Beach Park

4th Ave.

4th Ave.

Burrard St.

Balsam St.

Alma St.

8th Ave.

10th Ave.

Broadway

Macdonald St.

Connaught Park

12th Ave.

Granville St.

Hemlock St.

16th Ave.

Carnarvon Park

Shaughn
Park

Wallace St.

Dunbar St.

Blenheim St.

Trafalgar St.

Valley Dr.

Arbutus St.

Cypress St.

Matthews

Ave.

99

King Edward Ave.

Chaldercott Park

27th Ave.

McKenzie St.

Eddington Dr.

Quilchena Park

Memorial Park West

Balaclava Park

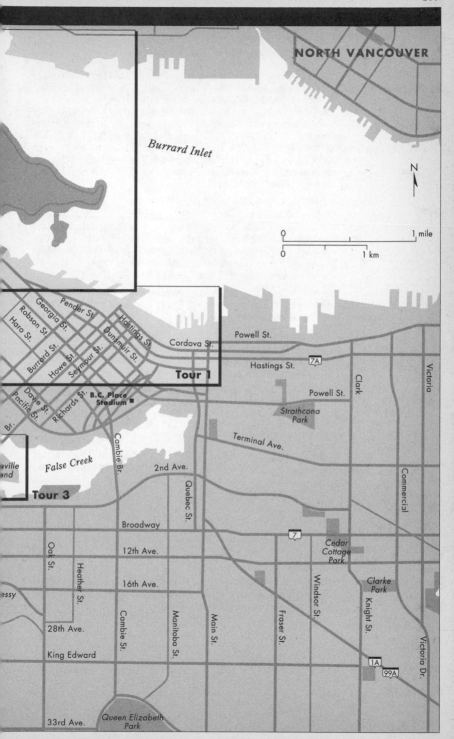

Essential Information

Arriving and Departing by Plane

Airport and Airlines International Airports Vancouver International Airport is on an island about 14 kilometers (9 miles) south of downtown. The main terminal building has three levels: departures, international arrivals, and domestic arrivals; a small south terminal building services flights to secondary destinations within the province. **American Airlines** (tel. 800/433–7300), **Continental** (tel. 604/222–2442), **Delta** (tel. 604/682–5933), **Horizon Air** (800/547–9308), and **United** (tel. 604/683–7111) fly into the airport. The two major domestic airlines are **Air Canada** (tel. 604/688–5515) and **Canadian Airlines** (tel. 604/279–6611).

Other Facilities **Air BC** (tel. 604/278–3800) offers 30-minute harbor-to-harbor service (downtown Vancouver to downtown Victoria) several times a day. Planes leave from near the Bayshore Hotel. Harbor-to-harbor service (Seattle to Vancouver) is run by **Lake Union Air** (tel. 800/826–1890). **Helijet Airways** (tel. 604/273–1414) has helicopter service from downtown Vancouver to downtown Victoria. The heliport is near Vancouver's Pan Pacific Hotel.

Between the Airport and Downtown The drive from the airport to downtown is 20–45 minutes, depending on the time of day. Airport hotels offer free shuttle service to and from the airport.

By Bus The **Airport Express** (tel. 604/273–9023) bus leaves the domestic arrivals level of the terminal building every 15 minutes, stopping at major downtown hotels and the bus depot. It operates from 5:30 AM until 12:30 AM. The fare is $7.25.

By Taxi There are taxi stands in front of the terminal building on the domestic and international arrivals levels. Taxi fare to downtown is about $20. Area cab companies are **Yellow** (tel. 604/681–3311), **Black Top** (tel. 604/731–1111), and **MacLures** (tel. 604/731–9211).

By Limousine Limousine service from **Airlimo** (tel. 604/273–1331) costs about the same as a taxi to downtown: The current rate is about $26.

Arriving and Departing

By Car From the south, I-5 from Seattle becomes **Highway 99** at the U.S.–Canada border. Vancouver is a three-hour drive from Seattle. Avoid border crossings during peak times: holiday weekends, Friday evenings, Saturday mornings, and Sunday afternoons and evenings.

Highway 1, the **Trans-Canada Highway,** enters Vancouver from the east. If you enter the city after rush hour (8:30 AM), you should not have a problem with traffic.

By Ferry **BC Ferries** operates two major ferry terminals outside Vancouver. From Tsawwassen to the south (an hour's drive from downtown), ferries sail 38 kilometers (24 miles) to Victoria on Vancouver Island and through the Gulf Islands (the small islands between the mainland and Vancouver Island). From Horseshoe Bay (30 minutes north from downtown), ferries sail a short distance up the coast and to Nanaimo on Vancouver Island. Call (tel. 604/685–1021) for departure and arrival times.

By Train The **VIA Rail** (tel. 800/561–8630) station is at Main Street and Terminal Avenue. VIA provides service through the Rockies to Banff. Passenger trains leave the **BC Rail** (tel. 604/631–3500) station in North Vancouver for Whistler and the interior of British Columbia. There is no Amtrak service from Seattle.

By Bus **Greyhound** (tel. 604/661–8747) is the biggest bus line servicing Vancouver. The **Vancouver bus depot** is at the corner of Dunsmuir and Cambie streets, a 10-minute walk from Georgia and Granville streets. **Quick Shuttle** (tel. 604/591–3571) bus service runs between Vancouver and Seattle four times a day.

Getting Around

By Car Although no freeways cross Vancouver, rush-hour traffic is not yet horrendous. The worst rush-hour bottlenecks are the North Shore bridges, the George Massey Tunnel on Highway 99 south of Vancouver, and Highway 1 through Coquitlam and Surrey.

By Subway Vancouver has a one-line, 25-kilometer (15-mile) rapid transit system called **SkyTrain** that travels underground downtown and is elevated for the rest of its route to New Westminster. Trains leave about every five minutes. Tickets must be carried with you as proof of payment. They are sold at each station from machines; correct change is not necessary. You may use transfers from Sky Train to Seabus and BC Transit buses (*see* below) and vice versa.

By Bus Exact change is needed to ride the buses: $1.25 adults, 65¢ for senior citizens and children 5–13. Books of 10 tickets are sold at convenience stores and newsstands; look for a red, white, and blue "Fare Dealer" sign. Day passes, good for unlimited travel after 9:30 AM, cost $3.50 for adults. They are available from fare dealers and any SeaBus or SkyTrain station.

By Taxi It is difficult to hail a cab in Vancouver; unless you're near a hotel, you'd have better luck calling a taxi service. Try **Yellow** (tel. 604/681–3311), **Black Top** (tel. 604/731–1111), or **MacLures** (tel. 604/731–9211).

By SeaBus The **SeaBus** is a 400-passenger commuter ferry that crosses Burrard Inlet from the foot of Lonsdale (North Vancouver) to downtown. The ride takes 13 minutes and costs the same as the transit bus. With a transfer, connection can be made with any BC Transit bus or SkyTrain.

Important Addresses and Numbers

Tourist Information **Vancouver Travel Infocentre** (1055 Dunsmuir St., tel. 604/683–2000) provides maps and information about the city, and is open in summer, daily 8–6; in winter, Monday–Saturday 9–5. A kiosk, located at Stanley Park in the Aquarium parking lot, is open mid-May–September, daily 10–6. The kiosk in Pacific Centre Mall is open daily in summer, Monday–Saturday 9:30–5, Sunday noon–5; in winter, Monday–Saturday 9–5. Eaton's department store downtown also has a tourist information counter that is open all year.

Embassies There are no embassies in Vancouver, only consulates and trade commissions: **United States** (1075 W. Georgia St., tel. 604/685–4311) and **United Kingdom** (800–1111 Melville St., tel. 604/

683–4421). For a complete listing, see the Yellow Pages under consulates.

Emergencies Call 911 for **police, fire department,** and **ambulance.**

Hospitals and Clinics **St. Paul's Hospital** (1081 Burrard St., tel. 604/682–2344), a major downtown hospital, has an emergency ward. **Medicentre** (1055 Dunsmuir St., lower level, tel. 604/683–8138) is a drop-in clinic on the lower level of the Bentall Centre.

Dentist The counterpart to Medicentre is **Dentacentre** (1055 Dunsmuir St., lower level, tel. 604/669–6700), and is next door.

Late-night Pharmacy **Shopper's Drug Mart** (1125 Davie St., tel. 604/685–6445) is open until midnight every night except Sunday, when it closes at 9 PM.

Road Emergencies **BCAA** (tel. 604/293–2222) has 24-hour emergency road service for members of AAA or CAA.

Travel Agencies **American Express Travel Service** (1040 W. Georgia St., tel. 604/669–2813), **Hagen's Travel** (210–850 W. Hastings St., tel. 604/684–2448), **P. Lawson Travel** (409 Granville St., tel. 604/682–4272).

Opening and Closing Times

Banks traditionally are open Monday–Thursday 10–3 and Friday 10–6, but many banks have extended hours and are open on Saturday, particularly in the suburbs.

Museums are generally open 10–5, including Saturday and Sunday. Most are open one evening a week as well.

Hours at **department stores** are Monday–Wednesday and Saturday 9:30–6, Thursday and Friday 9:30–9, and Sunday noon–5. Many smaller stores are also open Sunday. Robson Street and Chinatown are particularly good for Sunday shopping.

Guided Tours

Orientation **Gray Line** (tel. 604/681–8687), the largest tour operator, offers the 3½-hour Grand City bus tour year-round. Departing from the Hotel Vancouver, the tour includes Stanley Park, Chinatown, Gastown, English Bay, and Queen Elizabeth Park, and costs about $31. **City and Nature Sightseeing** (tel. 604/683–2112) accommodates up to 14 people in vans that run a 3½-hour City Highlights Tour for $25 (pick-up available from any downtown location). A short city tour (2½ hours) is offered by **Vance Tours** (tel. 604/222–1966) in their minibuses and costs $20.

North Shore tours usually include any or several of the following: a gondola ride up Grouse Mountain, a walk across the Capilano Suspension Bridge, a stop at a salmon hatchery, the Lonsdale Quay Market, and a ride back to town on the SeaBus. Half-day tours cost about $45 and are offered by **Landsea Tours** (tel. 604/687–5640), **Harbour Ferries** (tel. 604/687–9558), **Gray Line** (tel. 604/681–8687), **City and Nature** (tel. 604/683–2112), and **Pacific Coach Lines** (tel. 604/662–7575).

Air Tours Tour the mountains and fjords of the North Shore by helicopter for $149 per person for 45 minutes: **Vancouver Helicopters** (tel. 604/683–4354) flies from the Harbour Heliport downtown. Or see Vancouver from the air for $55 for 20 minutes: **Harbour Air**'s (tel. 604/688–1277) seaplanes leave from beside the Bayshore Hotel.

Boat Tours The Royal Hudson, Canada's only functioning steam train, heads along the mountainous coast up Howe Sound to the coastal logging town of Squamish. After a break to explore, you sail back to Vancouver via the M.V. *Britannia*. This highly recommended excursion costs $45, takes 6½ hours, and is organized by **Harbour Ferries** (tel. 604/687–9558). Reservations are necessary.

The **S.S.** *Beaver* (tel. 604/682–7284), a replica of a Hudson Bay fur-trading vessel that ran aground here in 1888, does two trips. One is the Harbour Sunset Dinner Cruise, a three-hour trip with a mesquite-grilled salmon dinner; the other is a daytime trip up Indian Arm with salmon for lunch. Each is about $35. Reservations are necessary.

Harbour Ferries (tel. 604/687–9558) takes a 1½-hour tour of the Burrard Inlet in a paddle wheeler. Including pick-up from a downtown hotel, the cost is $18.

Fraser River Tours (tel. 604/250–3458 or 604/584–5517) will take you on a 4-hour tour of a fascinating working river—past log booms, tugs, and houseboats. The cruiser, *Atria Star*, leaves from Westminster Quay Market (a handy destination from downtown via SkyTrain) and costs $25.

Personal Guides **Fridge's Early Motion Tours** (tel. 604/687–5088) covers Vancouver in a Model-A Ford convertible. Minimum charge is $45 or $18 per person for an hour-long trip around downtown, Chinatown, and Stanley Park.

AAA Horse & Carriage (tel. 604/681–5115) will pick you up at your downtown hotel and take you for a ride in Stanley Park for $100 an hour.

Walking Pick up "A Self-Guided Walking Tour of Downtown Vancouver," published by Tourism Vancouver (Vancouver Travel Infocentre, 1055 Dunsmuir St., tel. 604/683–2000).

Exploring Vancouver

Orientation

The heart of Vancouver—which includes the downtown area, Stanley Park, and the West End high-rise residential neighborhood—sits on a peninsula bordered by English Bay and the Pacific Ocean to the west; by False Creek, an inlet on which you will find Granville Island, to the south; and to the north by Burrard Inlet, the working port of the city, past which loom the North Shore mountains. The oldest part of the city—Gastown and Chinatown—lies at the edge of Burrard Inlet, around Main Street, which runs north–south and is roughly the dividing line between the east side and the west side. All the avenues, which are numbered, have east and west designations.

Highlights for First-time Visitors

Chinatown (*see* Tour 1: Downtown Vancouver)
English Bay (*see* Tour 2: Stanley Park)
Granville Island (*see* Tour 3: Granville Island)

Robson Street (*see* Shopping, below)
Stanley Park (*see* Tour 2: Stanley Park)

Tour 1: Downtown Vancouver

Numbers in the margin correspond to points of interest on the Tour 1: Downtown Vancouver map.

❶ You can logically begin your downtown tour in either of two ways. If you're in for a day of shopping, amble down **Robson Street** (*see* Shopping, below), where you'll find any item from souvenirs to high fashions, from espresso to muffins.

❷ If you opt otherwise, start at **Robson Square,** built in 1975 and designed by architect Arthur Erickson to be the gathering place of downtown Vancouver. The complex, which functions from the outside as a park, encompasses the Vancouver Art Gallery and government offices and courts that have been built under landscaped walkways, a block-long glass canopy, and a waterfall that helps mask traffic noise. An ice-skating rink and restaurants occupy the below-street level.

❸ The **Vancouver Art Gallery** that heads the Square was a neoclassical-style 1912 courthouse until Erickson converted it in 1980. Notice some original details: The lions that guard the majestic front steps and the use of columns and domes are features borrowed from ancient Roman architecture. In the back of the old courthouse, a more modest staircase now serves as a speakers' corner. *750 Hornby St., tel. 604/682-5621. Admission: $3.75 adults, $2.25 students and senior citizens; free Thurs. eve. Open Mon., Wed., Fri., and Sat. 10-5, Thurs. 10-9, Sun. noon-5.*

❹ Adjacent to the art gallery, on Hornby Street, is the **Hotel Vancouver** (1939), one of the last of the railway-built hotels. (The last one built was the Chateau Whistler, in 1989.) Reminiscent of a medieval French castle, this château style has been incorporated into hotels throughout every major Canadian city. With the onset of the Depression, construction was halted here, and the hotel was finished only in time for the visit of King George VI in 1939. It has been renovated twice: During the 1960s it was unfortunately modernized, but the more recent refurbishment is more in keeping with the spirit of what is the most recognizable roof on Vancouver's skyline. The exterior of the building has carvings of malevolent gargoyles at the corners, an ornate chimney, Indian chiefs on the Hornby Street side, and an assortment of grotesque mythological figures.

❺ **Christ Church Cathedral** (1895), across the street from the Hotel Vancouver, is the oldest church in Vancouver. The tiny church was built in a Gothic style with buttresses and pointed arched windows and looks like the parish church of an English village. By contrast, the cathedral's rough-hewn interior is that of a frontier town, with Douglas-fir beams and carpenter woodwork that offers excellent acoustics for the frequent vespers, carol services, and Gregorian chants presented here. *690 Burrard St., tel. 604/682-3848.*

❻ The **Marine Building** (1931), at the foot of Burrard Street, is Canada's best example of Art Deco style. Terra-cotta bas-reliefs depict the history of transportation: Airships, biplanes, steamships, locomotives, and submarines are figured. These motifs were once considered radical and modernistic adorn-

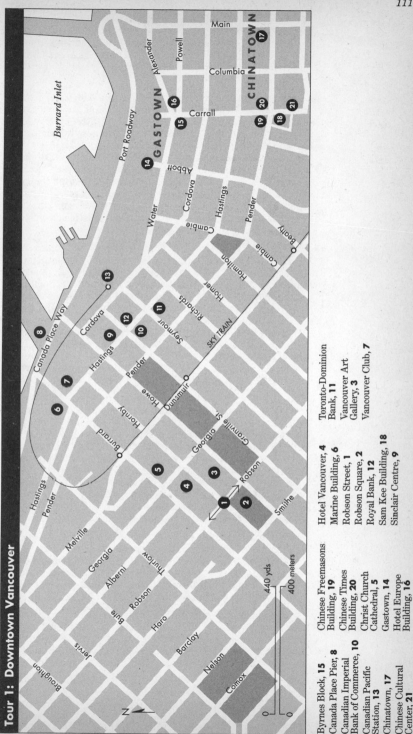

Tour 1: Downtown Vancouver

111

Byrnes Block, 15
Canada Place Pier, 8
Canadian Imperial
Bank of Commerce, 10
Canadian Pacific
Station, 13
Chinatown, 17
Chinese Cultural
Center, 21

Chinese Freemasons
Building, 19
Chinese Times
Building, 20
Christ Church
Cathedral, 5
Gastown, 14
Hotel Europe
Building, 16

Hotel Vancouver, 4
Marine Building, 6
Robson Street, 1
Robson Square, 2
Royal Bank, 12
Sam Kee Building, 18
Sinclair Centre, 9

Toronto-Dominion
Bank, 11
Vancouver Art
Gallery, 3
Vancouver Club, 7

ments since most buildings were still using classical or Gothic ornamentation. From the east, the Marine Building is reflected in bronze by 999 West Hastings, and in silver from the southeast by the Canadian Imperial Bank of Commerce. Stand on the corner of Hastings and Hornby streets for the best view of the Marine Building.

A nice walk is along Hastings Street—the old financial district. Until the 1966–1972 period, when the first of the bank towers and underground malls on West Georgia Street were developed, this was Canada's westernmost business terminus. The temple-style banks, businessmen's clubs, and investment houses survive as evidence of the city's sophisticated architec-
7 tural advances prior to World War I. The **Vancouver Club,** built between 1912 and 1914, was a gathering place for the city's elite. Its architectural design is reminiscent of private clubs in England that were inspired by Italian Renaissance palaces. The Vancouver Club is still a private businessmen's club. *915 W. Hastings St., tel. 604/685–9321.*

8 The foot of Howe Street, north of Hastings, is **Canada Place Pier.** Converted into Vancouver's Trade and Convention Center after Expo 86, Canada Place was originally built on an old cargo pier to be the off-site Canadian pavilion. It is dominated at the shore end by the luxurious Pan Pacific Hotel (*see* Lodging, below), with its spectacular three-story lobby and waterfall. The convention space is covered by a fabric roof shaped like 10 sails, which has become a landmark of Vancouver's skyline. Below is a cruise-ship facility, and at the north end are an Imax theater, restaurant, and outdoor performance space. A promenade runs along the pier's west side with views of the Burrard Inlet harbor and Stanley Park. *999 Canada Pl., tel. 604/682–1070.*

9 Walk back up to Hastings and Howe streets to the **Sinclair Centre.** Vancouver's outstanding architect, Richard Henriquez, has knitted four government office buildings (built 1905–1939) into an office-retail complex. The two Hastings Street buildings—the 1905 post office with the elegant clock tower and the 1913 Winch Building—are linked with the Post Office Extension and Customs Examining Warehouse to the north. Painstaking and very costly restoration involved finding master masons—the original terrazzo suppliers in Europe—and uncovering and refurbishing the pressed-metal ceilings.

Canada has a handful of old chartered banks; the oldest and
10 most impressive of these is the former **Canadian Imperial Bank of Commerce** headquarters (1906–1908) at Hastings and Granville streets; the columns, arches, and details are of typically
11 Roman influence. The **Toronto-Dominion Bank,** one block east, is of the same style, but was built in 1920.

Backtracking, directly across from the CIBC on Hastings
12 Street, is the more Gothic **Royal Bank.** It was intended to be half of a symmetrical building that was never completed, due to the Depression. Striking, though, is the magnificent hall, ecclesiastical in style, reminiscent of a European cathedral.

13 At the foot of Seymour Street is the **Canadian Pacific Station,** the third and most pretentious of three CPR passenger terminals. Built 1912–1914, this terminal replaced the other two as the western terminus for Canada's transcontinental railway. After Canada's railways merged, the station became obsolete

until a 1978 renovation turned it into an office-retail complex
and SeaBus Terminal. Murals in the waiting rooms show passengers what kind of scenery to expect on their journeys across
Canada.

From Seymour Street, pick up Water Street, on your way to
⑭ **Gastown.** Named after the original townsite saloon keeper,
"Gassy" Jack Deighton, Gastown is where Vancouver originated. Deighton arrived at Burrard Inlet in 1867 with his Indian wife, a barrel of whiskey, and few amenities. A statue of
Gassy Jack stands on the north side of Maple Tree Square, the
intersection of five streets, where he built his first saloon.

When the transcontinental train arrived in 1887, Gastown became the transfer point for trade with the Orient and was soon
crowded with hotels and warehouses. The Klondike gold rush
encouraged further development until 1912, when the "Golden
Years" ended. The 1930s–1950s saw hotels being converted
into rooming houses and the warehouse district shifting elsewhere. The area gradually became unattended and rundown.
However, both Gastown and Chinatown were declared historic
areas and revitalization projects are underway.

⑮ The **Byrnes Block** building was constructed on the corner of
Water and Carrall streets (the site of Gassy Jack's second saloon) after the 1886 Great Fire. The date is just visible at the
top of the building above the door where it says "Herman
Block," which was its name for a short time. The extravagantly
detailed Alhambra Hotel that was situated here was luxury
class for the time, at a cost of a dollar a night.

Tucked behind 2 Water Street is **Blood Alley** and **Gaoler's
Mews.** Once the site of the city's first civic buildings—the con-
stable's cabin and courthouse, and a two-cell log jail—today
the cobblestone street with antique streetlighting is the home
to architectural offices.

⑯ The **Hotel Europe** (1908–1909), a flatiron building at Powell and
Alexander streets, was billed as the best hotel in the city, and
was Vancouver's first reinforced concrete structure. Designed
as a functional commercial building, the hotel lacks ornamentation and fine detail, a style unusually utilitarian for the time.

From Maple Tree Square, walk three blocks up Carrall Street
⑰ to Pender Street, where **Chinatown** begins. There was already
a sizable Chinese community in British Columbia because of
the 1858 Cariboo gold rush in central British Columbia, but the
biggest influx from China occurred in the 1880s, during construction of the Canadian Pacific Railway, when 15,000 labor-
ers were imported. The Chinese were among the first
inhabitants of Vancouver, and some of the oldest buildings in
the city are in Chinatown.

Even while doing the hazardous work of blasting the railbed
through the Rocky Mountains, the Chinese were discriminated
against. The Anti-Asiatic Riots of 1907 stopped growth in Chinatown for 50 years and immigration from China was discour-
aged by more and more restrictive policies, climaxing in a $500
head tax during the 1920s.

In the 1960s the city council was planning bulldozer urban renewal for Strathcona, the residential part of Chinatown, and
freeway connections through the most historic blocks of China-

town were charted. Fortunately, plans were halted and today Chinatown is an expanding, vital district fueled by investment from Vancouver's most notable newcomers—immigrants from Hong Kong. It is best to view the buildings in Chinatown from the south side of Pender Street, where the Chinese Cultural Center stands. From here you'll get a better view of important details that adorn the upper stories. The style of architecture typical in Vancouver's Chinatown is patterned on that of Canton, and won't be seen in any other Canadian cities.

The corner of Carrall and East Pender streets, now the western boundary of Chinatown, is one of the neighborhood's most historic spots. Standing at 8 West Pender Street is the **Sam Kee Building,** recognized by *Ripley's Believe It Or Not!* as the narrowest building in the world. The 1913 structure still exists, with its bay windows overhanging the street and a basement that burrows under the sidewalk.

⑲ The **Chinese Freemasons Building** (1901) at 1 West Pender Street has two completely different styles of facades: The side facing Chinatown displays a fine example of Cantonese-imported recessed balconies; on the Carrall Street side, the standard Victorian style common throughout the British Empire is displayed. It was in this building that Dr. Sun Yat-sen hid for months from the agents of the Manchu dynasty while he raised funds for its overthrow, which he accomplished in 1911.

⑳ Directly across Carrall Street is the **Chinese Times Building,** constructed in 1902. Inside, there is a hidden mezzanine floor from which police officers could hear the clicking sounds of clandestine mah-jongg games played after sunset. Attempts by vice squads to enforce restrictive policies against the Chinese gamblers proved fruitless because police were unable to find the players who were hidden on the secret floor.

㉑ Planning for the **Chinese Cultural Center** and Dr. Sun Yat-sen Gardens (1980–87) began during the late-1960s; the first phase was designed by James Cheng, a former associate of Arthur Erickson. The cultural center has exhibition space, classrooms, and meeting rooms. The **Dr. Sun Yat-sen Gardens** located behind the cultural center, were built by 52 artisans from Suzhou, the Garden City of the People's Republic. The gardens incorporate design elements and traditional materials from several of that city's centuries-old private gardens and are the first living classical Chinese gardens built outside China. As you walk through the gardens, remember that no power tools, screws, or nails were used in the construction. *Dr. Sun Yat-sen Gardens. 578 Carrall St., tel. 604/689–7133. Admission: $3.50 adults, $2.50 senior citizens and students, $7 family. Open May–Sept., daily 10–8; Oct.–Apr., daily 10–4:30.*

Tour 2: Stanley Park

Numbers in the margin correspond to points of interest on the Tour 2: Stanley Park map.

A 1,000-acre wilderness park just blocks from the downtown section of a major city is a rarity, but is one of Vancouver's major attractions. In the 1860s, due to a threat of American invasion, the area that is now Stanley Park was set aside as a military reserve (though it was never needed). When the City of Vancouver was incorporated in 1886, the council's first act was to request that the land be set aside for a park. In 1888 permission was granted and the grounds were named Stanley Park after Lord Stanley, then Governor-General of Canada (the same person after whom hockey's Stanley Cup is named).

An afternoon in Stanley Park gives you a capsule tour of Vancouver that includes beaches, the ocean, the harbor, Douglas fir and cedar forests, and a good look at the North Shore mountains. The park sits on a peninsula and along the shore is a 9-kilometer (5½-mile) long pathway called the seawall. You can walk or bicycle all the way around, or follow the shorter route, suggested below.

Bicycles are for rent at the foot of Georgia Street near the park entrance. Cyclists must ride in a counterclockwise direction and stay on their side of the path. A good place for pedestrians
㉒ to start is at the foot of Alberni Street beside **Lost Lagoon.** Go through the underpass and veer right to the seawall.

㉓ The old wood structure that you pass is the **Vancouver Rowing Club,** a private athletic club (established 1903), a bit farther
㉔ along is the **Royal Vancouver Yacht Club.**

㉕ About ½ kilometer (⅛ mile) away is the causeway to **Deadman's Island,** a former burial ground for the local Salish Indians and the early settlers. It is now a small naval training base called the HMCS *Discovery* that is not open to the public. Just ahead
㉖ is the **Nine O'Clock Gun,** a cannonlike apparatus that sits by the water's edge. Originally used to alert fishermen of a curfew ending weekend fishing, now it automatically signals every night at 9.

㉗ Farther along is **Brockton Point,** and its small but functional lighthouse and foghorn. The **totem poles,** which are situated more inland, make a popular photo spot for tourists. Totem poles were not carved in the Vancouver area; these were brought to the park from the north coast of British Columbia and were carved by the Kwakiutl and Haida peoples late in the last century. These cedar poles with carved animals, fish, birds, or mythological creatures were like a family coat-of-arms or crest.

㉘ At kilometer 3 (mile 2) is **Lumberman's Arch,** a huge log archway dedicated to the workers in Vancouver's first industry. Beside the arch is an asphalt path that leads back to Lost Lagoon, for those who want a shorter walk. (This is about a third of the
㉙ distance.) This path also leads to the **Vancouver Public Aquarium,** with killer and beluga whale shows several times a day. Also part of this attraction is the humid Amazon rain-forest gallery, through which you can walk, with its piranhas, giant cockroaches, alligators, tropical birds, and jungle vegetation. Other displays show the underwater life of coastal British Columbia, the Canadian arctic, and other areas of the world. The Clamshell Gift Shop next to the aquarium is the best spot in town for quality souvenirs and gifts, most with an emphasis on natural history. *Aquarium, tel. 604/682–1118. Admission: $8 adults, $7 senior citizens and youths, $5 children 5–12. Open daily in summer 9:30–8; daily in winter 10–5:30. Clamshell open July–Labor Day, daily 9:30–8; rest of year, daily 10–6.*

㉚ Next to the aquarium is the **Stanley Park Zoo,** a friendly place, easily seen in an hour or two. Except for the polar bears, most

Tour 2: Stanley Park

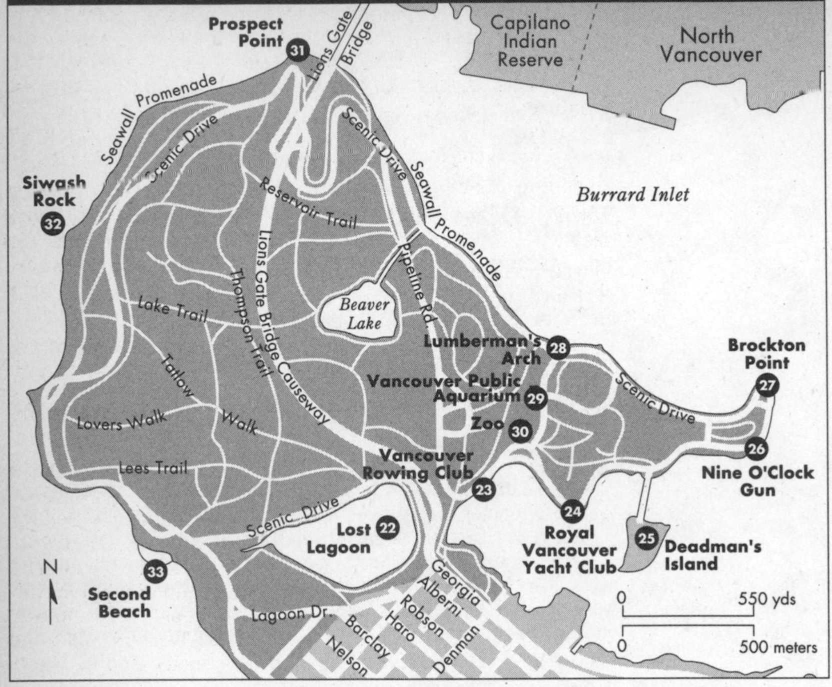

of the animals are small—monkeys, seals, exotic birds, penguins, and playful otters.

About 1 kilometer (¾ mile) farther is the **Lions Gate Bridge**—the halfway point of the seawall. On the other side of the bridge 31 is **Prospect Point,** where you can see cormorants in their seaweed nests on the ledges along the cliffs. The large black diving birds are recognized by their long necks and beaks; when not nesting, they often perch atop floating logs or boulders. Another remarkable bird found along the shore in the park is the beautiful great blue heron. Reaching up to 4-feet tall with a wing span of 6 feet, the heron preys on passing fish in the waters here. The oldest heron rookery in British Columbia is in the trees around the zoo.

Continuing around the seawall you will come to the **English Bay** side and the beginning of sandy beaches. The imposing 32 rock just off shore is **Siwash Rock.** Legend tells of a young Indian who, about to become a father, bathed persistently to wash his sins away so that his son could be born pure, and for his devotion he was blessed by the gods and immortalized in the shape of Siwash Rock. Two small rocks, said to be his wife and child, are just up on the cliff above the site.

Time Out Along the seawall is one of Vancouver's best restaurants, the **Ferguson Point Teahouse.** Set on the great lawn among Douglas fir and cedar trees, the restaurant is the perfect stopover for a summer weekend lunch or brunch. If you just want a snack, a park concession stand is also at Ferguson Point.

㉝ The next attraction along the seawall is the large saltwater pool
at **Second Beach.** In the summer it is a children's pool with life-
guards, but during winter the pool is drained and skate-
boarders perform stunts. At the pool you can take a shortcut
back to Lost Lagoon. To take the shortcut, walk along the per-
pendicular road behind the pool that cuts into the park. The
wood footbridge that's ahead will lead you to a path along the
south side of the lagoon and to your starting point at the foot of
Alberni or Georgia street.

If you continue along the seawall, it will emerge out of the park
into a high-rise residential neighborhood, the **West End.** You
can walk back to Alberni Street along Denman Street where
there are plenty of places to stop for coffee, ice cream, or a
drink.

Tour 3: Granville Island

*Numbers in the margin correspond to points of interest on the
Tour 3: Granville Island map.*

Granville Island was just a sandbar until World War I when the
nearby creek was dredged for access to the sawmills that lined
the shore. Sludge heaped on the sandbar gradually created the
island that was then used to house supplies for the logging industry. In 1971 the federal government bought the island with
an imaginative plan to refurbish it and introduce a public market, marine activities, and artisans' studios. The opposite
shore of False Creek was the site of the 1986 World's Fair and is
now part of the largest urban redevelopment plan in North
America.

The small island is almost strictly commercial except for a small
houseboat community. Most of the previously used industrial
buildings and tin sheds have been retained, but are painted in
upbeat reds, yellows, and blues. The government regulates the
types of businesses that settle on Granville Island; only businesses involving food, crafts, marine activities, and the arts
are permitted here.

Access on foot to Granville Island starts with a 15-minute walk
from downtown Vancouver to the south end of Thurlow Street.
From a dock behind the Vancouver Aquatic Center, the Granville Island ferry leaves every six minutes for the short trip
across False Creek to the Granville Island Public Market.
These pudgy boats are a great way to see the sights on False
Creek, but for a longer ride, go to the Maritime Museum (1905
Ogden St., tel. 604/737–2211). For more information call Granville Island Ferries (tel. 604/684–7781).

Another option is to take a 20-minute ride on a BC Transit (tel.
604/261–5100) bus. Take a UBC, Granville, Arbutus, Cambie,
or Oak bus from downtown to Granville and Broadway and
transfer to the Granville Island bus No. 51. Parking is limited,
but if you must take a car, go early in the week and early in the
day to avoid crowds. Parking is free for only three hours; an alternative is to use the pay parking buildings on the island if you
can find a space.

㉞ The ferry to Granville Island will drop you off at the **Granville
Island Public Market**. Although there are a few good food
stores outside, most stalls are enclosed in the 50,000-square-
foot building. Since the government allows no chains, each out-

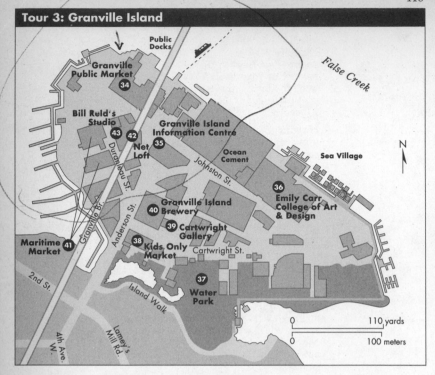

Tour 3: Granville Island

let is unique, and most are of good quality. You probably won't
be able to leave the market without a snack, espresso, or fix-
ings for a lunch out on the wharf. Don't miss the charcoal-
grilled oysters from **Sea-kist,** fish chowder or bouillabaisse
from the **Stock Market,** fresh fudge at **Olde World Fudge,** or
smoked salmon from the **Salmon Shop.** In the summer you'll see
mounds of raspberries, strawberries, blueberries, and even
more exotic fruits like persimmons and lychees. On the water
side of the market is lots of outdoor seating. *Public Market.
Tel. 604/666–5784. Open June–Aug., daily 9–6; closed Mon.
Sept.–May except holidays.*

③⑤ The **Granville Island Information Centre,** kitty-corner to the
market, is a good place to get oriented with the island. Maps
are available and a slide show depicts the evolution of Granville
Island. Ask here about special-events days; perhaps there's a
boat show, outdoor symphony concert, dance performance, or
some other happening. *1592 Johnston St., tel. 604/666–5784.
Open daily 10–6.*

Continue walking south on Johnston Street, along a clockwise
loop of the island. Next is **Ocean Cement,** one of the last of the
island's former industries; its lease does not expire until the
year 2004.

③⑥ Next door is the **Emily Carr College of Art and Design.** Just inside the front door, to your right, is the **Charles H. Scott Gallery.** This gallery hosts contemporary multi-media exhibits.
*1399 Johnston St., tel. 604/687–2345. Open daily 11–5, Thurs.
11–8.*

Past the art school, on the left, is one of the only **houseboat communities** in Vancouver; others have been banned by the city because of problems with sewage and property taxes. The owners of this community appealed the ban and won special status. Take the boardwalk that starts at the houseboats and continues partway around the island.

As you circle around to Cartwright Street, stop in **Kakali** at number 1249, where you can watch the process of making fine handmade paper from all sorts of materials like bluejeans, herbs, and sequins. Another unusual artisan on the island is the glassblower at 1440 Old Bridge Street, around the corner.

The next two attractions will make any child's visit to Granville Island a thrill. First, on Cartwright Street, is the children's
(37) **water park,** with a wading pool, sprinklers, and a fire hydrant made for children to shower each other. A bit farther down, be-
(38) side Isadora's restaurant, is the **Kids Only Market,** with two floors of small shops selling toys, arts-and-crafts materials, dolls, records and tapes, chemistry sets, and other sorts of kid stuff. *Water park. 1318 Cartwright St., tel. 604/665–3425. Admission free. Open June–Aug., daily 10–6. Kids Only Market. 1496 Cartwright St., tel. 604/689–8447. Open June–Aug., daily 10–6; Sept.–May, Tues.–Sun. 10–6.*

(39) Across from the Kids Only Market is the **Cartwright Gallery,** which hosts such temporary exhibits as native Indian and local crafts and intriguing traveling exhibits. *1141 Cartwright St., tel. 604/687–8266. Open Tues.–Sat. 10–5, Sun. 11–3.*

(40) At the **Granville Island Brewery,** next door, you can take a half-hour tour every afternoon; at the end of the tour, sample the Granville Island Lager that is produced here and sold locally in most restaurants. *Tel. 604/688–9927. Admission free. Tours run Mon.–Fri. at 2; Sat. and Sun. at 1 and 3.*

Cross Anderson Street and walk down Duranleau Street. On your left, the scuba diving pool in **Adrenalin Sports** marks the
(41) start of the **Maritime Market,** a string of businesses all geared to the sea. The first walkway to the left, Maritime Mews, leads to marinas and dry docks. There are dozens of outfits in the Maritime Market that charter boats (with or without skippers) or run cruise-and-learn trips.

Another way to take to the water is by kayak. Take a lesson or rent a kayak from **Ecomarine Ocean Kayak Center** (1668 Duranleau St., tel. 604/689–7575). Owner John Dowd is considered *the* expert on Pacific Northwest ocean kayaking.

Time Out   **Bridges** (1696 Duranleau St., tel. 604/687–4400), in the bright yellow building across from the market, is a good spot to have lunch, especially on a warm summer's day. Eat on the spacious deck that looks out on the sailboats, fishing boats, and other water activities.

The last place to explore on Granville Island is the blue building
(42) next to Ecomarine on Duranleau Street, the **Net Loft.** The loft is a collection of small, quality stores—good places to find a gift to take home: bookstore, crafts store/gallery, kitchenware shop, postcard shop, custom-made hat shop, handmade paper store, British Columbian native Indian gallery, do-it-yourself jewelry store, and more reside here.

Vancouver   *120*

(43) Behind Blackberry Books, in the Net Loft complex, is the **studio of Bill Reid,** British Columbia's most respected Haida Indian carver. His *The Raven and the First Men* (which took five carvers more than three years to complete) is in the Museum of Anthropology (*see* Other Museums, below). Reid's Pacific Northwest Coast Indian artworks are world-renowned. Although you can't visit the studio, there are large windows through which you can look.

Since you have come full circle, you can either take the ferry back to downtown Vancouver, or stay for dinner and catch a play at the **Arts Club** (tel. 604/687-1644) or **Waterfront Theater** (tel. 604/685-6217).

Other Museums

The **Maritime Museum** traces the history of marine activities on the west coast. Permanent exhibits depict the port of Vancouver, the fishing industry, and early explorers; the model ships on display are a delight. Traveling exhibits vary, but always have a maritime theme. Guided tours are led through the double-masted schooner, the *St. Roch*, the first ship to sail in both directions through the treacherous Northwest Passage. A changing variety of restored heritage boats, from different cultures, are moored behind the museum and a huge Kwakiutl totem pole stands out front. *North foot of Cypress St., tel. 604/ 737-2211. Admission: $4 adults, $2.50 children, students, and senior citizens, $8 families; free Wed. eve. Open daily 10-5, Wed. 10-9. Access available by the Granville Island ferries.*

The **Museum of Anthropology,** focusing on the arts of the Pacific Northwest Indians, is Vancouver's most spectacular museum. Situated on the campus of the University of British Columbia, the museum is housed in an award-winning glass and concrete structure designed by Arthur Erickson. In the Great Hall are large and dramatic totem poles, ceremonial archways, and dugout canoes—all adorned with carvings of frogs, eagles, ravens, bears, and salmon. Also showcased are exquisite carvings of gold, silver, and argillite (a black stone found in the Queen Charlotte Islands). Masks, tools, and costumes from many other cultures are also displayed. A ceramics wing, housing 600 pieces from 15th- to 19th-century Europe opened in 1990. *6393 N.W. Marine Dr., tel. 604/228-3825. Admission: $4 adults, $2 youths (13-18) and senior citizens, $1 children; free on Tues. Open Tues. 11-9, Wed.-Sun. 11-5.*

Science World is in a gigantic shiny dome that was built for Expo 86 for an Omnimax Theater—the world's largest dome screen. Science World is not a traditional museum, but is very much hands-on. Visitors are encouraged to touch and to participate in the theme exhibits. A special gallery, the Search Gallery, is aimed at younger children, as are the fun-filled demonstrations given in Center Stage. *1455 Québec St., tel. 604/687-7832. Admission to Science World: $7 adults, $4.50 senior citizens and children. Admission to Omnimax is the same; for admission to both you get a discount. Open daily 10-5, Saturday 10-9.*

Vancouver Museum displays permanent exhibits that focus on the city's early history and native art and culture. Life-size replicas of an 1897 CPR passenger car, trading post, Victorian parlor, and a real dugout canoe are highlights. Also on the site are the Planetarium and Observatory (*see* Off the Beaten Track, below). *1100 Chestnut St., tel. 604/736–7736. Admission: $5 adults, $2.50 senior citizens and children. Open Tues.–Sun. 10–5 in winter, daily 10–5 in summer.*

Parks and Gardens

Nitobe Garden is a small (2.4-acre) garden that is considered the most authentic Japanese garden outside Japan. The circular path around the park symbolizes the cycle of life and provides a tranquil view from every direction. In April and May cherry blossoms are the highlight, and in June the irises are magnificent. *1903 West Mall, Univ. of B.C., tel. 604/228–4208. Admission: $1.75 adults, $1 senior citizens and students, free Wed. and every day Oct. 11–Mar. 17. Open daily 10–dusk in summer; Mon.–Fri. in winter; phone for specific closing times.*

Pacific Spirit Park (W. 16th Ave., tel. 604/224–5739) is a 1,000-acre park that is bigger and more rugged than Stanley Park. Pacific Spirit's only amenities are 30 miles of trails, a few washrooms, and a couple of signboard maps. Go for a wonderful walk in the west coast woods—it's hard to believe that you are only 15 minutes from downtown Vancouver.

Queen Elizabeth Park has lavish gardens and lots of grassy picnicking spots. Illuminated fountains; the botanical Bloedel Conservatory, with tropical and desert zones and 20 species of free-flying tropical birds; and other facilities including 20 tennis courts, lawn bowling, pitch and putt, and a restaurant are on the grounds. *Cambie St. and 25th Ave., tel. 604/872–5513. Admission to conservatory: $2.70 adults, $1.35 senior citizens and students, $5.40 family ticket. Open May–Sept., daily 10–9; Oct.–Apr., daily 10–5.*

Van Dusen Botanical Garden was a 55-acre golf course, but is now the grounds of one of the largest collections of ornamental plants in Canada. Native and exotic plant displays include the shrubbery maze and the rhododendrons in May and June. *5251 Oak St. at 37th Ave., tel. 604/266–7194. Admission: $4.25 adults, $2.15 senior citizens and youths (13–18), $8.50 family ticket. Open 10–dusk.*

Vancouver for Free

Several public galleries and museums are free on certain days: The **Vancouver Art Gallery** (750 Hornby St., tel. 604/682–5621) is free on Thursday evenings; the **Maritime Museum** (1950 Ogden St., tel. 604/737–2211) is free Wednesday evenings for shanty-singing night; the **Museum of Anthropology** (6393 N.W. Marine Dr., tel. 604/228–3825) is free Tuesday. The **Vancouver Museum** (1100 Chestnut St., tel. 604/736–7736) is free on the first Thursday evening of every month. It is also free every Tuesday for senior citizens.

Also free is the **Beatles Museum** (456 Seymour St., tel. 604/685–8841), with memorabilia from the early years of the Fab Four.

What to See and Do with Children

Stanley Park Zoo (*see* Tour 2: Stanley Park, above).

The **miniature steam train** in Stanley Park, just five minutes northwest of the aquarium, is a big hit with children as it chugs through the forest.

Splashdown Park (Hwy. 17, just before the Tsawwassen Ferry causeway, tel. 604/943–2251), 38 kilometers (24 miles) outside Vancouver, is a giant water-slide park with 11 slides (for toddlers to adults), heated water, picnic tables, and minigolf.

Richmond Nature Park (No. 5 Rd. exit from Hwy. 99, tel. 604/273–7015), with its displays and games in the Nature House, is geared toward children. Guides answer questions and give tours. Since the park sits on a natural bog, rubber boots are recommended if it's been wet, but a boardwalk around the duck pond makes some of the park accessible to strollers and wheelchairs.

Maplewood Farms (405 Seymour River Pl., tel. 604/929–5610), a 20-minute drive from downtown Vancouver, is set up like a small farm, with all the barnyard animals for children to see and pet. Cows are milked every day at 1:15.

Kids Only Market (*see* Tour 3: Granville Island, above).

The Planetarium (1100 Chestnut St., tel. 604/736–3656), on the same site as the Vancouver Museum in Vanier Park, has astronomy shows each afternoon and evening, and laser rock music shows later in the night.

Science World (*see* Other Museums, above)

Off the Beaten Track

On the North Shore you can get a taste of the mountains and test your mettle at the **Lynn Canyon Suspension Bridge** (Lynn Headwaters Regional Park, North Vancouver, tel. 604/987–5922), which hangs 240 feet above Lynn Creek. Also on the North Shore is the **Capilano Fish Hatchery** (4500 Capilano Rd., tel. 604/987–1411), with exhibits about salmon.

If the sky is clear, the telescope at the **Gordon Southam Observatory** (1100 Chestnut St., in Vanier Park, tel. 604/738–2855) will be focused on whatever stars or planets are worth watching that night. While you're there, visit the planetarium on the site.

Shopping

Unlike many cities where suburban malls have taken over, Vancouver's downtown area is still lined with individual boutiques and specialty shops. Stores tend to be open every day and on Thursday and Friday nights.

Shopping Districts

The immense **Pacific Center Mall,** in the heart of downtown, connects Eaton's and The Bay department stores, which stand at opposite corners of Georgia and Granville streets. Pacific Center is on two levels and is mostly underground.

A new commercial center is developing around **Sinclair Center** (*see* Tour 1, above), which caters to sophisticated and upscale tastes.

On the opposite side of Pacific Center, stretching from Burrard to Bute streets, is **Robson Street**—the place for fashion-conscious clothing. Chockablock with small stores and cafés, it is Vancouver's liveliest street and provides many excellent corners for people-watching.

Two other shopping districts, one on **West 41st Avenue,** between West Boulevard and Larch Street, in Kerrisdale, and the other on **West 10th** from Discovery Street west, are both in upscale neighborhoods and have quality shops and restaurants.

Fourth Avenue, from Burrard to Balsam streets, offers an eclectic mix of stores (from sophisticated women's clothing to surfboards and Jams), with an emphasis on sports shops.

In addition to the Pacific Center Mall, **Oakridge Shopping Center** at Cambie Street and 41st Avenue has chic, expensive stores that are fun to browse.

Ethnic Districts **Chinatown** (*see* Tour 1, above)—centered around Pender and Main streets—is an exciting and animated place for restaurants, exotic foodstuffs, and distinctive architecture.

Commercial Drive (around East 1st Avenue) is the heart of the **Italian community,** here called Little Italy. You can sip cappuccino in coffee bars where you may be the only one speaking English, buy sun-dried tomatoes, real Parmesan, or an espresso machine.

The **East Indian shopping district** is on Main Street around 50th Avenue. Curry houses, sweet shops, grocery stores, and sari shops abound.

A small **Japantown** on Powell Street at Dunlevy Street is made up of grocery stores, fish stores, and a few restaurants.

Department Stores

The two biggest department stores in Vancouver, **Eaton's** and **The Bay,** are Canadian owned and located downtown and at most malls. The third, **Woodward's,** is a local chain and is found only in British Columbia and Alberta. The flagship store is in the Oakridge Shopping Center.

Flea Markets

A huge flea market (703 Terminal Ave., tel. 604/685–0666), with more than 300 stalls, is held Saturday, Sunday, and holidays from 8 to 4. This is easily accessible from downtown via SkyTrain.

Auctions

On Wednesday at noon and 7 PM, auctions are held at **Love's** (1635 W. Broadway, tel. 604/733–1157). **Maynard's** (415 W. 2nd Ave., tel. 604/876–6787) also has home furnishings auctions on Wednesday at 7 PM. Phone for times of art and antiques auctions.

Specialty Stores

Antiques A stretch of antiques stores runs along Main Street from 19th to 35th avenues. On 10th Avenue near Alma are a few antiques stores that specialize in Canadiana, including **Folkart Interiors** (3715 W. 10th Ave.), and **Old Country Mouse Factory** (3720 W. 10th Ave.). Also try **Canada West** (3607 W. Broadway). For very refined antiques, see **Artemis** (321 Water St.) in Gastown. For Oriental rugs, go to Granville Street between 7th and 14th avenues.

Art Galleries There are many private galleries throughout Vancouver. The best of them are: **Bau-Xi** (3045 Granville St., tel. 604/733–7011), **Buschlen-Mowatt** (1445 W. Georgia St., tel. 604/682–1234), **Diane Farris** (1565 W. 7th Ave., tel. 604/737–2629), **Equinox** (2321 Granville St., tel. 604/736–2405), and the **Heffel Gallery** (2247 Granville St., tel. 604/732–6505).

Books The best general bookstores are **Duthie's,** located downtown (919 Robson St.) and near the university (4444 W. 10th Ave.), and **Blackberry Books** (1663 Duranleau St.) on Granville Island.

Specialty bookstores include: **The Travel Bug** (2667 W. Broadway) and **World Wide Books and Maps** (736 Granville St., downstairs) for travel books, **Vancouver Kidsbooks** (3083 W. Broadway), **Sportsbooks Plus** (230 W. Broadway), and **Pink Peppercorn** (2686 W. Broadway) for cookbooks, and **William McCarley** (213 Carrall St.) for design and architecture.

Most of the secondhand and antiquarian dealers such as **William Hoffer** (60 Powell St.) and **Colophon Books** (407 W. Cordova St., upstairs), are in the Gastown area. A block or two away are **McLeod's** (455 W. Pender St.), **Ainsworth's** (321 W. Pender St.), and **Bond's** (319 W. Hastings St.). **Lawrence Books** (3591 W. 41st Ave.) is out of the way but is probably the best used bookstore in town.

Children's Stores An unusual children's store worth checking out is **The Imagination Market** (528 Powell St.), an oddball warehouse-type store selling recycled industrial goods for arts and crafts materials: barrels of metallic plastic, feathers, fluorescent-colored paper, buttons, bits of Plexiglas, and other materials by the bagful.

Clothing Several quality men's clothing stores are in the business dis-
Men trict: **Edward Chapman** (833 W. Pender St.) has conservative looks; **E.A. Lee** (466 Howe St.) is stylish; **Leone** (757 W. Hastings St.) is ultra-chic; and **Polo Country** (375 Water St.) offers a casual line of Ralph Lauren.

A few blocks away, at Pacific Center, are **Harry Rosen** and **Holt Renfrew,** both on the upper level. If your tastes are traditional, don't miss **George Straith** (900 W. Georgia St.) in the Hotel Vancouver.

On Robson Street, a more trendy shopping area, are **Ralph Lauren** (No.1123) and **Club Monaco** (No. 1153), for casual wear.

Outside downtown Vancouver there are two men's boutiques selling Italian imports: **Mondo Uomo** (2709 Granville St.) and **Boboli** (2776 Granville St.).

In Kerrisdale, two excellent men's clothing stores are **Finn's** (2159 W. 41st Ave.) and, across the street, **S. Lampman** (2126 W. 41st Ave.).

Women For women's fashions, visit **E.A. Lee** (466 Howe St.), **Wear Else?** (789 W. Pender St.), **Leone** (757 W. Hastings St.), and the more conservative **Chapy's** (833 W. Pender St.), all in the business district. Nearby is the casual **Polo Country** (375 Water St.).

On Robson Street, look for **Margareta** (No. 948), **Ralph Lauren** (No. 1123), **Alfred Sung** (No. 1143), **Club Monaco** (No. 1153), and a lingerie shop, **La Vie en Rose** (No. 1001). For shoes, try **Aldo** (No. 1016), **Pegabo** (No. 1137), and **Stephane de Raucourt** (No. 1024). Off Robson is **Morgan** (813 Hornby St.).

Two expensive and very stylish import stores in South Granville are: **Boboli** (2776 Granville St.) and **Bacci** (2788 Granville St.). Nearby, one of the largest and best shoe stores in town is **Freedman Shoes** (2867 Granville St.).

On the west side **Enda B.** (4346 W. 10th Ave.) and **Wear Else?** (2360 W. 4th Ave.) are the largest and best stores for high-quality fashions, but there's also **Bali Bali** for the more exotic (4462 W. 10th Ave.) and **Zig Zag** (4424 W. 10th Ave.) for fashion accessories.

Gifts Want something special to take home from British Columbia? The best places for quality souvenirs are the **Vancouver Art Gallery** (750 Hornby St.) and the **Clamshell Gift Shop** at the aquarium in Stanley Park. The **Salmon Shop** in the Granville Island Public Market will wrap smoked salmon for travel. Downtown, Haida and Salish Indian art is available at **Images for a Canadian Heritage** (779 Burrard St.). Near Granville Island is **Leona Lattimer** (1590 W. 2nd Ave.), where the inside of her shop is built like an Indian longhouse and is full of Indian arts and crafts ranging from cheap to priceless.

Sports and Outdoor Activities

Participant Sports

Biking **Stanley Park** (*see* Tour 2 in Exploring Vancouver, above) is the most popular spot for family cycling. Rentals are available here from **Bayshore Bicycles** (745 Denman St., tel. 604/688–2453) or around the corner at **Stanley Park Rentals** (676 Chilco St., tel. 604/681–5581).

Another biking route is along the north or south shore of **False Creek**. Rent bikes at **Reckless Rider** (1840 Fir St., tel. 604/736–7325), near Granville Island.

Fishing You can fish for salmon all year in coastal British Columbia. **Sewell's Landing Marina** (6695 Nelson St., Horseshoe Bay, tel. 604/921–7461) organizes a daily four-hour trip on Howe Sound or has hourly rates on U-drives. **Bayshore Yacht Charters** (1601 W. Georgia St., tel. 604/682–3377) has a daily five-hour fishing trip; boats are moored five minutes from downtown Vancouver. **Island Charters** (Duranleau St., Granville Island, tel. 604/688–6625) arranges charters or boat shares and supplies all gear.

Golf Lower Mainland golf courses are open all year. **Fraserview Golf Course** (tel. 604/327–3717), a spacious course with fairways well defined by hills and mature conifers and deciduous trees, is the busiest course in the country. Fraserview is also the most central, about 20 minutes from downtown. **Seymour Golf and Country Club** (tel. 604/929–5491), on the south side of Mt. Seymour, on the North Shore, is a semiprivate club that is open to the public on Monday and Friday. One of the finest public courses in the country is **Peace Portal** (tel. 604/538–4818), near White Rock, a 45-minute drive from downtown.

Health and Fitness Clubs Both the **YMCA** (955 Burrard St., tel. 604/681–0221) and the **YWCA** (580 Burrard St., tel. 604/683–2531) downtown have drop-in rates that let you participate in all activities for the day. Both have pools, weight rooms, and fitness classes; the YMCA has racquetball, squash, and handball courts. Two other recommended clubs are: **Chancery Squash Club** (202–865 Hornby St., tel. 604/682–3752) and **Tower Courts Racquet and Fitness Club** (1055 Dunsmuir St., lower level, tel. 604/689–4424), both with racquet courts, weight rooms, and aerobics.

Hiking **Pacific Spirit Park** is a 1,000-acre wilderness park, with 30 miles of hiking trails (*see* Parks and Gardens, above).

The **Capilano Regional Park,** (*see* Off the Beaten Track, in Exploring Vancouver, above), on the North Shore, provides a scenic hike.

Jogging The seawall around **Stanley Park** (*see* Tour 2 in Exploring Vancouver, above), is 9 kilometers (5½ miles) and gives an excellent minitour of the city. A shorter run of 4 kilometers (2½ miles) in the park is around **Lost Lagoon.**

Skiing
Cross-country The best cross-country skiing is at **Hollyburn Ridge** in Cypress Park (tel. 604/925–2704).

Downhill Vancouver is two hours away from **Whistler/Blackcomb** (Whistler Resort Association, tel. 604/685–3650; snow report, tel. 604/687–7507), one of the top ski spots in North America.

There are three ski areas on the North Shore mountains, close to Vancouver, with night skiing. The snow is not as good as at Whistler and runs are generally used by novice, junior, and family skiers or those who want a quick ski after work. **Cypress Park** (tel. 604/926–5612; snow report, tel. 604/926–6007) has the most and the longest runs; **Grouse Mountain** (tel. 604/986–0661; snow report, tel. 604/980–6262) has extensive night skiing, restaurants, and bars; and **Mt. Seymour** (tel. 604/986–2261; snow report, tel. 604/986–3444) is the highest in the area, so the snow is a little better.

Water Sports
Kayaking Rent a kayak from **Ecomarine** (tel. 604/689–7575) on Granville Island (*see* Tour 3 in Exploring Vancouver, above).

Rafting The Thompson, the Chilliwack, and the Fraser are the principal rafting rivers in southwestern British Columbia. The Fraser River has whirlpools and big waves, but for frothing white water, try the Thompson and Chilliwack rivers. Trips range from three hours to several days. Some well-qualified outfitters that lead trips are: **Kumsheen** (Lytton, tel. 604/455–2296; in B.C., tel. 800/482–2269), **Hyak** (Vancouver, tel. 604/734–8622), and **Canadian River Expeditions** (Vancouver, tel. 604/736–4449).

Sailing Several charter companies offer a cruise-and-learn vacation, usually to the Gulf Islands. The five-day trip is a crash course teaching the ins and outs of sailing. The **Westcoast School of Seamanship** (Granville Island, tel. 604/689–9440), **Sea Wing**

(Granville Island, tel. 604/669–0840), **Pacific Quest** (Granville Island, tel. 604/682–2205), and **Blue Orca** (Granville Island, tel. 604/687–4110) offer this package.

Windsurfing Rental shops clustered on the west side of town include: **Surf City** (420 W. 1st Ave., tel. 604/872–8585), **The Windsurfing Shop** (1793 W. 4th Ave., tel. 604/734–7245), and at **Windsure** (Jericho Beach, tel. 604/224–0615). Boards can also be rented at **Jericho Beach** or **English Bay Beach** (Davie and Denman Sts.).

Spectator Sports

The **Vancouver Canucks** (tel. 604/254–5141) of the National Hockey League play in the Coliseum October–April. The **Canadians** (tel. 604/872–5232) play baseball in an old-time outdoor stadium in the Pacific Coast League. Their season runs April–September. The **B.C. Lions** (tel. 604/681–5466) football team scrimmage at the B.C. Place Stadium downtown June–November. Tickets are available from Ticketmaster (tel. 604/280–4444).

Beaches

An almost continuous string of beaches runs from Stanley Park to the University of British Columbia. Children and hardy swimmers can take the cool water but most others prefer to sunbathe; these beaches are sandy with grassy areas running alongside. Note that liquor is prohibited in parks and on beaches. For information on beaches, call the **Parks Department of the City of Vancouver** (tel. 604/681–1141).

Kitsilano Beach. Kits Beach, with a lifeguard, is the busiest of them all—transistor radios, volleyball games, and sleek young bodies are ever-present. The part of the beach nearest the Maritime Museum is the quietest. Facilities include a playground, tennis courts, heated saltwater pool (good for serious swimmers to toddlers), concession stands, and many nearby restaurants to cafés.

Point Grey Beaches. Jericho, Locarno, and Spanish Banks begin at the end of Point Grey Road. This string of beaches has a huge expanse of sand, especially in the summer and at low tide. The shallow water here is warmed slightly by the sun and the sand and so is best for swimming. Farther out, toward Spanish Banks, you'll find the beach becomes less crowded, but the last concession stand and washrooms are at Locarno. If you keep walking along the beach just past Point Grey, you'll hit Wreck Beach, Vancouver's nude beach. It is also accessible from Marine Drive at the university but there is a fairly steep climb from the beach to the road.

West End Beaches. Second Beach and Third Beach, along Beach Drive in Stanley Park, are large family beaches. Second Beach has a guarded saltwater pool. Both have concession stands and washrooms. Farther along Beach Drive, at the foot of Jervis Street, is Sunset Beach, a surprisingly quiet beach considering the location. A lifeguard is on duty, but there are no facilities.

Dining

Among other allures, experiencing Vancouver's diverse gastronomical pleasures makes a visit to the city worthwhile. Restaurants appear throughout Vancouver—from the bustling downtown area to trendy beach-side neighborhoods—making the diversity of the establishment's surroundings as enticing as the succulent cuisine they serve. A new wave of Chinese immigration and Japanese tourism has brought a proliferation of upscale Chinese and Japanese restaurants, offering dishes that would be at home in their own leading cities. Restaurants featuring Pacific Northwest fare—including homegrown regional favorites such as salmon and oysters, accompanied by British Columbia and Washington State wines—have become some of the city's leading attractions.

Highly recommended restaurants are indicated by a star ★.

Category	*Cost
Very Expensive	over $41
Expensive	$31—$40
Moderate	$21—$30
Inexpensive	under $20

*per person, including appetizer, entrée and dessert; excluding drinks, service, and sales tax

American

Isadora's. Not only does Isadora's offer good coffee, a menu that ranges from samosas to lox and bagels, and children's specials, but there is also an inside play area packed with toys, and restrooms with changing tables accommodate families. In the summer, the restaurant opens onto Granville Island's water-park, so kids can entertain themselves. Service can be slow, but Isadora's staff is friendly. *1540 Old Bridge St., Granville Island, tel.604/681–8816. Reservations required for 6 or more. Dress: casual. Closed dinner Mon. Sept–May. MC, V. Inexpensive.*

Nazarre BBQ Chicken. The best barbecued chicken in several hundred miles comes from this funky storefront on Commercial Drive. Owner Gerry Moutal massages his chickens for tenderness before he puts them on the rotisserie, then bastes them in a mixture of rum and spices. Chicken comes with roasted potatoes and a choice of mild, hot, extra hot, or hot garlic sauce. You can eat in, at one of four rickety tables, or take out. *1408 Commercial Dr., tel. 604/251–1844. No reservations. Dress: casual. No credit cards. Inexpensive.*

Cambodian/ Vietnamese

Phnom Penh Restaurant. A block away from the bustle of Keefer Street, the Phnom Penh is part of a small cluster of Southeast Asian shops on the fringes of Chinatown. Simple, pleasant decor abounds: arborite tables, potted plants, and framed views of Ankor Wat on the walls. Hospitable staff serves unusually robust Vietnamese fare including crisp, peppery garlic prawns fried in the shell and slices of beef crusted with ground salt and pepper mixed in the warm beef salad. *244 E. Georgia St., tel. 604/682–5777. No reservations for lunch;*

advised for dinner. Dress: casual. MC, V. Closed Tues. Inex-pensive.

Chinese **Kirin Mandarin Restaurant.** Kirin, located two blocks from
★ most of the major downtown hotels, presents attentively
served Chinese food in posh, elegant surroundings. Live fish in
tanks set into the slate green walls remind one of aquariums
displayed in a lavishly decorated home. Drawn from a smatter-
ing of northern Chinese cuisines, dishes include Shanghai-style
smoked eel, Peking duck, and Szechuan hot-and-spicy scallops.
*1166 Alberni St., tel. 604/682–8833. Reservations advised.
Dress: neat but casual. AE, MC, V. Closed for 2 days, 15 days
after Chinese New Year. Moderate.*

★ **The Pink Pearl.** In the world of Cantonese restaurants, biggest
may very well be best: This 650-seat restaurant certainly wins
the prize in this city. The huge, noisy room features tanks of
live seafood—crab, shrimp, geoduck, oysters, abalone, rock
cod, lobsters, and scallops. Menu highlights include clams in
black bean sauce, crab sautéed with five spices (a spicy dish
sometimes translated as crab with peppery salt), and Pink
Pearl's version of crispy-skinned chicken. Arrive early for dim
sum on the weekend if you don't want to be caught in the lineup.
*1132 E. Hastings St., tel.604/253–4316. Reservations advised.
Dress: casual. AE, MC, V. Inexpensive.*

★ **Szechuan Chongqing.** Although fancier Szechuan restaurants
can be found, the continued popularity of this unpretentious
white tablecloth restaurant in a revamped fried chicken fran-
chise speaks for itself. Try the Szechuan-style fried green
beans, steamed and tossed with spiced ground pork or the
Chongqing chicken—a boneless chicken served on a bed of
spinach cooked in dry heat until crisp, giving it the texture of
dried seaweed and a salty, rich, and nutty taste. *2495 Victoria
Dr., tel. 604/254–7434. Reservations advised. Dress: casual.
AE, MC, V. Inexpensive.*

Continental **Chartwell.** Named after Sir Winston Churchill's country home
★ (a painting of which hangs over the green marble fireplace), the
flagship dining room at the Four Seasons Hotel (*see* Lodging,
below) looks like an upperclass British men's club. Floor-to-
ceiling dark wood paneling, deep leather chairs to sink back in
and sip claret, plus a quiet setting make this the city's top spot
for a power lunch. Chef Wolfgang von Weiser (formerly of the
Four Seasons in Toronto) cooks robust, inventive Continental
food. A salad of smoked loin of wild boar comes sprinkled with
hazelnuts; the seafood pot au feu is served with fennel bread
and aioli. Conclude the meal with port and Stilton. *791 W. Georgia St., tel. 604/689–9333. Reservations advised. Jacket required. AE, DC, MC, V. Expensive.*

Seasons in the Park. Seasons has a commanding view over the
park gardens to the city lights and the mountains beyond. A
comfortable room with lots of light wood, white tablecloths,
and deep-pile carpeting, this restaurant in Queen Elizabeth
Park serves a conservative Continental menu with standards
such as grilled salmon with fresh mint and roast duck with Bing
cherry sauce. *Queen Elizabeth Park, tel. 604/874–8008. Reservations advised. Dress: neat but casual. AE, MC, V. Closed
Christmas Day. Expensive.*

★ **The Teahouse Restaurant at Ferguson Point.** The best of the
Stanley Park restaurants is perfectly poised for watching sunsets over the water, especially from its newer wing, a glassed-
in room that conveys a conservatory-like ambience. Although

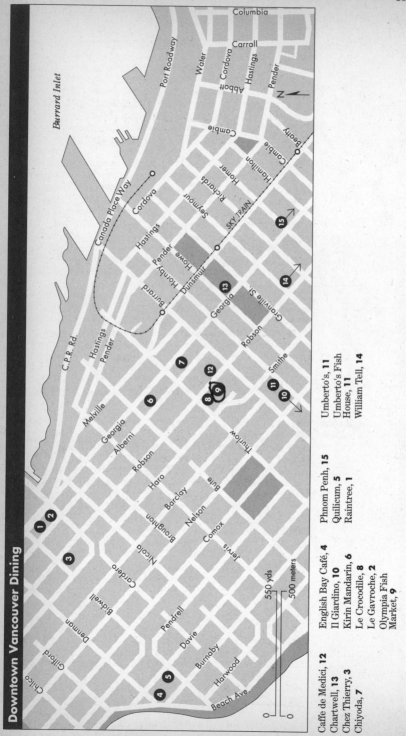

Downtown Vancouver Dining

130

Caffe de Medici, **12**
Chartwell, **13**
Chez Thierry, **3**
Chiyoda, **7**

English Bay Café, **4**
Il Giardino, **10**
Kirin Mandarin, **6**
Le Crocodile, **8**
Le Gavroche, **2**
Olympia Fish
Market, **9**

Phnom Penh, **15**
Quilicum, **5**
Raintree, **1**

Umberto's, **11**
Umberto's Fish
House, **11**
William Tell, **14**

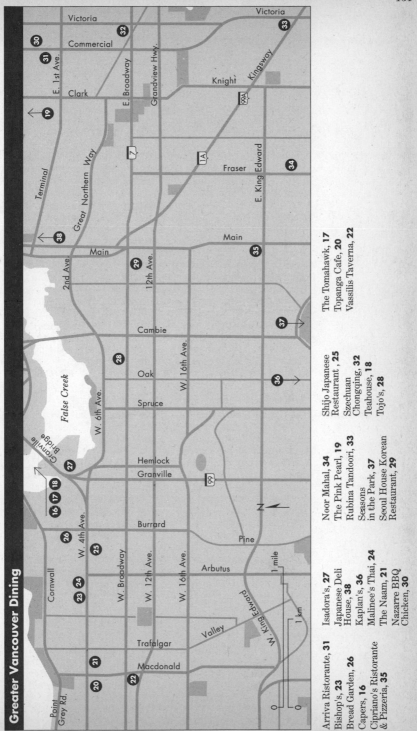

the teahouse has a less innovative menu than its sister restaurant, Seasons in the Park, certain features, including the cream of carrot soup, duck in cassis, and the perfectly grilled fish don't need any meddling. For dessert, there's baked Alaska—a natural for this restaurant. *Ferguson Point in Stanley Park, tel. 604/669–3281. Reservations required. Dress: neat but casual. AE, MC, V. Closed Christmas Day. Expensive.*

The William Tell. Silver underliners, embossed linen napkins, and a silver flower vase on each table set the tone of Swiss luxury. The William Tell's 27-year reputation for excellent Continental food continues at its quarters on the main floor of the Georgian Court Hotel, located 10 minutes from the central business district. Chef Pierre Dubrelle, a member of the gold medal-winning Canadian team at the 1988 Culinary Olympics, offers locally raised pheasant with glazed grapes and red wine sauce, sautéed veal sweetbreads with red onion marmalade and marsala sauce, as well as the Swiss specialty *Buendnerfleisch* (paper-thin slices of air-dried beef). Professional and discreet service contribute to the restaurant's excellence. *765 Beatty St., tel. 604/688–3504. Reservations advised. Jacket required at dinner. AE, DC, MC, V. Expensive.*

English Bay Café. Downstairs, the English Bay Café is a noisy tapas bistro serving nachos, crabcakes, and other grazing food. Upstairs, in the more serious dining room, you'll find the chef's fondness for venison and racks of lamb. Regardless of the level, however, when you look out the windows, it's all the same: With English Bay just two lanes of traffic away, you're guaranteed a glorious view of the sunset. Both bars are substantial; the bistro offers a large choice of imported beers, while the upstairs features jalapeño-pepper martinis. Valet parking is available and well worth the money. *1795 Beach Ave., tel. 604/669–2225. Reservations required. Dress: casual downstairs; neat but casual upstairs. AE, DC, MC, V. Moderate.*

Deli/Bakery **The Bread Garden Bakery, Café & Espresso Bar.** What began as a croissant bakery has taken over two neighboring stores, and is now the ultimate Kitsilano 24-hour hangout. Salads, smoked salmon pizzas, quiches, elaborate cakes and pies, giant muffins, and cappuccino bring a steady stream of the young and fashionable. The Bread Garden To Go, next door, serves over-the-counter, but you may still be subjected to an irritatingly long wait in line; things just don't happen fast here. *1880 W. 1st Ave., tel. 604/ 738–6684; 812 Bute St., tel. 604/688–3213. No reservations. Dress: casual. DC, MC, V. Inexpensive.*

★ **Kaplan's Deli, Restaurant and Bakery.** Tucked into a mini-mall on Oak Street (the road that leads to the Tsawwassen ferries and Seattle), Kaplan's is the traveler's last chance for authentic Jewish deli food before leaving town. Eat in at booths, or take your chopped liver, chopped herring, lox, and home-made corned beef with you. The bakery makes justly famous cinnamon buns. *5775 Oak St., tel. 604/263–2625. No reservations. Dress: casual. MC, V. Closed Jewish holidays. Inexpensive.*

East Indian **Rubina Tandoori.** If one must single out the best East Indian ★ food in the city, then Rubina Tandoori, 20 minutes from downtown, ranks as a top contender. The large menu spans most of the subcontinent's cuisines, and the especially popular *chevda* (East Indian salty snack,) gets shipped to fans all over North America. Maitre d' Shaffeen Jamal has a phenomenal memory for faces. Nonsmokers get the smaller, funkier back room with the paintings of coupling gods and goddesses; smokers get the big, upholstered banquettes in the new room. *1962 Kingsway, tel. 604/874-3621. Reservations advised on weekends. Dress: casual. AE, MC, V. Closed lunch Sun. Moderate.*

Noor Mahal. The only Lower Mainland restaurant that specializes in South Indian food, the Noor Mahal provides good-sized portions at a reasonable price in authentic surroundings. The pink walls help to create the light and airy decor. Try a *dosa*—a lacy pancake made from bean, rice, and semolina flour, stuffed with curried potatoes, shrimp, or chicken—for lunch. Owners Susan and Paul Singh double as staff so service can be slow and harried during busy periods. *4354 Fraser St., tel. 604/873-9263. Reservations advised on weekends. Dress: casual. AE, MC, V. Closed lunch Mon. and Tues. Inexpensive.*

French **Le Gavroche.** Time has stood still in this charming turn-of-the-
★ century house, where a woman dining with a man will be offered a menu without prices. Featuring classic French cooking, lightened—but by no means reduced—to nouvelle cuisine, Le Gavroche's menu also includes simple listings such as smoked salmon with blinis and sour cream. Other options may be as complex as smoked pheasant breast on a puree of celeriac, shallots, and wine with a light truffle sauce. The excellent wine list stresses Bordeaux. Tables by the front window promise mountains and water views. *1616 Alberni St., tel. 604/685-3924. Reservations advised on weekends. Jacket and tie advised. AE, DC, MC, V. Closed Dec. 24-Jan. 1. Expensive.*

Chez Thierry. This cozy bistro on the Stanley Park end of Robson Street adds pizzazz to a celebration: Owner Thierry Damilano stylishly slashes open champagne bottles with a sword on request. The country-style French cooking emphasizes seafood. Try watercress and smoked salmon salad; fresh tuna grilled with artichokes, garlic, and tomatoes; and apple tarte Tatin for dessert. During the week the intimate dining room promises a relaxing meal; on the weekend, however, with every one of the 16 tables jammed, the restaurant gets noisy. *1674 Robson St., tel. 604/688-0919. Reservations required on weekends. Dress: casual. AE, DC, MC, V. Closed lunch; Dec. 24-26. Moderate.*

★ **Le Crocodile.** Why do people want to sit packed tighter than sardines in this tiny bistro? Because chef Michael Jacob serves extremely well-cooked simple food at very moderate prices. His Alsatian background shines with the caramelly, sweet onion tart. Anything that involves innards is superb, and even old standards such as duck à l'orange are worth ordering here. The one flaw? A small, overpriced wine list. *818 Thurlow St., tel. 604/669-4298. Reservations required. Jacket advised. AE, MC, V. Closed lunch; Sat., Sun. Moderate.*

Greek **Vassilis Taverna.** The menu in this family-run restaurant, located in the heart of the city's small Greek community, is almost as conventional as the decor: checked tablecloths and mandatory paintings of white fishing villages and the blue Aegean Sea. At Vassilis, though, even standards become memorable due to the flawless preparation. The house specialty is a deceptively simple *kotopoulo* (a half-chicken, pounded flat, herbed, and charbroiled); the lamb fricassee with artichoke hearts and broad beans in an egg-lemon sauce is more complicated, though not necessarily better. Save room for a *navarino*, a creamy custard square topped with whipped cream and ground nuts. *2884 W. Broadway, tel. 604/733-3231. Reserva-*

tions advised on weekends. Dress: casual. AE, DC, MC, V. Closed lunch Mon.; Sat. and Sun. Moderate.

Health Food **Capers.** Hidden in the back of the most lavishly handsome health food store in the Lower Mainland, Capers (open for breakfast, lunch, and dinner), drips with earth-mother chic: wood tables, potted plants, and heady smells from the store's bakery. Breakfast starts weekdays at 7, weekends at 8. Eggs and bacon? Sure, but Capers serves free-range eggs, and bacon without additives. Feather-light blueberry pancakes, crammed with berries star here. The view of the water compensates for service that can be slow and forgetful. *2496 Marine Dr., W. Vancouver, tel. 604/925-3316. No reservations. Dress: casual. MC, V. Inexpensive.*

★ **The Naam Restaurant.** Vancouver's oldest alternative restaurant is now open 24 hours, so those needing to satisfy a late-night tofu burger craving, rest easy. The Naam has left its caffeine- and alcohol-free days behind, and now serves wine, beer, cappuccinos, and wicked chocolate desserts, along with the vegetarian stir-fries. Wood tables and kitchen chairs make for a homey atmosphere. On warm summer evenings, the outdoor courtyard at the back of the restaurant welcomes diners. *2724 W. 4th Ave., tel. 604/738-7151. Reservations required for 6 or more. Dress: casual. MC, V. Inexpensive.*

Italian **Caffe de Medici.** It takes shifting gears as you leave the stark ★ concrete walls of the Robson Galleria behind and step into this elegant restaurant with its ornate molded ceilings, rich green velvet curtains and chair coverings, and portraits of the Medici family. But after a little wine, an evening's exposure to courtly waiters, and a superb meal, you may begin to wish the outside world conformed more closely to this peaceful environment. Although an enticing antipasto table sits in the center of the room, consider the *Bresaola* (air-dried beef marinated in olive oil, lemon, and pepper) as a worthwhile appetizer. Try the rack of lamb in a mint, mustard, and Martini & Rossi sauce. Any of the pastas is a safe bet. *1025 Robson St., tel. 604/669-9322. Reservations advised. Jacket advised. AE, DC, MC, V. Closed lunch Sat. and Sun. Expensive.*

Arriva Ristorante. Commercial Drive Italian restaurants, like Chinese restaurants in Chinatown, are best looked at with a skeptical eye. The best of the breed are elsewhere, what's left is often found cranking out North Americanized travesties of the home country's food. Arriva is one Little Italy restaurant that's worth the drive, and a welcome find if you've spent the day shopping in Italian groceries. There's a version of spaghetti and meatballs on the menu, ziti with spicy squid sauce, and a fusili with wild game—"Bambi and Bugs Bunny," as the waiters have affectionately coined it. The antipasto plate includes a heaping order of octopus, shrimp, roasted red peppers, cheese, sausage, and fat lima beans in a herby marinade. Don't miss the orange sherbet served in a hollowed-out orange for dessert. *1537 Commercial Dr., tel. 604/251-1177. Reservations advised. Dress: casual. AE, MC, V. Closed lunch Sat. and Sun. Moderate.*

Il Giardino di Umberto, Umberto's. First came Umberto's, a Florentine restaurant serving classic northern Italian food, installed in a century-old Vancouver home at the foot of Hornby Street. Then, next door, Umberto Menghi built Il Giardino, a sunny, light-splashed restaurant styled after a Tuscan house. This restaurant features braided breast of pheasant with polenta and reindeer filet with crushed peppercorn sauce. Where Il Giardino attracts a regular young, moneyed crowd, Umberto's is more quiet and sedate. Fish is treated either Italian style—rainbow trout grilled and served with sun-dried tomatoes, black olives, and pine-nuts—or with a taste of the far east, as in yellow-fin tuna grilled with wasabi butter. *Il Giardino, 1382 Hornby St., tel. 604/669-2422. Umberto's, 1380 Hornby St., tel. 604/687-6316. Reservations advised. Dress: neat but casual. AE, DC, MC, V. Umberto's closed lunch and Sun. Moderate.*

Cipriano's Ristorante & Pizzeria. Formerly a Greek pizza parlor, Cipriano's has been transformed into an Italian restaurant, with green-white-and-red walls representing the Italian flag, Mama-mia!—inexpensive and hearty Italian food is the mainstay here, including good pizza, even better pasta, and the "Pappa" lasagna. *3995 Main St., tel. 604/879-0020. Reservations accepted. Dress: casual. V. Closed lunch. Inexpensive.*

Japanese **Tojo's.** Hidekazu Tojo is a sushi-making legend here. His hand-
★ some blond-wood tatami rooms, on the second floor of a new green-glass tower in the hospital district on West Broadway, provide proper ambience for intimate dining, but Tojo's 10-seat sushi bar stands as the centerpiece. With Tojo presiding, this is a convivial place for dinner, and a ringside seat for watching the creation of edible art. Although tempura and teriyaki dinners will satisfy, the seasonal menu is more exciting. In October, ask for *dobbin mushi,* a soup made from pine mushrooms that's served in teapot. In spring, try sushi made from scallops and pink cherry blossoms. *777 W. Broadway, No. 202, tel. 604/ 872-8050. Reservations advised on weekends. Dress: neat but casual. AE, MC, V. Closed Mon.; Dec. 24-26. Expensive.*

Chiyoda. The robata bar curves like an oversize sushi bar through Chiyoda's main room: On one side are the customers and an array of flat baskets full of the day's offerings; on the other side are the robata chefs and grills. There are 35 choices of things to grill, from squid, snapper, and oysters to eggplant, mushrooms, onions, and potatoes. The finished dishes, dressed with sake, soy, or *ponzu* sauce, are dramatically passed over on the end of a long wooden paddle. If Japanese food only means sushi and tempura to you, check this out. *1050 Alberni St., tel. 604/688-5050. Reservations accepted. Dress: casual. AE, MC, V. Closed lunch Sat. and Sun. Moderate.*

Shijo Japanese Restaurant. Shijo has an excellent and very large sushi bar, a smaller robata bar, tatami rooms, and a row of tables overlooking bustling Fourth Avenue. The epitome of modern urban Japanese chic is conveyed through the jazz music, handsome lamps with a patinated bronze finish, and lots of black wood. Count on creatively prepared sushi, eggplant *dengaku* topped with light and dark miso paste and broiled, and shiitake *foil yaki* (fresh shiitake mushrooms cooked in foil with *ponzu* sauce). *1926 W. 4th Ave., tel. 604/732-4676. Reservations advised. Dress: casual. AE, MC, V. Closed lunch, Sat. and Sun. Moderate.*

Japanese Deli House. The least expensive sushi in town is served in this high-ceilinged room on the main floor of a turn-of-the-century building on Powell Street, once the heart of Vancouver's Japantown. Along with the standard sushi-bar menu, Japanese Deli House makes a pungent but tender hot ginger squid appetizer from baby squid caught off the Thai coast, and a geoduck appetizer in mayonnaise worth wandering off the beaten path for. Food is especially fresh and good if you can make it an early lunch: Nigiri sushi and sushi rolls are made at 11 AM for the 11:30 opening. *381 Powell St., tel. 604/681–6484. No reservations. Dress: casual. No credit cards. Closed Mon. Inexpensive.*

Korean   **Seoul House Korean Restaurant.** The shining star in a desperately ugly section of East Broadway, Seoul House is a bright restaurant, decorated in Japanese style, that serves a full menu of Japanese and Korean food. The best bet is the Korean Barbecue, which you cook at your table. A barbecue dinner of marinated beef, pork, chicken, or fish comes complete with a half dozen side dishes—*kim chee* (Korea's national pickle), salads, stir-fried rice, and pickled vegetables—as well as soup and rice. Service can be chaotic in this very popular restaurant. *36 E. Broadway, tel. 604/874–4131. Reservations advised. Dress: casual. MC, V. Closed lunch Sun. Inexpensive.*

Mexican   **Topanga Cafe.** Arrive before 6:30 or after 8 PM to avoid waiting in line for this 40-seat Kitsilano classic. The California-Mexican food hasn't changed much in the 14 years the Topanga has been dishing up fresh salsa and homemade tortilla chips. Quantities are still huge and prices are low. Kids can color blank menu covers while waiting for food; a hundred or more of the clientele's best efforts are framed and on the walls. *2904 4th Ave., tel. 604/733–3713. No reservations. Dress: casual. MC, V. Closed Sun. Inexpensive.*

Nouvelle   **Bishop's.** John Bishop established Vancouver's most influential
★   restaurant seven years ago, serving a variety of cuisines from northern Italian to nouvelle and East–West crossover. Penne with grilled eggplant, roasted peppers, and basil pasta cohabits the menu with marinated loin of lamb with ginger and sesame. The small white rooms—their only ornament some splashy, expressionist paintings—are favored by Robert de Niro when he's on location in Vancouver. *2183 W. 4th Ave., tel. 604/738–2025. Reservations required. Dress: casual. AE, DC, MC, V. Closed 1st week in Jan. Expensive.*

Pacific Northwest   **Quilicum.** Only a few blocks from English Bay, this downstairs "longhouse" serves the original Northwest Coast cuisine: bannock bread, baked sweet potato with hazelnuts, alder-grilled salmon, and soap-berries for dessert. Try the authentic, but odd dish—oolichan grease—that's prepared from candlefish. Native music is piped in, and Northwest Coast masks (for sale) peer out from the walls. *1724 Davie St., tel. 604/681–7044. Reservations advised. Dress: casual. AE, MC, V. Closed lunch Sat. and Sun. Moderate.*

★   **The Raintree.** This cool, spacious restaurant offers a local menu and wine list; the latter won a 1988 award from the *Wine Spectator* for its British Columbia, Washington, and Oregon choices. Raintree bakes its own bread, makes luxurious soups, and has pumped-up old favorites such as a slab of apple pie for dessert. With main courses, which change daily depending on market availability, the kitchen teeters between willfully eccentric and exceedingly simple. Specials could include Queen Charlotte abalone and side-stripe shrimps stir fried with scallions and spinach in chamomile essence, or grilled lamb chops with a mint and pear puree. *Leon's Bar and Grill*, on the ground floor, stocks local beers and a respectable number of single malt scotches. The pub-food menu, under the direction of chef Rebecca Dawson, includes organic-beef burgers and vegetarian chili. *1630 Alberni St., tel. 604/688-5570. Reservations advised on weekends. Dress: casual. AE, DC, MC, V. Closed Dec. 24-26. Moderate.*

The Tomahawk. North Vancouver was mostly trees 65 years ago, when the Tomahawk first opened. Over the years, the original hamburger stand grew and mutated into part Northwest Coast Indian kitsch museum, part gift shop, and part restaurant. Renowned for its Yukon breakfast—five slices of back bacon, two eggs, hash browns, and toast—the Tomahawk also serves gigantic muffins, excellent French toast, and pancakes. The menu switches to burgers named after Indian chiefs for lunch and dinner. *1550 Philip Ave., tel. 604/988-2612. No reservations. Dress: casual. AE, MC, V. Inexpensive.*

Seafood **Olympia Fish Market and Oyster Co. Ltd.** Some of the city's best fish and chips are fried in this tiny shop located behind a fish store in the middle of the Robson Street shopping district. The choice is halibut, cod, prawns, calamari, and whatever's on special in the store, served with genuine—never frozen—french fries. *1094 Robson St., tel. 604/685-0716. No reservations. Dress: casual. No credit cards. Inexpensive.*

excellent

Thai **Malinee's Thai.** The city's most consistently interesting Thai
★ food can be found in this typically Southeast Asian–style room, tapestries adorning the walls. The owners, two Canadians who lived several years in Thailand, can give you detailed descriptions of every dish on the menu. Steamed fish with ginger, pickled plums, and red chili sauce is on the regular menu; a steamed whole red snapper, marinated in oyster sauce, ginger, cilantro, red pepper, and lime juice is a special worth ordering when available. *2153 W. 4th Ave., tel. 604/737-0097. Reservations advised. Dress: casual. AE, DC, MC, V. Closed lunch Sat. and Sun.; Mon. Moderate.*

Lodging

Lodging has become a major business for Vancouver, a fairly young city that hosts a lot of Asian businesspeople who are used to an above-average level of service. Although by some standards pricey, properties here are highly competitive, and you can expect the service to reflect this trend.

Highly recommended lodgings are indicated by a star ★.

Category	Cost*
Very Expensive	over $180
Expensive	$120–$180
Moderate	$80–$119
Inexpensive	under $80

All prices are for a standard double room for two, excluding 10% provincial accommodation tax, 15% service charge, and 7% goods and services tax. Non-Canadians are eligible for a rebate on the goods and services tax paid for hotel accommodations.

Very Expensive **Four Seasons.** The 28-story hotel is adjacent to the Vancouver Stock Exchange and is attached to the Pacific Centre shopping

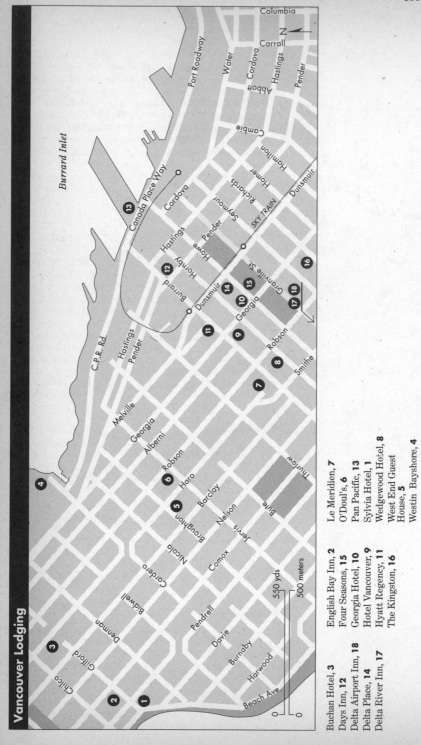

Vancouver Lodging

Columbia

Carrall

N

Burrard Inlet

Port Roadway

Water
Cordova
Hastings
Pender

Abbott

Cambie

Hamilton

Homer

Richards

SKY TRAIN

Dunsmuir

Canada Place Way

Cordova

Seymour

Pender

Howe

Hastings

Hornby

Burrard

Dunsmuir

Granville St.

Georgia

Robson

Smithe

Hastings

Pender

C.P.R. Rd.

Melville

Georgia

Alberni

Robson

Haro

Barclay

Nelson

Comox

Thurlow

Bute

Jervis

Broughton

Nicola

Cardero

Pendrell

Davie

Burnaby

Harwood

Beach Ave.

Bidwell

Denman

Gilford

Chilco

550 yds

500 meters

0

Buchan Hotel, **3**
Days Inn, **12**
Delta Airport Inn, **18**
Delta Place, **14**
Delta River Inn, **17**

English Bay Inn, **2**
Four Seasons, **15**
Georgia Hotel, **10**
Hotel Vancouver, **9**
Hyatt Regency, **11**
The Kingston, **16**

Le Meridien, **7**
O'Doul's, **6**
Pan Pacific, **13**
Sylvia Hotel, **1**
Wedgewood Hotel, **8**
West End Guest
House, **5**
Westin Bayshore, **4**

mall. Standard rooms are not large; corner deluxe or deluxe Four Seasons rooms are recommended. Expect tasteful and stylish decor in the rooms and hallways that provide a calm mood despite the bustling hotel. A huge sun deck and indoor-outdoor pool are part of the complete health club facilities. Service is outstanding and the Four Seasons has all the amenities. The formal dining room, Chartwell (*see* Dining, above), is one of the best in the city. *791 W. Georgia St., V6C 2T4, tel. 604/689-9333; in Canada, 800/268-6282; in the U.S., 800/332-3442; fax 604/684-4555. 317 doubles, 68 suites. Facilities: restaurant, café, bars, indoor-outdoor pool, sun deck, weight room, aerobics classes, sauna, Jacuzzi, ping-pong. AE, DC, MC, V.*

★ **Le Meridien.** The Meridien feels more like an exclusive guest house than a large hotel. The lobby has sumptuously thick carpets, enormous displays of flowers, and a newsstand situated discreetly down the hall. The rooms are even better, furnished with rich, dark wood, in a style that is reminiscent of 19th-century France. Despite the size of this hotel, the Meridien in Vancouver has achieved and maintained a level of intimacy and exclusivity. The **Café Fleuri** serves the best Sunday brunch in town (plus a chocolate buffet on Friday and Saturday evenings), and **Gerard,** a formal French restaurant, is a special-occasion place. The bar has lots of leather, dark wood, wingback chairs, and a fireplace. *845 Burrard St., V6Z 2K6, tel. 604/682-5511 or 800/543-4300, fax 604/682-5513. 350 doubles, 47 suites. Facilities: restaurant, café, bar, business center, handicapped rooms, health club with pool, Jacuzzi, sauna, steam room, tanning bed, masseur, hairdresser, weights, exercise equipment, adjoining apartment hotel. AE, DC, MC, V.*

★ **Pan Pacific.** Canada Place sits on a pier right by the financial district and houses the luxurious Pan Pacific Hotel (built in 1986 for the Expo), the Vancouver Trade and Convention Centre, and a cruise ship terminal. The lobby has a dramatic three-story atrium with a waterfall, and the lounge, restaurant, and café all have huge expanses of glass, so that you are rarely without a harbor view or mountain backdrop. Earth tones and Japanese detail give the rooms an understated elegance. Make sure you get a room that looks out on the water. The health club has a $10 fee that's well worth the price. The Pan Pacific is a grand, luxurious, busy hotel, but it is not a pick for an intimate weekend getaway. *300-999 Canada Pl., V6C 3B5, tel. 604/662-3223; in Canada, 800/663-1515; in the U.S., 800/937-1515; fax 604/685-8690. 468 doubles, 40 suites. Facilities: 3 restaurants, bar, health club with indoor track, sauna, steam room, state-of-the-art aerobics equipment, weights, massage and Shiatsu, sports lounge with wide-screen TV, squash, racquetball, and paddle-tennis courts, heated outdoor pool. AE, DC, MC, V.*

Expensive–
Very Expensive
Westin Bayshore. This hotel is the closest thing to a resort that you'll find in the downtown area. Because the Bayshore is perched right on the best part of the harbor, because it is a five-minute walk from Stanley Park, because of the truly fabulous view, and because of its huge outdoor pool, sun deck, and grassy areas, it is the perfect place to stay during the summer, especially for a family. The tower is the newer section, so rooms there are better furnished, larger, and offer the best view of the water. The café is okay but avoid the dining room, Trader Vic's; you can do much better at several neighborhood restaurants. People commuting from Seattle via Lake Union Air

(downtown-to-downtown service) will find it handy that the floatplanes land at the Bayshore. *1601 W. Georgia St., V6G 2V4, tel. 604/682–3377 or 800/228–3000; fax 604/687–3102. 481 doubles, 38 suites, 2 handicapped floors. Facilities: restaurant, café, bars, free shuttle service downtown, bicycle rentals, marina with fishing and sailing charters, health club with indoor and outdoor pools, Jacuzzi, sun deck, masseur, sauna, pool table. AE, DC, MC, V.*

Expensive **Delta Airport Inn.** It's not a view or a shoreline that make this place (five minutes from the airport) a resort, it's the facilities on the 12-acre site: three swimming pools (one indoor), four all-year tennis courts with a pro (matching list for partners), an outdoor fitness circuit, squash courts, aqua-exercise classes, outdoor volleyball nets, golf practice net, a play center for children, summer camps for 5- to 12-year-olds, and a playground. In spite of its enormity, the atmosphere is casual and friendly. There are two guest-room towers and a few low-rise buildings for convention facilities. The rooms are nothing special, but all the extras, and the hotel's close proximity to the airport, make it worthwhile. The Japanese restaurant is expensive and all show. *10251 St. Edwards Dr., V6X 2M9, tel. 604/278–9611; in Canada, 800/268–1133; in the U.S., 800/877–1133; fax 604/276–1122. 460 doubles, 4 suites. Facilities: restaurant, café, bar, free shuttle to airport and shopping center, meeting rooms. AE, DC, MC, V.*

Delta Place. This 18-story hotel was built in 1985 by the luxurious Hong Kong Mandarin chain but was sold to Delta Hotels in 1987. The rates have gone down but the surroundings have not changed. The lobby is restrained and tasteful—one has to look for the registration desk. A slight Oriental theme is given to the deluxe furnishings and dark, rich mahogany is everywhere. Most rooms have small balconies and the studio suites are recommended since they are much roomier and only slightly more expensive than a standard room. The business center has secretarial services, work stations, cellular phones for rent, and small meeting rooms. The restaurant and bar are adequate and the location is perfect; the business and shopping district is a five-minute walk away. *645 Howe St., V6C 2Y9, tel. 604/687–1122; in Canada, 800/268–1133; in the U.S., 800/877–1133; fax 604/689–7044. 181 doubles, 16 suites. Facilities: restaurant, bar, squash and racquetball courts, lap pool, weight room. AE, DC, MC, V.*

Delta River Inn. This hotel, on the edge of the Fraser River, is two minutes from the airport. Rooms on the south side get the best view. Although renovations began in 1990, the River Inn still has a way to go to compete with others in the price range. The rooms do not have the style and pizzazz that some have. All the dark wood in the hotel gives it an out-of-date feel, but the hotel is convenient. The marina attached to the hotel organizes fishing charters. Food does not seem to be a priority with Delta. *3500 Cessena Dr., V7B AC7, tel. 604/278–1241; in Canada, 800/268–1133; in the U.S., 800/877–1133; fax 604/276–1975. 410 doubles, 6 suites. Facilities: jogging route, free shuttle to airport, shopping center, and extensive health club at the nearby Delta Airport Inn. AE, DC, MC, V.*

★ **Hotel Vancouver.** The Hotel Vancouver, built in 1939 by the Canadian National Railway, is a grand old lady of the château-style hotels that appear in Canadian cities. It commands a regal position in the center of things across from the fountains of the art gallery. Standard rooms are nothing special, but are decorated in a more classic style than those of the Hyatt or the Four Seasons. But the hotel has a category called Entré Gold: two floors with all the extra services and amenities. Entré Gold suites have a luxurious amount of space, French doors, graceful wingback chairs, and fine mahogany furniture. The style and elegance of the Hotel Vancouver leaves its mark here. The hotel's restaurants and bars are adequate. *900 W. Georgia St., V6C 2W6, tel. 604/684–3131; in Ontario and Quebec, 800/268–9420; rest of Canada, 800/268–9411; in the U.S., 800/828–7447; fax 604/662–1937. 466 doubles, 42 suites, handicapped rooms. Facilities: 2 restaurants, 2 bars, two-line telephones, health club with lap pool, exercise machines, tanning bed, sun deck. AE, DC, MC, V.*

Hyatt Regency. The 17-year-old Hyatt is in the midst of a badly needed $11-million renovation, but the location is still perfect. The Hyatt's standard rooms are the largest in the city, and are decorated in deep, dramatic colors and dark wood. Ask for a corner room with a balcony on the north or west side. The lobby, however, can't escape the feel of a large convention hotel. The Hyatt has two special features: Camp Hyatt and the Regency Club. The Camp Hyatt has organized evening activities for children. For a small fee, the Regency Club gives you the exclusivity of two floors accessed by keyed elevators, your own concierge, a private lounge with a stereo and large TV, complimentary breakfast, 5 PM hors d'oeuvres, and evening pastries. Robes and special toiletries are also in the Regency Club rooms. For a hotel restaurant, Fish & Co. is unusual in that the room is casual, the atmosphere fun, and the food good. The Gallery Lounge is one of the most pleasant in town. Health club facilities are available, but they leave much to be desired. *655 Burrard St., V6C 2R7, tel. 604/687–6543 or 800/233–1234, fax 604/689–3707. 612 doubles, 34 suites. Facilities: restaurant, café, 2 bars, health club. AE, DC, MC, V.*

O'Doul's. Set on a lively street with loads of shops and restaurants, this hotel is a five-minute walk from either the heart of downtown or Stanley Park. This is a great location if you're traveling with teenagers who want time on their own. It was built in 1986 in a long, low style and feels like a very deluxe motel. The rooms are what you'd expect from any mid-range hotel, with modern decor and pastel color schemes, but the place is very well maintained. The deluxe rooms (with king-size beds) face Robson Street, and are worth the price, especially off-season when rates plummet. *1300 Robson St., V6E 1C5, tel. 604/684–8461 or 800/663–5491, fax 604/684–8326. 119 doubles, 11 suites. Facilities: 3 telephones in every room, pool, Jacuzzi, steam rooms, exercise machines. AE, DC, MC, V.*

★ **Wedgewood Hotel.** This hotel upholds a reputation for being a small, elegant hotel run by an owner who fervently cares about her guests. The intimate lobby is decorated in fine detail with polished brass, a fireplace, and tasteful artwork. All the extra touches are here, too: nightly turn-down service, afternoon ice delivery, dark-out drapes, flowers growing on the balcony, terry-cloth robes, and morning newspaper. No tour groups or conventions stop here; the Wedgewood's clients are almost exclusively corporate, except on weekends when it turns into a honeymoon retreat. Health facilities are next door at the excellent Chancery Squash Club. The lounge and restaurants couldn't be better. It's a treasure. *845 Hornby St., V6Z 1V1, tel. 604/689–7777 or 800/663–0666, fax 604/688–3074. 60 dou-*

bles, 33 suites. Facilities: 2 restaurants, bar, use of the adjacent Chancery Squash Club with 7 squash courts, weight room, aerobics, sauna, and whirlpool. AE, DC, MC, V.

Moderate **Days Inn.** For the businessperson looking for a bargain, this location is tops. The six-story, 71-year-old Days Inn (formerly the Abbotsford) is the only moderately priced hotel in the business core, and the recent renovations of the guest rooms and the lobby have made this accommodation even more agreeable. This is a basic accommodation but rooms are bright, clean, and functional. Standard rooms are very large but there is no room service and few amenities. Suites 310, 410, 510, and 610 have a harbor view. The bar, the **Bombay Bicycle Club,** is a favorite with businesspeople. *921 W. Pender St., V6C 1M2, tel. 604/681–4335 or 800/663–1700, fax 604/681–7808. 74 doubles, 11 suites. Facilities: restaurant, 2 bars, free parking. AE, DC, MC, V.*

★ **English Bay Inn.** The English Bay Inn, in a newly renovated 1930s house, is two blocks from the ocean and Stanley Park in a quiet residential part of the West End. The five small guest rooms—each with private bath—have wonderful sleigh beds with matching armoires and brass lighting fixtures. The common areas are generous and elegantly furnished: The sophisticated but cozy parlor has wingback chairs, a fireplace, and French doors opening onto the front garden. A sunny English country garden graces the back of the inn. Breakfast is served in a rather formal dining room furnished with a Gothic dining room suite and an 18th-century grandfather clock. *1968 Comox St., V6G 1R4, tel. 604/683–8063. 5 rooms. Facilities: off-street parking. AE, MC, V.*

★ **Georgia Hotel.** Across from the Four Seasons, this hotel is a five-minute walk from the business district. This handsome 12-story hotel, built in 1927, has such Old-World features as an oak-paneled lobby, ornate brass elevators, and a subdued, genteel atmosphere. Although it's lacking in special amenities, the Georgia is a reliable and satisfactory deal. Rooms are small but well furnished, with nothing worn around the edges. Executive rooms have an almost-separate seating area. Rooms facing the art gallery have the best views. *801 W. Georgia St., V6C 1P7, tel. 604/682–5566 or 800/663–1111, fax 604/682–8192. 310 doubles, 4 suites. Facilities: restaurant, 3 bars. AE, DC, MC, V.*

★ **West End Guest House.** The bright-pink exterior of this delightful Victorian house may throw you: The gracious front parlor with its early 1900s furniture is more indicative of the charm of the place. Most of the rooms are small but are extraordinarily handsome because of the high brass beds, antiques, gorgeous linen, and dozens of old framed pictures of Vancouver. All rooms have phones, TVs, and new bathrooms. There's a veranda for people-watching, and a back deck for sunbathing. A full breakfast is included and can be served in bed. The inn's genial hosts, Charles and George, have learned that it is the little things that make the difference, including an evening glass of sherry, duvets and feather mattress-pads, and a pantry where guests can help themselves to tea or snacks. The inn is in a residential neighborhood that is a 15-minute walk from downtown and Stanley Park and two minutes from Robson Street. This is a nonsmoking establishment. *1362 Haro St., V6E 1G2, tel. 604/681–2889. 7 rooms. Facilities: off-street parking. MC, V.*

Inexpensive **Buchan Hotel.** This three-story 1930s building is conveniently ★ set in a tree-lined residential street a block from Stanley Park, a block from shops and restaurants on Denman Street, and a 15-minute walk from the liveliest part of Robson Street. The hallways appear a bit institutional, but the rooms are bright and clean. Furnishings, in good condition, consist of a color TV, and a wood-grained arborite desk and chest of drawers. The rooms are small and the bathrooms tiny. None of the rooms have phones and you have to park on the street, but with this location you probably won't use your car much. Rooms on the east side are brightest and overlook a park; front corner rooms are the biggest. A popular restaurant with an eclectic menu is in the basement and is open for dinner. *1906 Haro St., V6G 1H7, tel. 604/685–5354. 60 rooms, 30 with private bath. Facilities: TV lounge, laundry room. AE, DC, MC, V.*

The Kingston. The Kingston is a small budget hotel in a location convenient for shopping. It is an old-style, four-story hotel, with no elevator—the type of establishment you'd find in Europe. The spartan rooms are small, immaculate, and share a bathroom down the hall. All rooms have phones but no TVs. Rooms on the south side are brighter. Continental breakfast is included. *757 Richards St., V6B 3A6, tel. 604/684–9024. 60 rooms, 7 with bath. Facilities: sauna, coin-op laundry, TV lounge, free nighttime parking. AE, MC, V.*

★ **Sylvia Hotel.** Perhaps the Sylvia Hotel is the best bargain in Vancouver, but don't count on staying here June–August unless you've booked six months ahead. What makes this hotel so popular are its low rates and near-perfect location: about 25 feet from the beach, 200 feet from Stanley Park, and a 20-minute walk from downtown. Vancouverites are particularly fond of the eight-story ivy-covered brick building—it was once the tallest building in the West End and the first to open a cocktail bar in the city, in 1954. It's part of the local history and was declared a protected heritage building in the 1970s. Rooms are unadorned and have basic plain furnishings that have probably been around for 20 years—not much to look at but the view and price make it worthwhile. Suites are huge and all have kitchens, making this a perfect family accommodation. There is little difference between the old and new wings. *1154 Gilford St., V6G 2P6, tel. 604/681–9321. 97 doubles, 18 suites. Facilities: restaurant, lounge, free parking. AE, DC, MC, V.*

The Arts and Nightlife

For information on events, look in the entertainment section of the *Vancouver Sun;* also, Thursday's paper has complete listings in the "What's On" column, and the **Arts Hotline** (tel. 604/684–ARTS). For tickets to major events, book through **Ticketmaster** (tel. 604/280–4444).

The Arts

Theater The **Vancouver Playhouse** (Hamilton St., tel. 604/872–6722) is the most established venue in Vancouver. The **Arts Club Theatre** (tel. 604/687–1644), with two stages on Granville Island (1585 Johnston St.) and performances all year, is the most active. Both feature mainstream theatrical shows. **Carousel Theater** (tel. 604/669–3410), which performs off-off Broadway shows at the **Waterfront Theatre** (1405 Anderson St.) on Granville Island, and **Touchstone** (tel. 604/687–8737), at the Firehall Theater (280 E. Cordova St.), are smaller but lively companies.

The **Back Alley Theatre** (751 Thurlow St., tel. 604/688–7013) hosts **Theatresports,** a hilarious improv event. The **Vancouver East Cultural Centre** (1895 Venables St., tel. 604/254–9578) is a multipurpose performance space that always hosts high-caliber shows.

Music The **Vancouver Symphony Orchestra** (tel. 604/684–9100) and the **CBC Orchestra** (tel. 604/662–6000) play at the restored **Orpheum Theatre** (601 Smithe St.). Choral groups like the **Bach Choir** (tel. 604/921–8012), the **Cantata Singers** (no tel.), and the **Vancouver Chamber Singers** (tel. 604/738–6822) play a major role in Vancouver's classical music scene. The **Early Music Society** (tel. 604/732–1610) performs medieval, renaissance, and baroque music throughout the year, and hosts the summer concerts of the most important Early Music Festival in North America. Concerts by the **Friends of Chamber Music** (no tel.) and the **Vancouver Recital Society** (tel. 604/736–6034) are always of excellent quality.

Vancouver Opera (tel. 604/682–2871) stages four productions a year, usually in October, January, March, and May at the **Queen Elizabeth Theatre** (600 Hamilton St.). Productions are high caliber with both local and imported talent.

Dance The **Dance Hotline** (tel. 604/872–0432) has information on upcoming events. Watch for **Ballet BC's Dance Alive!** series, presenting visiting or local ballet companies (from the Kirov to Ballet BC), as well as the modern dance series, **Discover Dance.** Most performances by these companies can be seen at the Orpheum or the Queen Elizabeth Theatre (*see* above). Local modern dance companies worth seeing are **Karen Jamison, Judith Marcuse,** and **Anna Wyman.**

Film Two theaters have distinguished themselves by avoiding the regular movie fare: **The Ridge** (3131 Arbutus St., tel. 604/738–6311), which generally plays foreign films; and **Pacific Cinématèque** (1131 Howe St., tel. 604/688–3456), which goes for even more esoteric foreign and art films. The **Vancouver International Film Festival** (tel. 604/685–0260) is held in September and October in several theaters around town.

Nightlife

Bars and Lounges The **Gérard Lounge** (845 Burrard St., tel. 604/682–5511) at Le Meridien Hotel is probably the nicest in the city because of the fireplaces, wingback chairs, dark wood, and leather. The **Bacchus Lounge** (845 Hornby St., tel. 604/689–7777) in the Wedgewood Hotel is stylish and sophisticated. The **Gallery Lounge** (655 Burrard St., tel. 604/687–6543) in the Hyatt is a genteel bar, with lots of windows letting in the sun and views of the action on the bustling street. The **Garden Lounge** (791 W. Georgia St., tel. 604/689–9333) in the Four Seasons is bright and airy with greenery and a waterfall, plus big soft chairs you won't want to get out of. For a more lively atmosphere, try **Joe Fortes** (777 Thurlow St., 604/669–1940), or **Night Court** (801 W. Georgia St., tel. 604/682–5566) in the Georgia Hotel.

The **English Bay Cafe** (1795 Beach Ave., tel. 604/669–2225) is the place to go to catch the sunset over English Bay. **La Bodega** (1277 Howe St., tel. 604/684–8815) beneath the Chateau Madrid is a popular Spanish tapas bar.

Two bars on Granville Island catering to the after-work crowd are **Bridges** (tel. 604/687–4400), near the Public Market, and the upscale **Pelican Bay** (tel. 604/683–7373) in the Granville Island Hotel, at the other end of the island.

Music While discos come and go, lines still form every weekend at
Discos **Richard's on Richards** (1036 Richards St., tel. 604/687–6794) for live and taped Top-40 music.

Jazz A jazz and blues hotline (tel. 604/682–0706) gives you current information on concerts and clubs. **Carnegie's** (1619 W. Broadway, tel. 604/733–4141), **Café Django** (1184 Denman St., tel. 604/689–1184), and the **Alma Street Cafe** (2505 Alma St., tel. 604/222–2244), all restaurants, are traditional venues with good mainstream jazz.

Rock The **Town Pump** (66 Water St., tel. 604/683–6695) is the main venue for local and touring rock bands. The **Soft Rock Cafe** (1925 W. 4th Ave., tel. 604/736–8480) is decidedly more upscale. There's live music, dinners, and weekend lineups. The **86th Street Music Hall** (750 Pacific Blvd., tel. 604/683–8687) serves up big-name bands.

Casinos A few casinos have been licensed recently in Vancouver and proceeds go to local charities and arts groups. Downtown there is the **Royal Diamond Casino** (535 Davie St., tel. 604/685–2340) and the **Great Canadian Casino** (2477 Heather St., tel. 604/872–5543) in the Holiday Inn.

Comedy **Yuk Yuks** (750 Pacific Blvd., tel. 604/687–5233) is good for a few laughs.

Excursion 1: Victoria

Introduction

Victoria, originally Fort Victoria, was the first European settlement on Vancouver Island and is the oldest city on Canada's west coast. It was chosen in 1842 by James Douglas to be the Hudson's Bay Company's most western outpost. Today it's a compact seaside town laced with tea shops and gardens. Though it's quite touristy during the high summer season, it's also at its prettiest, with flowers hanging from turn-of-the-century building posts and strollers feasting on the beauty of Victoria's natural harbor.

Tourist Information

Tourism Victoria (812 Wharf St., tel. 604/382–2127; mailing address, 612 View St., Victoria V8W 1J5) is open 9–9 June–Sept. 4 and 9–5 the rest of the year.

Arriving and Departing by Plane

BC Air (tel. 604/688–5515) provides both airport and harbor-to-harbor service from Vancouver to Victoria. Flights from Vancouver's international airport to Victoria's depart every hour from 8:15 AM. Harbor-to-harbor service runs every half hour from Coal Harbour in downtown Vancouver to Empress Harbour in Victoria. Both flights take about 35 minutes.

Arriving and Departing by Ferry

The **British Columbia Ferry Corporation** runs frequent ferry service from Vancouver to Victoria year-round. For information call 604/669–1211.

Getting Around

By Bus The **BC Transit System** runs a fairly extensive service throughout Victoria and the surrounding areas. Tourists may want to consider an all-day pass that allows passengers unlimited rides during the day at a cost of $3 for adults, $2 for students and senior citizens. Passes are sold at many outlets in downtown Victoria, including Eaton Centre and Harbour Square Ticket Centre.

For more information about passes and schedules, call 604/382–6161.

By Taxi Taxis are readily available throughout Victoria and can always be hailed outside hotels.

Exploring Victoria

Numbers in the margin correspond to points of interest on the Downtown Victoria map.

❶ For the most part, **Victoria** is a walker's city; most of its main attractions are located downtown or are a few blocks from the core. Attractions on the outskirts of downtown can easily be reached by bus or a short cab ride (though taxis can be alarmingly expensive). In the summer you have the added option of horse-drawn carriages, bicycle, boat, or double-decker bus tours.

❷ A logical place to begin this tour is at the **Visitors Information Centre,** located along the waterfront. Pick through numerous leaflets, maps, and tourism information concerning Victoria, Vancouver Island, ferries, entertainment, and accommodations. *812 Wharf St., tel. 604/382–2127. Open July, Aug., daily 9–9; May, June, Sept., Oct., daily 9–7; Nov.–Apr., daily 9–5.*

❸ Just across the way is the recently renovated **Empress Hotel,** a symbol both of the city and of the Canadian Pacific Railway. Originally opened in 1908, the hotel was designed by Francis Rattenbury, whose works dot Vancouver. The Empress is another of the great châteaus built by Canadian Pacific, the still-current owners who also built the Chateau Frontenac in Québec City, Chateau Laurier in Ottawa, and Chateau Lake Louise. The $55 million facelift has been a hot topic of discussion in traditional Victoria, though not all of the comments have been positive; criticism aside, the ingredients that made the 488-room hotel a tourist attraction in the past are still alive. Stop in for high tea—served at hour-and-a-half intervals during the afternoon. The experience may lend to your appreciation of the lobby's high-beamed ceiling and wood floors. In the basement of the hotel is an informative collection of historical photos and items from the hotel's early days. *721 Government St., tel. 604/ 384–8111. Proper dress required; no jeans, shorts, or T-shirts.*

Also, in the north wing of the Empress is **Miniature World,** where small replicas of people, trains, and historical events are displayed. The exhibit seems at times like a mix of fact and fic-

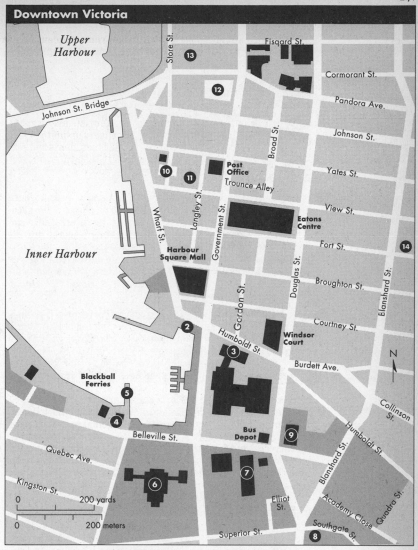

Downtown Victoria

Upper Harbour

Fisgard St.

Cormorant St.

Pandora Ave.

Johnson St. Bridge

Broad St.

Johnson St.

Store St.

13

12

Yates St.

Post Office

10 **11**

Trounce Alley

View St.

Langley St.

Government St.

Eatons Centre

Wharf St.

Harbour Square Mall

Fort St.

14

Inner Harbour

Broughton St.

Blanshard St.

Gordon St.

Courtney St.

2

Humboldt St.

Windsor Court

Douglas St.

3

Burdett Ave.

Blackball Ferries

Collinson St.

5

4

Belleville St.

Bus Depot

9

Humboldt St.

Quebec Ave.

7

Kingston St.

6

Elliot St.

Academy Close

Blanshard St.

Quadra St.

0   200 yards

0   200 meters

Superior St.

Southgate St.

8

N

Bastion Square, **10**
Beacon Hill Park, **8**
Chinatown, **13**
Craigdarroch Castle, **14**
Crystal Gardens, **9**

Empress Hotel, **3**
Legislative/Parliament Buildings, **6**
Maritime Museum, **11**
Market Square, **12**
Pacific Undersea Garden, **5**

Royal British Columbia Museum, **7**
Royal London Wax Museum, **4**
Visitors Information Centre, **2**

tion, though many of the models are delicately laid out. *649 Humbolt St., tel. 604/385–9731. Admission: $6 adults, $5 children 12–17, $4 children under 12; children under 10 and disabled persons with escort free. Open mid-June–mid-Sept., daily 8:30–10 PM; mid-Sept.–mid-June, daily 9–5:30.*

A short walk around the harbor leads you to the old CPR Steamship Terminal, also designed by Rattenbury and com- **4** pleted in 1924. Today it is the **Royal London Wax Museum,** housing more than 200 wax figures, including replicas of Queen Victoria, Elvis, and Marilyn Monroe. *470 Belleville St., tel. 604/388–4461. Admission: $6 adults, $5 students and senior citizens, $3 children 5–12. Open May–end of July, daily 8 AM–9 PM; end of July–Aug., daily 8 AM–11:30 PM; Sept.–Apr., daily 9:30–5.*

5 Next to the wax museum is the **Pacific Undersea Garden,** where more than 5,000 marine specimens are on display in their natural habitat. You also get performing scuba divers and Armstrong the giant octopus. Unfortunately, there are no washrooms, and the site is not wheelchair accessible. *490 Belleville St., tel. 604/382–5717. Admission: $6 adults, $5.50 senior citizens, $4.50 children 12–17, $2.75 children 5–11. Open Oct.– end of May, daily 10–5; summer, daily 9–9; closed Christmas. Shows run about every 45 minutes.*

6 Across Belleville Street is the **Legislative Parliament Buildings** complex. The stone exterior building, completed in 1897, dominates the inner harbor and is flanked by two statues: Sir James Douglas, who chose the location of Victoria, and Sir Matthew Baille Begbie, the man in charge of law and order during the gold-rush era. Atop the central dome is a gilded statue of Captain George Vancouver, who first sailed around Vancouver Island; a statue of Queen Victoria stands in front of the complex; and outlining the building at night are more than 3,000 lights. Another of Rattenbury's creations, the complex gives a good example of the rigid symmetry and European elegance that characterize much of the city's architecture. The public can watch the assembly, when it's in session, from the galleries overlooking the Legislative Chamber. *501 Belleville St., tel. 604/387–3046. Admission free. Tours run several times daily, and are conducted in at least 4 languages in summer and 3 in winter. Open Sept.–June, weekdays 8:30–5; summer, daily 8:30–5:30.*

7 Follow Belleville Street one block east to reach the **Royal British Columbia Museum.** Adults and children can wander for hours through the centuries, beginning with the present and going back 12,000 years. In the prehistoric exhibit, you can actually smell the pines and hear the calls of mammoths and other ancient wildlife. Other exhibits allow you to explore a turn-of-the-century town, with trains rumbling past; in the Kwakiutl Indian Bighouse, the smell of cedar envelopes you, while piped-in potlatch songs tell the origins of the genuine ceremonial house before you. Also explored in this museum are the industrial era, fur trading, pioneering, and the effects of modern history on native Indian cultures. *675 Belleville St., tel. 604/387–3014. Admission: $5 adults, $3 students and senior citizens, $2 children 6–18 and disabled persons, children under 6 free. Open Oct.–Apr., daily 10–5:30; May–Sept., daily 9:30–7; closed Christmas and New Year's Day.*

A walk east on Belleville Street to Douglas Street will lead you
⑧ to the **Beacon Hill Park,** a favorite place for joggers, walkers,
and cyclists. The park's southern lawns offer one of the best
views of the Olympic Mountains and the Strait of Juan de Fuca.
There are also athletic fields, lakes, walking paths, abundant
flowers, and a wading pool and petting farm for children.

From the park, go north on Douglas Street and stop off at the
⑨ **Crystal Gardens.** Opened in 1925 as the largest swimming pool
in the British Empire, this glass-roof building—now owned by
the provincial government—is home to flamingos, macaws, 75
varieties of other birds, hundreds of blooming flowers, walla-
bies, and monkeys. At street level there are several boutiques
and Rattenbury's Restaurant, one of Victoria's well-fre-
quented establishments. *713 Douglas St., tel. 604/381–1213.
Admission: $6 adults, $4 children 6–16 and senior citizens.
Open Oct.–Apr., daily 10–5:30; summer, daily 9–9.*

From Crystal Gardens continue on Douglas Street going north
⑩ to View Street, west to **Bastion Square,** with its gas lamps, restaurants, cobblestone streets, and small shops. This is the spot
James Douglas chose as the original Fort Victoria in 1843 and
the original Hudson's Bay Company trading post. Today fashion boutiques and restaurants occupy the old buildings. At the
Wharf Street end of the square are some benches where you
can rest your feet and catch a great view of the harbor. While
you're here, you may want to stop in at what was Victoria's
⑪ original courthouse, but is now the **Maritime Museum of British
Columbia.** Dugout canoes, model ships, Royal Navy charts,
photographs, uniforms, and ships bells chronicle Victoria's
seafaring history. A seldom-used 100-year-old cage lift, believed to be the oldest in North America, ascends to the third
floor. *28 Bastion Sq., tel. 604/385–4222. Admission: $4 adults,
$3 senior citizens, $1 children 6–18, children under 6 free.
Open Sept. 16–June 16, daily 9:30–4:30; June 17–Sept. 15, daily 9:30–6:30; closed Christmas and New Year's Day.*

West of Government Street, between Pandora Avenue and
⑫ Johnson Street is **Market Square,** offering a variety of specialty
shops and boutiques and considered one of the most picturesque shopping districts in the city. At the turn of the century
this area—once part of Chinatown—provided everything a visitor desired: food, lodging, entertainment. Today the square
has been restored to its original, pre-1900s character.

Just around the corner from Market Square is Fisgard Street,
⑬ the heart of one of the oldest **Chinatowns** in Canada. It was the
Chinese who were responsible for building much of the Canadian Pacific Railway in the 19th century; and their influences still
mark the region. If you enter Chinatown from Government
Street, you'll walk under the elaborate Gate of Harmonious Interest, made from Taiwanese ceramic tiles and decorative pan-
els. Along the street, merchants display fragile paper lanterns,
embroidered silks, imported fruits, and vegetables. **Fan Tan
Alley,** situated just off Fisgard Street, holds claim not only to
being the narrowest street in Canada but also to having been
the gambling and opium center of Chinatown, where mah-
jongg, fantan, and dominoes games were played.

A 15-minute walk, or short drive, east on Fort Street will take
⑭ you to Joan Crescent, where **Craigdarroch Castle** stands. This
lavish mansion was built as the home of British Columbia's first

millionaire, Robert Dunsmuir, who oversaw coal mining for the
Hudson's Bay Company (he died before the castle's completion
in about 1890). Recently converted into a museum depicting
turn-of-the-century lifestyle, the castle is strikingly authentic,
with elaborately framed landscape paintings, stained-glass
windows, carved woodwork—precut in Chicago for Dunsmuir
and sent by rail—and rooms for billiards and smoking. The location offers a wonderful view of downtown Victoria from the
fifth-floor tower; guided tours are given. *1050 Joan Crescent,
Victoria, tel. 604/592-5323. Admission: $5 adults, $4 senior
citizens and children 12 and older. Open mid-June–Aug., daily 9–7:30; Sept.–mid-June, daily 10–5.*

What to See and Do with Children

Anne Hathaway's Cottage, tucked away in a unique English-vil-
lage complex, is a full-size replica of the original thatched home
in Stratford-Upon-Avon, England. The building and the 16th-
century antiques inside are typical of Shakespeare's era. The
Olde England Inn, on the grounds, is a pleasant spot for tea or a
traditional English-style meal. You can also stay in one of the 50
antiques-furnished rooms, some complete with four-poster
beds. *429 Lampson St., Victoria, V9A 5Y9, tel. 604/388-4353.
Admission: $4.50 adults, $2.95 senior citizens and children 8–
17, children under 8 free. Open June–Sept., daily 9–9; rest of
year, daily 10–4. Guided tours leave from the inn during the
winter, and directly from the cottage in summer. From downtown Victoria, take the Munro bus to the door.*

Dominion Astrophysical Observatory, maintained by the National Research Council of Canada, has a 72-inch telescope that
transmits pictures of planets, star clusters, and nebulae. A museum display around the inside of the domed building provides
a quick lesson in astrophysics, and video monitors are set up for
visitors' easy viewing. *Off W. Saanich Rd. (Hwy. 17), 16 km
(10 mi) from Victoria on Little Saanich Mt., tel. 604/383-0001.
Admission: free. Open Mon.–Fri. 9–4:30; Apr.–Oct., Mon.–
Fri. 9–4:30, Sat. 9 PM–11 PM.*

Sealand of the Pacific. Featured at this aquarium are Orcas
(killer whales), seals, and sea lions, with poolside shows every
hour. The setting itself is an attraction, offering one of the finest views of the Strait of Juan de Fuca in the Victoria area. *1327
Beach Dr., Oak Bay, tel. 604/598-3373. Admission: $6.50
adults, $5 children 12–17, $2.75 children 5–11. Open June–
Sept., daily 10–6; Sept.–May, daily 10–5; closed Mon. and
Tues. in Nov., Jan., Feb.*

Shopping

Shopping in Victoria is easy. Virtually everything can be found
in the downtown area, beginning at the Empress and walking
north along Government Street. In succession you'll hit **Roger's
Chocolates and English Sweet Shop** (tel. 604/384-7021), for fine
chocolates; **George Straith Ltd.** (tel. 604/384-6912) for woolens;
Piccadilly Shoppe British Woolens (tel. 604/384-1288) for
women's woolens; **Gallery of the Arctic** (tel. 604/382-9012), for
quality Inuit art; **Munro's Books** (tel. 604/382-2464), for the
best selection of Victoriana in the city; and **Old Morris Tobacco-
nist, Ltd.** (tel. 604/382-4811) for unusual pipe tobacco blends.

The **Eaton's Centre** at Government and Fort streets is both a department store and a series of small boutiques, with a total of 140 shops and restaurants. For upscale boutiques, visit **Bastion Square** and **Windsor Court,** at the corner of Douglas and Humboldt. Market Square, between Johnson and Pandora, has three stories of specialty shops.

At last count, Victoria had 60-plus **antiques shops** specializing in coins, stamps, estate jewelry, rare books, crystal, china, furniture, or paintings and other works of art. A short walk on Fort Street going away from the harbor will take you to **Antique Row** between Blanshard and Cook streets. **Waller Antiques** (tel. 604/388–6116) and **Newberry Antiques** (tel. 604/388–7732) offer a wide selection of furniture and collectibles. You will also find antiques on the west side of Government Street near the **Old Town.**

Chinatown is marked by the red Gate of Harmonious Interest. On Fisgard Street shops offer merchandise and meals straight from the Orient. You must visit the little shops of **Fan Tan Alley,** a walkway between two buildings so small that two people have a difficult time passing without one giving way.

Sports and Outdoor Activities

Golf Though **Victoria Golf Club** (1110 Beach Dr., Victoria, tel. 604/595–2433) is private, it's open to other private-club members. This windy course is the oldest (built in 1893) in British Columbia and offers a spectacular view of the Strait of Juan de Fuca. **Uplands Golf Club** (3300 Cadboro Bay Rd., Victoria, tel. 604/592–1818) is a flat, semi-private course (it becomes public after 2). **Cedar Hill Municipal** (1400 Derby Rd., Victoria, tel. 604/595–3103) is a public course with up-and-down terrain. **Royal Oak Inn Golf Club** (4680 Elk Lake Dr., Victoria, tel. 604/658–1433) is the newest nine-hole course in the area. **Gorge Vale Golf Club** (1005 Craigflower Rd., Victoria, tel. 604/386–3401) is a semiprivate course, but is open to the public. It has punitive traps and a deep gorge that eats up golf balls. **Glen Meadows Golf and Country Club** (1050 McTavish Rd., Sidney, tel. 604/656–3921), situated near the ferry terminal, is a semiprivate course that's open to the public at select times.

Dining and Lodging

Dining **Chez Daniel.** One of Victoria's old standbys, Chez Daniel offers dishes that are rich, though the nouvelle influence has found its way into a few of the offerings. The interior, following a burgundy color scheme, seems to match the traditional rich, caloric cuisine. The wine list is varied and the menu has a wide selection of basic dishes: rabbit, salmon, duck, steak. This is a restaurant where you linger for the evening in the romantic atmosphere. *2524 Estavan Ave., tel. 604/592-7424. Reservations advised. Jacket advised. AE, MC, V. Closed lunch and Sun.-Mon. Expensive.*

★ **La Ville d'Is.** This seafood house is one of the best bargains in Victoria in terms of quality and price. Run by Michel Duteau, a Brittany native, the restaurant is cozy and friendly, with an outside café open May–October. An extensive, imaginative wine list features bottles from the Loire Valley that go well with the seafood, rabbit, lamb, and beef tenderloin specials. Try the *perche de la nouvelle Zelande* (orange roughie in muscadet with herbs) or lobster soufflé for a unique taste. *26 Bastion Sq., tel. 604/388–9414. Reservations advised. Dress: casual but neat. AE, MC, V. Closed Sun. and Jan. Expensive.*

Chez Pierre. Established in 1973, this is the oldest French restaurant in Victoria; and the downtown location, combined with an intimate, rustic decor, creates a pleasant ambience. House specialties include canard à l'orange (duckling in orange sauce), rack of lamb, and British Columbia salmon. Although a tourist destination, this restaurant has managed to maintain its quality over the years. *512 Yatos, tol. 604/388 7711. Reservations advised. Dress: casual but neat. AE, MC, V. Closed lunch and Sun.–Mon. Moderate–Expensive.*

Camilles. This restaurant is romantic, intimate, and one of the few West Coast-cuisine restaurants in Victoria. House specialties such as Zinfandel chicken, papaya brochettes (prawns wrapped around chunks of papaya in a lime and jalapeño marinade), phyllo-wrapped salmon (fresh fillet of salmon in phyllo pastry) are all served in generous portions. Camilles also has an extensive wine cellar, uncommon in Victoria. *45 Bastion Sq., tel. 604/381–3433. Reservations advised. Dress: casual but neat. AE, MC, V. Closed lunch and Sun.–Mon. Moderate.*

French Connection. Located in one of Victoria's Heritage homes, built in 1884, the restaurant has maintained the character of the time. From the outside, ornate details indicate the French tradition that you will find in the service and on the menu. The food is prepared with care, with an emphasis on the sauces. *512 Simcoe St., tel. 604/385–7014. Reservations required. Dress: casual. AE, MC, V. Closed Sat.–Mon. lunch and Sun. Moderate.*

★ **Pagliacci's.** If you want Italian food, Pagliacci's is a must. Featured are dozens of pasta dishes, quiches, veal, and chicken in marsala sauce with fettuccine. The pastas are freshly made in-house. The orange-color walls are covered with photos of Hollywood stars, so there's always something to look at here. *1011 Broad St., tel. 604/386–1662. No reservations. Dress: casual. MC, V. Moderate.*

Le Petite Saigon. This is a small, intimate café-style restaurant, offering a quiet dining experience with beautifully presented meals and a fare that is primarily Vietnamese, with a touch of French. The crab, asparagus, and egg swirl soup is a specialty of the house, and combination meals are a cheap and tasty way to learn the menu. *1010 Langley St., tel. 604/386–1412. Dress: casual. AE, MC, V. Closed Sat. lunch and Sun. Inexpensive–Moderate.*

Cafe Mexico. This is a spacious, red-brick dining establishment just off the waterfront, serving hearty portions of Mexican food, such as pollo chipolte (grilled chicken with melted cheddar and spicy sauce, on a bed of rice). Bullfight ads and cactus plants decorate the restaurant, reinforcing its character and theme. *1425 Store St., tel. 604/386–5454. Reservations accepted. Dress: casual. AE, MC, V. Inexpensive.*

Periklis. Standard Greek cuisine is offered in this warm, Taverna-style restaurant, but there are also steaks and ribs on the menu. On the weekends you can enjoy Greek and belly dancing, but be prepared for the hordes of people who come for the entertainment. *531 Yates St., tel. 604/386–3313. Reservations accepted. Dress: casual. Closed weekend lunch; during summer, open Sat. lunch. AE, MC, V. Inexpensive.*

★ **Six-Mile-House.** This 1855 carriage house is a Victoria landmark. The brass, carved oak moldings, and stained glass, set a festive mood for the evening. The menu is constantly changing, but always features seafood selections and burgers. Try the cider or one of many international beers offered. *494 Island Hwy., tel. 604/478–3121. Reservations accepted. Dress: casual. MC, V. Inexpensive.*

★ **Wah Lai Yuen.** Although Chinatown seems to be offering less-interesting restaurants than before, this one has managed to maintain its character. It's a small corner of authenticity, combining Cantonese cuisine with wonderful baked goods including pork and curry beef buns. The portions are enormous and the price is right. *560 Fisgard St., tel. 604/381–5355. Reservations accepted. Dress: casual. No credit cards. Closed Mon. Inexpensive.*

Lodging **The Bedford Hotel.** This European-style hotel, located in the heart of downtown, is reminiscent of San Francisco's small hotels, with personalized service and strict attention to details. In keeping with the theme, rooms follow an earthen color scheme, and many have goose-down comforters, fireplaces, and Jacuzzis. Meeting rooms and small conference facilities are available also, making this a good businessperson's lodging. Gourmet breakfast is included in the room rate. *1140 Government St., V8W 1Y2, tel. 604/384–6835 or 800/665–6500; fax 604/386–8930. 40 rooms. Facilities: restaurant, pub. AE, MC, V. Very Expensive.*

★ **The Empress Hotel.** This is Victoria's dowager queen with a face-lift. First opened in 1908, it recently underwent a multimillion dollar renovation that has only enhanced its Victorian charm. In the renovation process, stained glass, carved archways, and hardwood floors were rediscovered and utilized effectively. Forty-six new rooms were added and the others were brought up to modern standards, something the hotel desperately needed. A new entrance has been constructed, in addition to the new rooms and re-landscaped grounds. The Empress dominates the inner-harbor area and is the city's primary meeting place for politicians, locals, and tourists. This is one of Victoria's top tourist attractions, so don't expect quiet strolls through the lobby. *721 Government St., V8W 1W5, tel. 604/384–8111, or 800/268–9411 in Canada, and 800/828–7447 in U.S.; fax 604/381–4334. 488 rooms. Facilities: 2 restaurants, café, 2 lounges, conference center, indoor pool, sauna, health club, in-room movies, cable TV, Christmas discount, family discount. AE, DC, MC, V. Very Expensive.*

★ **Hotel Grand Pacific.** This is a new hotel and one of Victoria's finest, with modern motifs and international service standards. Overlooking the harbor, and adjacent to the legislative buildings, the hotel accommodates business and vacationing people looking for comfort, convenience, and great scenery; all rooms have terraces, with views of either the harbor or the Olympic Mountains. The health club is elaborate, equipped with Nautilus, racquetball court, and sauna. *450 Québec St., V8V 1W5, tel. 604/386–0450 or 800/663–7550; fax 604/383–7603. 149 rooms. Facilities: restaurant, lounge, sauna, whirlpool, fitness center, convention facilities, underground parking, indoor pool. AE, DC, MC, V. Very Expensive.*

★ **Holland House Inn.** Two blocks from the inner harbor, legislative buildings, and ferry terminals, this nonsmoking hotel has a sense of casual elegance. Some of the individually designed rooms have original fine art created by the owner, and some have four-poster beds and fireplaces. All rooms have private baths and all but two have their own balconies. A gourmet breakfast is served and included in room rates. You'll recognize the house by the picket fence around it. *595 Michigan St., V8V 1S7, tel. and fax 604/384–6644. 10 rooms. Facilities: lounge. AE, DC, MC, V. Expensive–Very Expensive.*

Victoria Regent Hotel. Originally built as an apartment, this is a posh, condo-living hotel that offers views of the harbor or city. The outside is plain, with a glass facade, but the interior is sumptuously decorated with warm earth tones and modern furnishings; each apartment has a living room, dining room, deck, kitchen, and one or two bedrooms with bath. *1234 Wharf St., V8W 3H9, tel. 604/386–2211 or 800/663–7472; fax 604/386–2622. 47 rooms. Facilities: restaurant, free parking, laundromat. AE, DC, MC, V. Expensive–Very Expensive.*

Captain's Palace Hotel and Restaurant. This is a unique lodging, contained within three Victorian-era mansions, and located only one block from the legislative buildings. Once a one-bedroom B&B, it has expanded to 16 guest rooms and a restaurant. Rooms, decorated in florals and pastels, offer different extras: some have private baths with claw-foot tubs, others have balconies. Although the restaurant provides ample breakfasts—included in the room price—don't overlook offerings in the neighborhood for dinner. Ask about special honeymoon, holiday, and blossom-time packages. *309 Belleville St., V8V 1X2, tel. 604/388–9191; fax 604/388–7606. 16 rooms. Facilities: restaurant, money exchange, bicycles. AE, MC, V. Moderate–Very Expensive.*

Oak Bay Beach Hotel. This Tudor-style hotel, located in Oak Bay, on the southwest side of the Saanich Peninsula, is well removed from the bustle of downtown. There's a wonderful atmosphere here, though; the hotel, situated oceanside, overlooks the Haro Strait, and catches the setting sun. The interior decor is as dreamy as the grounds, with antiques and flower prints decorating the rooms. The restaurant, Tudor Room by the Sea, is average, but the bar with its cozy fireplace is truly romantic. *1175 Beach Dr., V8S 2N2, tel. and fax 604/598–4556. 51 rooms. Facilities: restaurant, pub, yacht for cruises, access to health club. AE, DC, MC, V. Moderate–Very Expensive.*

★ **Abigail's.** A Tudor country inn with gardens and crystal chandeliers, Abigail's is not only posh, but also conveniently located four blocks east of downtown. All guest rooms are lavishly detailed with a rose, peach, and mint color scheme. Down comforters, and Jacuzzis and fireplaces in some add to the luxurious atmosphere. There's a sense of elegant formality about the hotel, noticed especially in the guest library and sitting room, where you'll want to spend an hour or so in the evening relaxing. Breakfast, included in the room rate, is served from 8 to 9:30 in the downstairs dining room. *906 McClure St., V8V 3E7, tel. 604/388–5363; fax 604/361–1905. 16 rooms. MC, V. Expensive.*

★ **The Beaconsfield Inn.** Built in 1875 and restored in 1984, the Beaconsfield has a feel of Old World charm. Dark mahogany wood appears throughout the house; down comforters and some canopy beds and claw-foot tubs adorn the rooms, reinforcing the Victorian style of this residentially situated inn. Some of the rooms have fireplaces and Jacuzzis. An added plus is the guest library and conservatory/sun room. One block away, a new addition—the Humboldt House—offers three more romantic rooms. Full breakfast, with homemade muffins, and a cocktail hour (6–7 PM), with sherry, cheese, and fruit, are included in the room rates. *998 Humboldt St., V8V 2Z8, tel. 604/ 384–4044; fax 604/384–4044. 12 rooms. Facilities: library, Jacuzzi. MC, V. Expensive.*

Chateau Victoria. This 19-story hotel, situated across from Victoria's new Conference Centre, near the inner harbor and the Royal British Columbia Museum, promises wonderful views from its upper rooms and its rooftop restaurant. Following a Victorian motif, the rooms are warm and spacious, some with balconies or sitting areas and kitchenettes. *740 Burdett Ave., V8W 1B2, tel. 604/382–4221 or 800/663–5891; fax 604/380– 1950. 178 rooms. Facilities: restaurants, lounge, indoor pool, whirlpool, meeting rooms, courtesy vans to ferry, access to health club. AE, MC, V. Expensive.*

Dashwood Manor. One of those small, intimate places for which you're always on the lookout, Dashwood Manor is on the waterfront next to Beacon Hill Park and is truly a find. Be aware, however, that this inn is a modestly furnished inn, and sloping ceilings and sometimes peculiar layout reflect its age. This Heritage Tudor mansion, built in 1912 on property once owned by Governor Sir James Douglas, offers panoramic views of the Strait of Juan de Fuca and the Olympic Mountains. Three rooms in this B&B have fireplaces. In the afternoon, join the other guests for sherry or brandy, or relax in the small library. *1 Cook St., V8V 3W6, tel. 604/385–5517. 14 rooms. MC, V. Moderate–Expensive.*

Admiral Motel. Located on the Victoria harbour and along the tourist strip, this motel is right where the action is, although it is relatively quiet in the evening. If you're looking for a basic, clean lodging, the Admiral is just that. The amicable owners take good care of the newly refurbished rooms, and small pets are permitted. *257 Belleville St., V8V 1X1, tel. 604/388–6267. 29 rooms, 23 with kitchens. Facilities: cable TV, free parking, laundry. AE, MC, V. Inexpensive–Moderate.*

★ **Craigmyle Guest House.** In the shade of Craigdarroch Castle, about 2 kilometers (1 mile) from the downtown core, this lodge, built in 1913, has a special view of the castle. The rooms are quietly elegant and simple, with decor reminiscent of Laura Ashley prints; most units have private bath. The Edwardian touches are best felt in the main lounge, where you'll find high ceilings and a huge fireplace. A hearty English-style breakfast, with homemade preserves, porridge, and eggs, is a main attraction here. *1037 Craigdarroch Rd., V8S 2A5, tel. 604/595– 5411, fax 604/370–5276. 19 rooms, 15 with private bath. MC, V. Inexpensive–Moderate.*

The Arts and Nightlife

The Arts **The Art Gallery of Greater Victoria** is considered one of Cana-
Galleries da's finest art museums and is home to large collections of Chinese and Japanese ceramics and other art, and also to the only authentic Shinto shrine in North America. The gallery hosts about 40 different temporary exhibitions yearly. *1040 Moss St., Victoria, tel. 604/384–4101. Admission: $3 adults, $1.50 students and senior citizens, children under 12 free; free Thurs. after 5, though donations are accepted. Open Mon.–Wed., and Fri.–Sat. 10–5, Thurs. 10–9, Sun. 1–5.*

Geert Maas Sculpture Gardens, Gallery, and Studio. World-class sculptor Geert Maas exhibits his art in an indoor gallery and a one-acre garden, in the hills above Kelowna. Maas, who works in bronze, stoneware, and mixed media, creates distinctive abstract figures with a round and fluid quality. He also sells medallions, original paintings, and etchings. *R.R. #1, 250 Reynolds Rd., Kelowna, V1Y 7P9, tel. 604/860–7012. Admission free. Open year-round, call for exact hours.*

Music The **Victoria Symphony** has a winter schedule and a summer season, playing out of the weathered **Royal Theatre** (805 Broughton St., Victoria, tel. 604/383–9711) and at the **University Centre Auditorium** (Finnerty Rd., Victoria, tel. 604/721–8559). The **Pacific Opera Victoria** performs three productions a year in the 800-seat **McPherson Playhouse** (3 Centennial Sq., tel. 604/386–6121), adjoining the Victoria City Hall. The **Victoria International Music Festival** (tel. 604/736–2119) features internationally acclaimed musicians, dancers, and singers each summer from the first week in July through late August.

Theater Live theater activity includes the **Belfry Theatre** (1291 Gladstone Ave., Victoria, tel. 604/385–6815), **Phoenix Theatre** (Finnerty Rd., tel. 604/721–8000) at the University of Victoria, **Victoria Theatre Guild** (805 Langham Ct., tel. 604/384–2141), **McPherson Playhouse** (3 Centennial Sq., tel. 604/386–6121).

In Prince George visit the **Prince George Playhouse** (2833 Recreation Place, tel. 604/563–8401). In Kelowna the **Sunshine Theatre Company** (1304 Ellis, tel. 604/763–4025) stages productions.

In Kamloops call the **Sagebrush Theatre Company** (821 Munro St., tel. 604/372–0966) or the **Western Canada Theatre Company** (1025 Lorne St., tel. 604/372–3216) for schedule information.

Nightlife After 8 PM, **Tudor House Hotel Pub** (533 Admirals Rd., tel. 604/389–9943) becomes a pub attracting the younger set. There's a dance floor and large screen for disco and video entertainment nightly.

Harpo's (15 Bastion Sq., tel. 604/385–5333) features live music, with visits from internationally recognized bands.

Excursion 2: Mayne Island

Introduction

The Gulf Islands lie in the Gulf of Georgia, between Vancouver and Victoria. The southern islands Galiano, Mayne, Saturna, Pender, and Salt Spring (the most commercialized) are warmer, have half the rainfall of Vancouver, and are graced with smooth sandstone rocks and beaches. Marine birds are numerous, and unusual vegetation such as arbutus trees (a leafy evergreen with red peeling bark) and Garry oaks make the islands very different from other areas around Vancouver. Writers, artists, craftspeople, weekend cottagers, and retirees take full advantage of the undeveloped islands.

For a first visit to the Gulf Islands, make a stopover on Mayne, the most agricultural of the group. In the 1930s and 1940s the island produced vegetables for Vancouver and Victoria until the Japanese farmers who worked the land were interned during World War II. Mayne's close proximity to Vancouver and its

manageable size (even if you're on a bicycle) make it accessible
and feasible for a one- or two-day trip. A free map, published by
the islanders, is available on the ferry or from any store on
Mayne.

Arriving and Departing by Ferry

BC Ferry (tel. 604/685–1021 for recorded message; for reservations, 604/669–1211) runs frequent service from outside Vancouver and Victoria to the Gulf Islands. The trip to Mayne
Island takes about 1½ hours, and a couple of sailings run each
day. Call for a 24-hour recorded phone message of crossings. If
you plan on taking a car, it is often necessary to make reservations a couple of weeks in advance, especially if you are traveling on the weekend. Go mid-week if possible.

Getting Around

By Bicycle Because Mayne Island is so small (20 sq km, or 8 sq mi) and scenic, it is great territory for a vigorous bike ride, though the
small hills make it not-quite-a-piece-of-cake. Renting a bike in
Vancouver is a good idea, unless the weather looks iffy; then it
would be worth taking a car. Some B&Bs have bicycles; ask for
them to be set aside for you when making your reservation. A
few bicycles are for rent at the island's only gas station (604/
539–5411) at Miners Bay.

By Car The roads on Mayne Island are narrow and winding.

Exploring Mayne Island

Mayne Island saw its heyday around the turn of the century
when passenger ships traveling from Victoria and Vancouver
stopped to enjoy Mayne's natural beauty. Late-19th-century
wood houses, hotels, and a church still stand today among the
newer A-frames, log cabins, and split level homes. Although
there is no real town on Mayne, except for a few commercial
buildings and homes around Miners Bay, you will find eagles,
herons, and rare ducks; sea lions and black-tail deer; quiet
beaches, coves, and forest paths; and warm, dry weather in the
summer.

Starting at the ferry dock at **Village Bay,** head toward Miners
Bay via Village Bay Road. A small white sign on your left will
indicate the way to **Helen Point,** previously an Indian reservation, which presently has no inhabitants. Indian middens at
Village Bay show that the island had been inhabited for 5,000
years by Cowichan Indians from Vancouver Island who paddled
to Mayne Island in dugout canoes. If you choose to go all the
way to Helen's Point (about a two-hour, round-trip walk), you
can look north across **Active Pass** (named for the turbulent waters).

If you continue on Village Bay Road, head toward **Miners Bay,** a
little town about 2 kilometers (1.2 miles) away. This commercial hub has a post office, restaurant, health-food store, gas station, bakery (with espresso), a general store, and a secondhand
bookstore. Look for the House of Taylor (tel. 604/539–5283), an
arts-and-crafts gallery that features local works. Also, visit
the **Plumbers Pass Lockup;** formerly a jail, it is now a minuscule
museum with local history exhibits.

Time Out Stop at the **Springwater Lodge** (tel. 604/539–5521), built in 1892 and the oldest operating hotel in British Columbia. The deck of the Springwater overlooks the bay and is a fine place for a cold soda or beer on a sunny day.

From Miners Bay head east on Georgina Point Road. About a mile away is **St. Mary Magdalene Church,** which doubles as an Anglican and United church. If Pastor Larry Grieg is around, he'll show you the century-old building, but the cemetery next to the church is even more interesting. Generations of islanders—the Bennetts, Georgesons, Maudes, and Deacons—whose names are all over the Mayne Island map—are buried here. Across the road, a stairway leads down to the beach.

At the end of Georgina Point Road is the **Active Pass Lighthouse.** The grassy grounds, open to the public every day from 1 to 3, are great for picnicking. Bald eagles are often on the shore along with many varieties of ducks (waterfowl is most abundant in spring and fall).

Head back down Georgina Point Road a short way and turn left on Waugh Road, left on Porter Road, and right to the end of Edith Point Road. A path leads off into the woods to **Edith Point,** an hour's walk away. The path is a bit steep in parts—not recommended for small children—but the sunny smooth sloping sandstone at the point is a real enticement. Many of the beaches on Mayne are on the north or east side, but at Edith Point you can take advantage of the full southern exposure. If the tide is out, beachcomb your way back to your car.

From Edith Point Road, go back along Waugh Road a short distance to Campbell Bay Road. Take this to Fernhill Road (which becomes Bennett Bay Road), heading east to **Bennett Bay,** the island's most popular beach. Just past the junction of Bennett Bay and Wilkes roads, beyond the Marisol Cottages, a small green sign on the right indicates beach access. The beach is wide and long and the bay is shallow, so the water warms up nicely. (Don't expect washrooms or concession stands in the Gulf Islands.) The mountain looming in the distance is Washington State's Mt. Baker. The nicest part of the beach is to your left if you are facing the water.

The last stop on the tour is **Mount Parke,** which was declared a wilderness park in 1989. Access is from Village Bay Road, where you will see a timber archway naming Mt. Parke. Drive up as far as you can until you see the sign that says "No Vehicles Beyond This Point." It is then about a 15-minute walk to the highest point on the island and a stunning, almost 360-degree view of Vancouver, Active Pass, and Vancouver Island. You may be face-to-face with eagles using the updraft to maintain their cruising altitude.

Dining and Lodging

Dining **Mayne Mast.** A nautical theme in blues and grays is appropriate for the Mayne Mast, ensconsed in a 1940s house with a large sunny deck facing Miners Bay. This family restaurant is open every day for breakfast, lunch, and dinner. Fish and chips made with red snapper is the most popular item on the menu, followed closely by the steak, prawn, and scallop dinner. *Village Bay Rd., tel. 604/539–3056. MC, V. Moderate.*

Dining and Lodging

Fernhill Lodge and Herb Farm. The lodge has built its reputation on friendly service, distinctive rooms, and historical dinners. Odds are the chef and owner, Brian Crumblehume, will be serving the Cleopatra, Chaucer, or Roman dinners. If you're not staying at the lodge, you must make a dinner reservation by 1 PM. Breakfasts are more traditional and are fabulous. They feature fresh-squeezed orange juice, freshly baked buns and muffins, good coffee, and eggs and sausages. In the summer, reserve in advance. You have a choice of seven rooms: the Jacobean, Oriental, Canadiana, Moroccan, East Indian, 18th-century French, or Victorian. *Fernhill Rd., Box 140, V0N 2J0, tel. 604/539-2544. Facilities: bicycles, sauna under the trees, sun room, library, piano, herb garden. MC, V. Moderate.*

Lodging

Oceanwood Country Inn. Set in 10 wooded acres on the waterfront, The Oceanwood offers eight deluxe rooms. Seven of them have a view of Navy Channel, which separates Mayne Island from North Pender. All have private bath and some have whirlpools, French doors, fireplaces, or terraces. Each room is individually decorated but features Canadian pine, Victorian mahogany, and romantic chintzes. During the winter, theme weekends are built around wine tastings, nature outings, murder mysteries, and the like. Room rates include breakfast and afternoon tea. The inn is open to the public daily for dinner and Sunday brunch. The menu focuses on wines and seasonal foods from the Pacific Northwest such as grilled salmon or warm scallop salad. No children or pets allowed. *630 Dinner Bay Rd., V0N 2J0, tel. 604/539-5074, fax 604/539-3002. Facilities: bicycles, sauna, hot tub, conference room, library, games room with bridge tables. AE, MC, V. Expensive.*

Blue Vista Resort. The sizable '60s-style cabins, decorated with rumpus room–style family furnishings, are about 100 feet from the beach at Bennett Bay. This is the best family accommodation on the island, because units are complete with kitchens and there are no restrictions on pets. Owners Gerry and Naomi Daignault can also provide bicycles, barbecues, and a rowboat. *Arbutus Rd., V0N 2J0, tel. 604/539-2463. MC, V. Inexpensive.*

Root Seller Inn. This warm and friendly country-style bed-and-breakfast is in a 1924 clapboard house a mile from the ferry dock. The location is popular with people getting around on foot or by bicycle because it is in the heart of activity at Miners Bay—within walking distance of stores and the pub. The four large rooms in this rustic house are furnished in old Canadiana oak and share two baths. The honeymoon suite has a fireplace and the family room sleeps five people. Guest rooms on the south side overlook the huge front deck and Miners Bay. There are picnic facilities for guests in the shady backyard. The lounge has a TV and a VCR. Breakfast is served in the dining room at a long communal table. *Box 5, Village Bay Rd. V0N 2J0, tel. 604/539-2621. Inexpensive.*

Index

Abigail's (B&B), *154*
Active Pass
  Lighthouse, *158*
Admiral Motel, *155*
Ainsworth's (shop),
  104
Air tours, *108–109*
A. Jay's (restaurant),
  65
Aldo (shop), *125*
Alexis (hotel), *71*
Alfred Sung (shop),
  125
All-City Dance Club,
  84
Allegro Dance
  Company, *81*
Alma Street Cafe,
  145
American Express, *7*
Amusement parks,
  122
Anne Hathaway's
  Cottage, *150*
Annie Steffen's
  (shop), *92*
Anthony's Home Port
  (bar), *82*
Antique Importers,
  57
Antiques shops
Seattle, *57*
Vancouver, *124*
Victoria, *151*
Aquariums
Seattle, *48–49*
Vancouver, *115*
Victoria, *150*
Arboretums, *52*
Armadillo & Co.
  (shop), *56*
Arnie's (bar), *82*
Arriva Ristorante,
  134
Artemis (shop), *124*
Art galleries and
  museums
Gallery Walk
  program, *53*
Puget Sound/San Juan
  Islands, *92*
Seattle, *48, 52, 53, 57*
Vancouver, *110, 118,
  119, 120, 124*
Victoria, *155–156*

Art Gallery of
  Greater Victoria,
  155
Arts Club Theatre,
  143
Arts festivals, *5*
ATMs (automated
  teller machines), *7–8*
Auctions, *123*
Avalon Ballroom, *84*

Baby-sitting services,
  14
Bacchus Lounge, *144*
Bacci (shop), *125*
Back Alley Theatre,
  144
Backstage (club), *82*
Bahn Thai
  (restaurant), *70*
Bainbridge Island
  Chamber of
  Commerce, *84*
Bainbridge Island
  Vineyard and
  Winery, *85*
Bali Bali (shop), *125*
Ballard Firehouse
  (club), *82*
Ballard Locks, *55*
Balloon flights, *45*
Ballroom dancing, *84*
Bank buildings, *112*
Baren Haus
  (restaurant), *100*
Bars and lounges
Seattle, *82*
Vancouver, *144–145*
Victoria, *156*
Baseball, *28*
Seattle, *59*
Vancouver, *127*
Basketball, *28*
Seattle, *59*
Bathhouse Theater,
  80
Bathtub races, *6*
Bau-Xi Gallery, *124*
Beaches, *29*
Mayne Island, *158*
Puget Sound/San Juan
  Islands, *94*
Vancouver, *117, 127*
Beacon Hill Park,
  149

Beaconsfield Inn,
  154–155
Bead Works (shop),
  56
Beatles Museum, *121*
Bed-and-breakfasts,
  30
Mayne Island, *159*
Puget Sound/San Juan
  Islands, *95, 96–97*
Vancouver, *142*
Victoria, *154–155*
Bedford Hotel, *153*
Beeliner Diner, *61*
Belfry Theatre, *156*
Bellevue Square
  shopping center, *57*
Bennett Bay, *158*
Bergman Luggage
  Co., *57*
Best Western
  Greenwood Hotel,
  79
Bicycling, *26*
Mayne Island, *157*
Puget Sound/San Juan
  Islands, *92*
Seattle, *58*
Vancouver, *125*
Big Time Brewery,
  54
Bilbo's Festivo
  (restaurant), *94*
Bishop's (restaurant),
  136
Bite of Seattle
  festival, *5*
Blackberry Books,
  124
Blair House (B&B),
  96
Blues/R&B clubs,
  82–83
Blue Vista Resort,
  159
Boating and sailing,
  26
Puget Sound/San Juan
  Islands, *93*
Seattle, *59*
Vancouver, *126–127*
Boat racing, *59*
Boboli (shop), *124,
  125*
Boeing Field, *52*

Bombay Bicycle Club
(bar), *142*
Bond's (shop), *124*
Bookshops, *124*
Books on Pacific
North Coast, *17–18*
Border-crossing
procedures, *8–9, 20,
22*
Borderline (club), *84*
Boutique Europa, *57*
Bread Garden
Bakery, Café &
Espresso Bar, *132*
Breweries
Seattle, *53, 55*
tours, *55*
Vancouver, *119*
Brew pubs, *54–55*
Bridges (restaurant),
119, 145
British Camp, *92*
British Columbia
Ferry Corporation,
23
Brockton Point, *115*
Bruce Lee's grave
site, *56*
Buchan Hotel,
142–143
Bumbershoot
festival, *5*
Buschlen-Mowat
Gallery, *124*
Bus travel, *20*
disabled travelers,
accommodations for,
15
Leavenworth, *99*
older travelers,
programs for, *17*
passes, *12*
regional service, *22*
Seattle, *42, 43*
Vancouver, *107*
Victoria, *146*
Byrnes Block
building, *113*

Cabezon Gallery, *92*
Cafe Alexis, *68*
Cafe Dilettante, *57*
Café Django, *145*
Cafe Juanita, *66*
Cafe Mexican, *152*
Cafe Sport, *68*
Caffe de Medici
(restaurant), *134*
Camilles
(restaurant), *152*

Campagne
(restaurant), *65*
Camping, *31*
Canada Day, *6*
Canada Place Pier,
112
Canada West (shop),
124
Canadian Imperial
Bank of Commerce
headquarters, *112*
Canadian Pacific
Station, *112–113*
Canlis (restaurant),
60
Canrailpass, *12*
Cantata Singers, *144*
Capers (restaurant),
134
Capilano Fish
Hatchery, *122*
Captain's Palace
Hotel and
Restaurant, *154*
Captain Whidbey
Inn, *98*
Carnegie's (club), *145*
Carousel Theater,
143
Carpenter's Hall, *84*
Car rentals, *11–12*
Car travel, *19–20*
ferry transport, *85*
insurance, *22*
Leavenworth, *98–99*
Mayne Island, *157*
Puget Sound/San Juan
Islands, *88*
Seattle, *42, 43*
service organizations,
22–23
speed limits, *22*
Vancouver, *106, 107*
winter driving, *22*
Cartwright Gallery,
119
Cash machines, *7–8*
Casinos, *145*
Catamaran service,
23
Caveman Kitchen
(restaurant), *61*
Celebrity (club), *84*
Cemeteries, *56*
Central Tavern, *83*
Chapy's (shop), *125*
Charles and Emma
Frye Art Museum,
53
Charles H. Scott

Gallery, *118*
Chartwell
(restaurant), *129*
Chateau Victoria,
155
Chau's Chinese
Restaurant, *61, 65*
Chez Daniel
(restaurant), *151*
Chez Pierre
(restaurant), *152*
Chez Thierry
(restaurant), *133*
Chicago's (club), *82*
Childers/Proctor
Gallery, *92*
Children, traveling
with
festivals and events,
5, 14
hotel services, *14*
safety seats, *14*
Seattle attractions,
53–54
Vancouver attractions,
5, 14, 119, 122
Victoria attractions,
150
Chimera Gallery,
92
Chinese Cultural
Center, *114*
Chinese Freemasons
Building, *114*
Chinese Times
Building, *114*
Chiyoda (restaurant),
135
Chocolate shops, *57*
Christ Church
Cathedral, *110*
Christina's
(restaurant), *94*
Churches
Mayne Island, *158*
Vancouver, *110*
Cipriano's Ristorante
& Pizzeria, *135*
Civic Light Opera,
81
Clamshell Gift Shop,
125
Cliff House (B&B),
97
Climate, *4–5*
Clothing shops
Seattle, *57–58*
Vancouver, *124–125*
Club Monaco (shop),
124, 125

Colleges and universities
Seattle, *52, 79*
Vancouver, *118*
Colophon Books, *124*
Comedy clubs
Seattle, *83–84*
Vancouver, *145*
Comedy Underground (club), *83*
A Contemporary Theater, *80*
Cooper's Northwest Alehouse, *54–55*
Cornish College of the Arts, *79*
Cougar Inn, *99–100*
Coupeville, WA, *90*
Crafts shops, *57*
Craigdarroch Castle, *149–150*
Craigmyle Guest House, *155*
Credit cards, *7, 31*
Cruises, *3, 23–24*
dinner cruises, *44*
Vancouver excursions, *109*
Crystal Gardens, *149*
Cucina! Cucina! (restaurant), *66–67*
Cuisine of Pacific North Coast, *29*
Currencies of Canada and United States, *8*
Currency exchange services, *7*
Customs regulations, *9–10*

Daily Planet (shop), *56*
Dance
Seattle, *81*
Vancouver, *144*
Dance clubs, *84*
Danish Bakery, *100*
Darvill's Rare Print Shop, *92*
Dashwood Manor (B&B), *155*
Days Inn, *142*
Deadman's Island, *115*
Deception Pass State Park, *90*

Deer Harbor Inn, *97*
Delaurenti Wine Shop, *57*
Delta Airport Inn, *140*
Delta Place (hotel), *140*
Delta River Inn, *140*
Der Ritterhof (hotel), *100*
Diane Farris Gallery, *124*
Dimitriou's Jazz Alley, *83*
Dinner cruises, *44*
Disabled travelers, hints for, *14–16*
Doc Maynard's (club), *82–83*
Dr. Sun Yat-sen Gardens, *114*
Doe Bay Village Resort, *96*
Dog House Backdoor Restaurant, *95*
Dominion Astrophysical Observatory, *150*
Doubletree Inn, *77*
Doubletree Suites, *77*
Dragon Boat Festival, *5*
Duck Soup Inn, *94*
Du Maurier International Jazz Festival, *5*
Dusty Strings (shop), *56*
Duthie's (shop), *124*

E. A. Lee (shop), *124, 125*
Early Music Guild (Seattle), *81*
Early Music Society (Vancouver), *144*
Eastsound Village, WA, *91, 94, 95, 98*
Ebey's Landing National Historical Reserve, *90*
Ecomarine Ocean Kayak Center, *119*
Eddie Bauer (shop), *57*
Edelweiss Hotel, *101*
Edenwild (B&B), *95*
Edgewater (hotel),

71, 74
Edith Point, *158*
Edward Chapman, (shop), *124*
86th Street Music Hall, *145*
Elderhostel program, *16*
Elliott Bay Book Company, *53*
El Puerco Lloron (restaurant), *68*
Emergencies
Seattle, *43*
Vancouver, *108*
Emily Carr College of Art and Design, *118*
Emmet Watson's Oyster Bar, *69*
Empress Hotel, *146, 153*
Empty Space Theater, *80*
Enda B. (shop), *125*
English Bay, *116*
English Bay Café, *132, 144*
English Bay Inn, *142*
Equinox Gallery, *124*
Evergreen Motel, *101*
Evergreen Theater Company, *80*

Fernhill Lodge and Herb Farm, *159*
Ferry service, *23*
for cars, *85*
Mayne Island, *157*
Puget Sound/San Juan Islands, *88*
Seattle, *43*
Vancouver, *106, 107*
Victoria, *146*
Winslow, *84–85*
Festivals and seasonal events, *5–6*
Fifth Avenue Musical Theater Company, *80*
Film
Seattle, *49*
Vancouver, *144*
Finn's (shop), *124*
Fireworks Gallery, *57*
Fishing, *26–27*
Puget Sound/San Juan Islands, *92–93*
Seattle, *58*

Vancouver, *125*
Fish Ladder, *55*
Fitzgerald's on Fifth
 (club), *84*
Flea markets, *123*
Flying Shuttle Ltd.
 (shop), *57*
Folkart Interiors
 (shop), *124*
Folk clubs, *82*
Football, *28*
Seattle, *59*
Vancouver, *127*
Ft. Casey State Park,
 90
Four Seasons (hotel,
 Vancouver), *137, 139*
Four Seasons
 Olympic Hotel
 (Seattle), *71*
Frank & Dunya
 Gallery, *56*
Freedman Shoes
 (shop), *125*
French Connection
 (restaurant), *152*
Friday Harbor, WA,
 91, 92, 96–97, 98
Friends of Chamber
 Music, *144*
F. X. McRory's (bar),
 82

Gallery Lounge, *144*
Gallery Walk
 program, *53*
Gambits (club), *83*
Garden Court (bar),
 82
Garden Lounge, *144*
Gardens
Puget Sound/San Juan
 Islands, *90*
Seattle, *52, 55*
Vancouver, *114, 121*
Victoria, *148, 149*
Garibyan Brothers
 Café Langley, *94–95*
Geert Maas
 Sculpture Gardens,
 Gallery, and Studio,
 155–156
George Straith
 (shop), *124*
Georgia Hotel, *142*
Gérard Lounge, *144*
Gift shops, *125*
Giggles (club), *83–84*
Glass House (shop),
 57

Glass Knight (shop),
 92
Golf, *27*
Leavenworth, *99*
Seattle, *58*
Vancouver, *125–126*
Victoria, *151*
Gordon Southam
 Observatory, *122*
Granville Island,
 117–121
Granville Island
 Brewery, *119*
Granville Island
 Information Centre,
 118
Granville Island
 Public Market,
 117–118
Grayling Gallery, *92*
Great Canadian
 Casino, *145*
Great Gallery, *52*
Great Windup (shop),
 57
Greenbank, WA, *90*
Group Theater, *80*
Guess Where (shop),
 56
Guest House
 Cottages (B&B), *97*
Gun control laws, *10*

Han Il (restaurant),
 67–68
Harpo's (club), *156*
Harry Rosen (shop),
 124
Health and fitness
 clubs, *126*
Health concerns, *10*
Health insurance, *11*
Heffel Gallery, *124*
Helen Point, *157*
Helicopter tours, *108*
Hendrix, Jimi, *55–56*
Henry Art Gallery,
 52
The Herbfarm
 (restaurant), *86–87*
Hien Vuong
 (restaurant), *70*
Hiking, *27*
Leavenworth, *99*
Vancouver, *126*
Hillside House
 (B&B), *96–97*
Hiram's at the Locks
 (bar), *82*
Hockey, *28*

Vancouver, *127*
Holiday Inn Sea-Tac
 (hotel), *78*
Holland House Inn,
 153–154
Hollywood
 Underground (club),
 84
Holt Renfrew (shop),
 124
Home exchanges, *31*
Horse and carriage
 rides, *109*
Horseback riding, *99*
Horse racing, *28*
Hotel Europe, *113*
Hotel Grand Pacific,
 153
Hotels, *29–30*
Leavenworth,
 100–101
Mayne Island, *159*
Puget Sound/San Juan
 Islands, *95–98*
Seattle, *70–79*
Snoqualmie Falls area,
 87
Vancouver, *137–143*
Victoria, *153–155*
Hotel Vancouver,
 110, 140–141
Houseboat
 communities, *119*
Hunt Club
 (restaurant), *68*
Hunting, *27*
Hyatt Bellevue
 (hotel), *78–79*
Hyatt Regency
 (hotel), *141*

Il Giardino di
 Umberto
 (restaurant),
 134–135
Images for a
 Canadian Heritage,
 125
Imagination Market,
 124
Indian artworks, *120,
 125*
Inn at Langley,
 97–98
Inn at the Market,
 74–75
Inns, *30*
Insurance
automobile, *22*
health, *11*

Insurance
(*continued*)
luggage, *11*
International
Bathtub Race, *6*
International
Student Identity
Card, *13*
Intiman Theater, *80*
Isadora's
(restaurant), *128*
Island County
Historical Museum,
90

J&M Cafe (bar), *82*
Japanese Deli House,
135–136
Jazz clubs
Seattle, *83*
Vancouver, *145*
Jazz festivals, *5*
Jeffrey-Michael
(shop), *57*
Jewelry shops, *57*
Jimi Hendrix's grave
site, *56*
Joe Fortes (bar), *144*
Jogging. *See* Running
and jogging

Kakali (shop), *119*
Kamloops, B.C., *156*
Kaplan's Deli,
Restaurant and
Bakery, *132*
Kayaking
instruction in, *119*
Seattle, *59*
Vancouver, *126*
Kells (restaurant),
66, 82
Keystone, WA, *90*
Kids Only Market,
119
Kingdome stadium,
49
Kingston (hotel), *143*
Kirin Mandarin
Restaurant, *129*
Kitsilano Beach, *127*
Klondike Gold Rush
National Historical
Park, *49*

La Bodega (bar), *144*
Ladies Musical Club,
81
Lakeside (bar), *82*
Landau's

(restaurant), *60*
Langley, WA
hotels, *97–98*
restaurants, *94–95*
shopping, *92*
sightseeing, *88, 90*
Languages, *10*
Larry's (club), *83*
Latona Tavern, *83*
La Vie en Rose
(shop), *125*
La Ville d'Is
(restaurant),
151–152
Lawrence Books, *124*
Leavenworth, WA, *98*
hotels, *100–101*
restaurants, *99–100*
sports, *99*
tourist information, *98*
transportation, *98–99*
Le Crocodile
(restaurant), *133*
Lee, Bruce, *55–56*
Le Gavroche
(restaurant), *133*
Legislative
Parliament
Buildings, *148*
Le Meridien (hotel),
139
Leona Lattimer
Gallery, *125*
Leone (shop), *124,
125*
Le Petite Saigon
(restaurant), *152*
Le Tastevin
(restaurant), *65–66*
Lighthouses, *158*
Lime Kiln Point
State Park, *91*
Linyen (restaurant),
61
Lions Gate Bridge,
116
Littler's (shop), *58*
Local Brilliance
(shop), *58*
Lofurno's (club), *83*
Loganberry Farm, *90*
Lopez Island, *91, 92,
93, 95*
Lost Lagoon, *115*
Luggage
airline rules on, *6–7*
insurance for, *11*
Luggage shops, *57*
Lumberman's Arch,
115

Lynn Canyon
Suspension Bridge,
122

Maas, Geert, *155–156*
Mackaye Harbor Inn,
95
McLeod's (shop), *124*
McPherson
Playhouse, *150*
Magic Mouse Toys,
57
Mail service, *24*
Malinee's Thai
(restaurant), *137*
Mansions, *149–150*
Maplewood Farms,
122
Margareta (shop),
125
Marine Building,
110, 112
Marine state parks,
93
Mario's (shop), *57*
Maritime Market,
119
Maritime Museum
(Vancouver), *120*
Maritime Museum of
British Columbia
(Victoria), *149*
Mayflower Park
Hotel, *75*
Mayne Island,
156–157
hotels, *159*
restaurants, *158–159*
sightseeing, *157–158*
transportation, *157*
Mayne Mast
(restaurant), *158*
Meany Hall for the
Performing Arts, *81*
Meany Tower Hotel,
76–77
Medical services
Seattle, *43*
Vancouver, *108*
Meerkerk
Rhododendron
Gardens, *90*
Metropolitan Grill,
70
Michael Pierce
Gallery, *57*
Miners Bay, B.C.,
157
Miniature World,
146, 148

Mirabeau (bar), *82*
Mondo Uomo (shop), *124*
Money, *7–8*
Monorail, *43*
Moore Theater, *81*
Moran State Park, *91*
Morgan (shop), *125*
Motels/motor inns, *30*
Mountaineering, *26*
Mt. Constitution, *91*
Mount Parke, *158*
Murphy's Pub, *82*
Museum of Anthropology, *120*
Museum of Flight, *52*
Museum of History and Industry, *52*
Museums. *See also* Art galleries and museums
anthropology, *52, 120*
astronomy, *150*
aviation, *52*
Beatles, *121*
children's, *53–54*
history, *52, 90, 91, 120–121, 148, 157*
maritime history, *120, 149*
in Mayne Island, *157*
natural history, *52, 148*
Oriental history and culture, *51*
in Puget Sound/San Juan Islands area, *90, 91*
science, *120*
in Seattle, *51, 52, 53–54*
in Vancouver, *108, 120–121*
in Victoria, *148, 149, 150*
whales, *91*
Music, classical
Seattle, *81*
Vancouver, *144*
Victoria, *156*
Music, popular
festivals, *5*
Seattle, *82–83*
Vancouver, *145*

Naam Restaurant, *134*
National Historic Civil Engineering Landmark, *86*

Nazarre BBQ Chicken, *128*
Net Loft, *119*
New City Arts Center, *80*
New Melody Tavern, *82*
New Orleans Creole Restaurant, *83*
Nightclubs. *See* Bars and lounges
Night Court (bar), *144*
Nine O'Clock Gun, *115*
Nippon Kan Theater, *51*
Nitobe Garden, *121*
Noggins (brew pub), *54*
Noor Mahal (restaurant), *133*
Northgate Mall, *56*
Northwest Chamber Orchestra, *81*
Northwest Folklife Festival, *5*

Oak Bay Beach Hotel, *154*
Oak Harbor, WA, *90*
Oakridge Shopping Center, *123*
Oceanwood Country Inn, *159*
Odlin County Park, *91*
O'Doul's (hotel), *141*
Okazuya (restaurant), *51*
OK Hotel (club), *83*
Old Country Mouse Factory (shop), *124*
Older travelers, hints for, *16–17*
Old Timer's Cafe, *83*
Olympia Fish Market and Oyster Co. Ltd. (restaurant), *137*
Omnidome Film Experience, *49*
On the Boards (dance company), *81*
Opening and closing times, *25*
Opera
Seattle, *81–82*
Vancouver, *144*
Victoria, *156*
Orcas Hotel, *95–96*

Orcas Island, *91, 92, 93, 94, 95–96, 97, 98*
Orcas Performing Arts Center, *98*
Out to Lunch Series, *53*
Owl Cafe & Tavern, *83*

Pacifica (restaurant), *69*
Pacific Center Mall, *122*
Pacific London Wax Museum, *148*
Pacific National Exhibition, *6*
Pacific Northwest Ballet, *81*
Pacific Northwest Brewing Co., *54–55*
Pacific Opera Victoria, *156*
Pacific Plaza (hotel), *75–76*
Pacific Spirit Park, *121*
Pacific Undersea Garden, *148*
Package deals, *3–4*
Packing, *6*
Pagliacci's (restaurant), *152*
Pan Pacific (hotel), *139*
Paramount Theater, *81*
Parker's (club), *83*
Park Inn Club & Breakfast, *76*
Parks, historical
Puget Sound/San Juan Islands, *91–92*
Seattle, *49*
Parks, state
marine state parks, *93*
Puget Sound/San Juan Islands, *90, 91, 93*
Passports, *8–9*
Pegabo (shop), *125*
Pelican Bay (bar), *145*
Pension Anna, *100–101*
Periklis (restaurant), *152*
Phnom Penh Restaurant, *128–129*
Phoenix Theatre, *156*

Photographers, tips
for, *10*
Pier 70 (club), *84*
Pike & Western Wine
Merchants, *57*
Pike Place Market,
48
Pink Pearl
(restaurant), *129*
Pink Peppercorn
(shop), *124*
Pioneer Park, *49*
Place Pigalle
(restaurant), *60*
The Planetarium, *122*
Planetariums and
observatories
Vancouver, *122*
Victoria, *150*
Plane travel, *18–19*
airfares, *20*
airlines, *18, 20, 21*
charter flights, *21*
discount flights, *18–19*
Leavenworth, *98*
luggage, rules on, *6–7*
Puget Sound/San Juan
Islands, *88*
regional service, *21*
Seattle, *42*
smoking, *19*
tips on, *18*
from United Kingdom,
20–21
Vancouver, *106*
Victoria, *145*
Plumbers Pass
Lockup (museum),
157
Point Grey Beaches,
127
Polo Country (shop),
124, 125
Powerboating, *28*
Prescription drugs, *6,
10*
Prices, *8*
Prince George, B.C.,
156
Prince George
Playhouse, *156*
Prospect Point, *116*
Puget Sound and
Snoqualmie Valley
Railway, *86*
Puget Sound/San
Juan Islands, *87*
the arts, *98*
beaches, *94*
guided tours, *88*

hotels, *95–98*
restaurants, *94–95,
97–98*
shopping, *92*
sightseeing, *88–92*
sports, *92–94*
tourist information, *87*
transportation, *88*

Queen Elizabeth
Park, *121*
Queen Elizabeth
Theatre, *144*
Quilicum
(restaurant), *136*

Rafting
Leavenworth, *99*
Vancouver, *126*
Rail passes, *12*
Railroads
Snoqualmie Falls area,
86
Vancouver, *122*
Rainier Brewery, *53*
The Raintree
(restaurant),
136–137
Ralph Lauren (shop),
124, 125
Ravenhouse Art, *92*
Ray's Boathouse
(restaurant), *69, 82*
Recreational
Equipment, Inc., *53*
Red Barn (airplane
factory), *52*
Red Lion Bellevue
(hotel), *78*
Red Lion/Sea-Tac
(hotel), *77*
REI (shop), *57*
Reid, Bill, studio of,
120
Reiner's Gasthaus
(restaurant), *100*
Resorts, *31*
Restaurants, *29*
American, *60–61,
99–100, 128*
Asian, *51, 61*
Cambodian, *128–129*
Chinese, *61, 65, 129,
153*
Continental, *60–61,
129, 132*
Danish, *100*
delis, *65, 132*
East Indian, *132–133*
French, *65–66, 133,*

152
German, *100*
Greek, *94–95,
133–134, 152*
health food, *94, 134*
Hungarian, *100*
Irish, *66*
Italian, *66–67,
134–135, 152*
Japanese, *67–68,
135–136*
Korean, *67–68, 136*
in Leavenworth,
99–100
in Mayne Island,
158–159
Mexican, *68, 94, 136,
152*
nouvelle, *136*
Pacific Northwest,
*68–69, 86–87,
136–137, 152*
in Puget Sound/San
Juan Islands area,
94–95, 97–98
seafood, *69, 94, 137,
151–152, 158*
in Seattle, *51, 60–70*
Snoqualmie Falls area,
86–87
Southwest, *69–70*
steak houses, *70*
teahouses, *116, 129*
Thai, *70, 137*
in Vancouver, *116,
119, 128–137*
in Victoria, *151–153*
Vietnamese, *70,
128–129, 152*
Richard's on
Richards (disco), *145*
Richmond Nature
Park, *122*
Roche Harbor, WA,
92, 96
Roche Harbor
Resort, *96*
Rock clubs
Seattle, *83*
Vancouver, *145*
Root Seller Inn, *159*
Rosario Spa
& Resort, *95*
Rover's (restaurant),
66
Royal Bank building,
112
Royal British
Columbia Museum,
148

Royal Diamond
Casino, *145*
Royal London Wax
Museum, *148*
Royal Theatre, *156*
Royal Vancouver
Yacht Club, *115*
Rubina Tandoori
(restaurant),
132–133
Running and jogging
Seattle, *58*
Vancouver, *126*

Sagebrush Theatre
Company, *156*
Sailboarding, *59*
Sailing. *See* Boating
and sailing
Ste. Michelle
Winery, *55*
St. Mary Magdalene
Church, *158*
Saleh Al Lago
(restaurant), *66*
Salish (hotel), *87*
Salmon, *25*
Salmon Shop, *125*
Salvatore Ristorante
Italiano, *67*
Sam Kee Building,
114
San Juan Community
Theatre, *98*
San Juan Historical
Museum, *91*
San Juan Inn, *97*
San Juan Island,
91–93, 94, 96–97
San Juan Island
National Historic
Park, *91–92*
San Juan Islands. *See*
Puget Sound/San
Juan Islands
Santa Fe Cafe, *69–70*
Scarlet Tree (club),
83
Science World, *120*
Seafair festival, *5*
Sealand of the
Pacific (aquarium),
150
Seasons in the Park
(restaurant), *129*
Seattle, WA, *41–42*
the arts, *79–82*
children, attractions
for, *53–54*
climate, *4*

downtown, *45–51*
emergencies, *43*
excursions, *84–101*
festivals, *5*
free attractions, *53*
Fremont area, *56*
guided tours, *44–45*
hotels, *70–79*
International District,
44, 49, 51
nightlife, *82–84*
Pioneer Square, *49*
restaurants, *51, 60–70*
shopping, *56–58*
Skid Row, *49*
sports, *58–59*
tourist information,
43, 45
transportation in, *43*
transportation to, *42*
Underground Tour,
44–45
Seattle Airport
Hilton (hotel), *77*
Seattle Aquarium,
48–49
Seattle Art Museum,
48
Seattle Center, *51*
Seattle Children's
Museum, *53–54*
Seattle Children's
Theater, *54*
Seattle Hilton
(hotel), *75*
Seattle International
Youth Hostel, *76*
Seattle/King County
Convention and
Visitors Bureau, *43*
Seattle Mariners, *59*
Seattle Marriott
(hotel), *77–78*
Seattle Opera, *81–82*
Seattle Repertory
Theater, *80*
Seattle Seahawks, *59*
Seattle Sheraton
Hotel and Towers,
74
Seattle SuperSonics,
59
Seattle Symphony, *81*
Seattle-Tacoma
International
Airport, *42*
Seattle Visitor
Information Center,
45
Second Beach, *117*

Seoul House Korean
Restaurant, *136*
Shaw Island, *91*
Shijo Japanese
Restaurant, *135*
Ship travel. *See*
Cruises
Shopping, *25–26. See
also specific types of
shops*
Puget Sound/San Juan
Islands, *92*
Seattle, *56–58*
Vancouver, *108,
122–125*
Victoria, *150–151*
Sinclair Centre, *112,
123*
Siwash Rock, *116*
Six-Mile-House
(restaurant),
152–153
Sixth Avenue Inn, *76*
Skating, *58*
Skid Row, *49*
Skiing, *27–28*
Leavenworth, *99*
Seattle, *59*
Snoqualmie Falls area,
86
Vancouver, *126*
S. Lampman (shop),
124
Snoqualmie Falls,
85–87
Snoqualmie Falls
Forest Theater, *86*
Snoqualmie Pass, *86*
Snoqualmie Winery,
86
Soft Rock Cafe, *145*
Sorrento (hotel), *74*
Southcenter Mall, *56*
Space Needle, *51, 82*
Space Needle
Lounge, *51*
Spencer Spit State
Park, *91*
Splashdown Park,
122
Sports. *See also
specific sports*
Leavenworth, *99*
participant, *26–28*
Puget Sound/San Juan
Islands, *92–94*
Seattle, *58–59*
spectator, *28*
Vancouver, *125–127*
Victoria, *151*

Sportsbooks Plus, 124
Springtree Eating Establishment and Farm, 94
Springwater Lodge, 158
Square on Yesler (club), 83
Squid Row Tavern, 83
Stanley Park, 114–117
Stanley Park Zoo, 115–116
Star Bistro, 95
Steam train, miniature, 122
Stephane de Raucourt (shop), 125
Stouffer Madison Hotel, 71
Student and youth travel, 13–14
Sunshine Theatre Company, 156
Swiftsure Race Weekend, 5
Swimming, 28
Sylvia Hotel, 143
Szechuan Chongqing (restaurant), 129

Takara (restaurant), 67
Taxes, 8, 25–26
Taxis
Seattle, 43
Vancouver, 107
Victoria, 146
Teahouse Restaurant at Ferguson Point, 116, 129, 132
Telephone service, 24
Tennis, 59
Theater
children's, 54
Seattle, 54, 80
Snoqualmie Falls area, 86
Vancouver, 143–144
Victoria, 156
Theater buildings, 51
Theatresports, 144
Thomas Burke Memorial Washington State Museum, 52
Three Girls Bakery, 65

Tipping, 24
Tojo's (restaurant), 135
The Tomahawk (restaurant), 137
Topanga Cafe, 136
Toronto-Dominion Bank building, 112
Totem poles, 115
Touchstone Theatre, 143
Tour groups, 2–3
Tourist information, 2
Puget Sound/San Juan Islands, 87
Seattle, 43, 45
Vancouver, 107
Victoria, 145
Winslow, 84
Town Pump (club), 145
Toy shops, 57
Train travel, 20. See also Railroads
disabled travelers, accommodations for, 15
older travelers, programs for, 17
rail passes, 12
regional service, 21
Seattle, 42
Vancouver, 107
Trattoria Mitchelli (restaurant), 67
Travel Bug (shop), 124
Traveler's checks, 7, 8
Trolleyman (brew pub), 54
Trolleys, 43
Tudor House Hotel Pub, 156
Turgeon-Raine Jewelers, 57
Turtleback Farm (B&B), 96

Umberto's (restaurant), 134–135
University of Washington, 52
University Plaza Hotel, 77
USA Rail Passes, 12
Uwajimaya (Japanese store), 51

Vancouver, B.C., 103–105
the arts, 143–144
beaches, 117, 127
Blood Alley, 113
children, attractions for, 5, 14, 119, 122
Chinatown, 113–114, 123
climate, 5
consulates, 107–108
downtown, 110–114
East Indian shopping district, 123
emergencies, 108
festivals, 5–6
free attractions, 121
Gaoler's Mews, 113
Gastown area, 113
Granville Island, 117–121
guided tours, 108–109
hotels, 137–143
Italian community, 123
Japantown, 123
nightlife, 144–145
restaurants, 116, 119, 128–137
Robson Square, 110
shopping, 108, 122–125
sightseeing, 109–122
sports, 125–127
Stanley Park, 114–117
subway system, 107
tourist information, 107
transportation in, 107
transportation to, 106–107
travel agencies, 108
West End, 117
Vancouver Art Gallery, 110
Vancouver Chamber Singers, 144
Vancouver Children's Festival, 5, 14
Vancouver Club, 112
Vancouver East Cultural Centre, 144
Vancouver International Airport, 106
Vancouver Kidsbooks, 124
Vancouver Museum, 120–121
Vancouver Opera, 144

Vancouver
Playhouse, *143*
Vancouver Public
Aquarium, *115*
Vancouver Recital
Society, *144*
Vancouver Rowing
Club, *115*
Vancouver Sea
Festival, *6*
Vancouver Symphony
Orchestra, *144*
Van Dusen Botanical
Garden, *121*
Vassilis Taverna
(restaurant),
133–134
Vic & Mick's Nine-10
Cafe, *60–61*
Victoria, B.C., *145*
the arts, *155–156*
Bastion Square, *149*
children, attractions
for, *150*
Chinatown, *149, 151*
hotels, *153–155*
Market Square, *149*
restaurants, *151–153*
shopping, *150–151*
sightseeing, *146–150*
sports, *151*
tourist information,
145
transportation,
145–146
Victoria Day, *5*
Victoria
International Music
Festival, *156*
Victoria Regent
Hotel, *154*
Victoria Symphony,
156
Victoria Theatre
Guild, *156*
Village Bay, B.C.,
157, 158
Village Theater, *80*
Visas, *8–9*
Vogue (club), *83*

Wah Lai Yuen
(restaurant), *153*
Wah Mee Club, *51*
Walking, *58*
Warwick Hotel, *75*
Washington Dance
Club, *84*
Washington Park
Arboretum, *52*
Washington State
Ferry System, *23*
Waterfalls, *85–86*
Waterfront Theatre,
143
Waterworks Gallery,
92
Wax museums, *148*
Wear Else? (shop),
125
Weather information,
5
Wedgewood Hotel,
141–142
WestCoast Camlin
Hotel, *76*
West End Beaches,
127
West End Guest
House, *142*
Western Canada
Theatre Company,
156
Western Union, *7*
Westin Bayshore
(hotel), *139–140*
Westin Hotel, *75*
Westlake Center, *48,
56*
Whale Museum, *91*
Whale-watching,
91
Whidbey Island, *87*
beaches, *94*
hotels, *97–98*
restaurants, *94–95,
97–98*
shopping, *92*
sightseeing, *88, 90*
sports, *93*
transportation, *88*

Whidbey Island
Naval Air Station,
90
Wild Ginger
(restaurant), *61*
Wildlife viewing, *28*
William Hoffer
(shop), *124*
William McCarley
(shop), *124*
William Tell
(restaurant), *132*
Windmills, *90*
Windsurfing, *127*
Wineries
Seattle, *55*
Snoqualmie Falls area,
86
Winslow, *85*
Wine shops, *57*
Wing Luke Museum,
51
Winslow, WA, *84–85*
Woodland Park Zoo,
52
Woodmark Hotel,
78
Working abroad,
13–14
World Wide Books
and Maps, *124*

Yacht races, *5*
YMCAs/YWCAs, *31*
Seattle, *76*
Youth hostels, *13*
Puget Sound/San Juan
Islands, *96*
Seattle, *76*
Youth International
Educational
Exchange (YIEE)
Card, *13*
Yuk Yuks (club),
145

Zig Zag (shop), *125*
Zoos
Seattle, *52*
Vancouver, *115–116*

Personal Itinerary

Departure   *Date*

                 Time

Transportation

Arrival   *Date*   *Time*

Departure   *Date*   *Time*

Transportation

Accommodations

Arrival   *Date*   *Time*

Departure   *Date*   *Time*

Transportation

Accommodations

Arrival   *Date*   *Time*

Departure   *Date*   *Time*

Transportation

Accommodations

Personal Itinerary

Arrival *Date*   *Time*

Departure *Date*   *Time*

Transportation

Accommodations

Arrival *Date*   *Time*

Departure *Date*   *Time*

Transportation

Accommodations

Arrival *Date*   *Time*

Departure *Date*   *Time*

Transportation

Accommodations

Arrival *Date*   *Time*

Departure *Date*   *Time*

Transportation

Accommodations

Personal Itinerary

Arrival *Date*   *Time*

Departure *Date*   *Time*

Transportation

Accommodations

Arrival *Date*   *Time*

Departure *Date*   *Time*

Transportation

Accommodations

Arrival *Date*   *Time*

Departure *Date*   *Time*

Transportation

Accommodations

Arrival *Date*   *Time*

Departure *Date*   *Time*

Transportation

Accommodations

Addresses

Name	_Name_
Address	_Address_
Telephone	_Telephone_
Name	_Name_
Address	_Address_
Telephone	_Telephone_
Name	_Name_
Address	_Address_
Telephone	_Telephone_
Name	_Name_
Address	_Address_
Telephone	_Telephone_
Name	_Name_
Address	_Address_
Telephone	_Telephone_
Name	_Name_
Address	_Address_
Telephone	_Telephone_
Name	_Name_
Address	_Address_
Telephone	_Telephone_

Fodor's Travel Guides

U.S. Guides

Alaska
Arizona
Boston
California
Cape Cod, Martha's
  Vineyard, Nantucket
The Carolinas & the
  Georgia Coast
The Chesapeake
  Region
Chicago
Colorado
Disney World & the
  Orlando Area
Florida
Hawaii

Las Vegas, Reno,
  Tahoe
Los Angeles
Maine, Vermont,
  New Hampshire
Maui
Miami & the
  Keys
National Parks
  of the West
New England
New Mexico
New Orleans
New York City
New York City
  (Pocket Guide)

Pacific North Coast
Philadelphia & the
  Pennsylvania
  Dutch Country
Puerto Rico
  (Pocket Guide)
The Rockies
San Diego
San Francisco
San Francisco
  (Pocket Guide)
The South
Santa Fe, Taos,
  Albuquerque
Seattle &
  Vancouver

Texas
USA
The U. S. & British
  Virgin Islands
The Upper Great
  Lakes Region
Vacations in
  New York State
Vacations on the
  Jersey Shore
Virginia & Maryland
Waikiki
Washington, D.C.
Washington, D.C.
  (Pocket Guide)

Foreign Guides

Acapulco
Amsterdam
Australia
Austria
The Bahamas
The Bahamas
  (Pocket Guide)
Baja & Mexico's Pacific
  Coast Resorts
Barbados
Barcelona, Madrid,
  Seville
Belgium &
  Luxembourg
Berlin
Bermuda
Brazil
Budapest
Budget Europe
Canada
Canada's Atlantic
  Provinces

Cancun, Cozumel,
  Yucatan Peninsula
Caribbean
Central America
China
Czechoslovakia
Eastern Europe
Egypt
Europe
Europe's Great Cities
France
Germany
Great Britain
Greece
The Himalayan
  Countries
Holland
Hong Kong
India
Ireland
Israel
Italy

Italy 's Great Cities
Jamaica
Japan
Kenya, Tanzania,
  Seychelles
Korea
London
London
  (Pocket Guide)
London Companion
Mexico
Mexico City
Montreal &
  Quebec City
Morocco
New Zealand
Norway
Nova Scotia,
  New Brunswick,
  Prince Edward
  Island
Paris

Paris (Pocket Guide)
Portugal
Rome
Scandinavia
Scandinavian Cities
Scotland
Singapore
South America
South Pacific
Southeast Asia
Soviet Union
Spain
Sweden
Switzerland
Sydney
Thailand
Tokyo
Toronto
Turkey
Vienna & the Danube
  Valley
Yugoslavia

Wall Street Journal Guides to Business Travel

Europe   International Cities   Pacific Rim   USA & Canada

Special-Interest Guides

Bed & Breakfast and
  Country Inn Guides:
  Mid-Atlantic Region
New England
The South
The West

Cruises and Ports
  of Call
Healthy Escapes
Fodor's Flashmaps
  New York

Fodor's Flashmaps
  Washington, D.C.
Shopping in Europe
Skiing in the USA &
  Canada

Smart Shopper's
  Guide to London
Sunday in New York
Touring Europe
Touring USA